# THE
# AGE OF CHIVALRY

# THE
# AGE OF CHIVALRY

## CULTURE AND POWER IN
## MEDIEVAL EUROPE 950-1450

### HYWEL WILLIAMS

Quercus

# CONTENTS

PREVIOUS PAGE *A pastoral scene is shown in this image
from the* Très Riches Heures du Duc de Berry,
*a 15th-century book of hours.*

EUROPE
*c.*1050

NORWAY

SWEDEN

ESTONIANS

SCOTLAND

NORTH
SEA

DENMARK

BALTIC
SEA

LITHUANIANS

PRUSSIANS
(BALTIC)

IRELAND

Durham
York

WESTERN
SLAVIC
PEOPLES

Gniezno

POLAND

WALES ENGLAND

FRISIA

SAXONY

Hildesheim
Magdeburg

London

LOWER
LOTHARINGIA
Cologne

GERMAN
KINGDOM

Winchester

FLANDERS

FRANCONIA

BOHEMIA

Aachen

Prague

MOROVIA

MONTREUIL
PONTHIEU
PICARDY

Frankfurt

VERMANDOIS
BEAUVAIS
VEXIN

Trier
Worms

UPPER
Speyer
LOTHARINGIA

Regensburg

ATLANTIC

NORMANDY

Paris

Esztergom

TROYES

ÎLE-DE-FRANCE

ALSACE

BAVARIA

BRITTANY
MAINE
Tours
ANJOU
TOURAINE
Bourges

BLOIS

AUXERRE
Autun

SWABIA

Salzburg

HUNGARY

NEVERS
BURGUNDY

Cluny

OCEAN

AQUITAINE

KINGDOM
OF
BURGUNDY

CARINTHIA

Milan
Pavia
Venice

CROATIA

BYZANTINE EMPIRE

AUVERGNE

Canossa

Bologna

GEVAUDAN

Genoa

Santiago de
Compostela

Oviedo

GASCONY

TOULOUSE

Montpellier
Arles
Marseille

ITALY

SPOLETO

SERBIA

ADRIATIC SEA

Pisa

PATRIMONY OF ST PETER

LEÓN

Burgos

NAVARRE

ARAGÓN

BARCELONA

Rome

SOUTH ITALIAN
PRINCIPALITIES

PUGLIA

CASTILE

Barcelona

CORSICA

Toledo

ISLAMIC TAIFAS
(PRINCIPALITIES)

SARDINIA

CALABRIA

MEDITERRANEAN

N

Seville
Córdoba

Palermo
SICILY

SEA

0          300 km

0          300 miles

# Introduction

Three distinctive civilizations developed in western Eurasia and North Africa following the fifth century collapse of the Western Roman empire's authority. The Greek empire of Byzantium was centred on the eastern Mediterranean while the civilization of Islam became predominant across North Africa and in the Middle East. European civilization incorporated the western Mediterranean territories but it also acquired a new axis which extended northwards to include areas that had been peripheral to classical Roman antiquity. These three cultures were the sibling civilizations of ancient Rome, and western Europe came to define itself as the bastion of Latin Christendom as opposed to the Greeks' eastern Orthodoxy. Up until at least the year 1000 Europe's level of cultural, intellectual and material development was clearly inferior to that attained by Byzantium and the Islamic states. During the central or 'high' Middle Ages that extended from the 11th to the 13th centuries the continent started to rival its two neighbouring powers in terms of political effectiveness, military success and cultural expansiveness. By the 15th century Europeans were asserting supremacy over their erstwhile rivals and superiors. The means by which this great transformation came to pass form the subject matter of this book.

Social structures were reorganized at a profound level in western Europe from *c*.500 onwards: the traditions of imperial Rome now yielded to those of the Germanic peoples, such as the Franks and the Lombards, who had migrated to the south and west. New kingdoms were thereby established in western Europe, and monarchy's institutional authority turned former citizens into subjects. A process of Christianization was encouraged by missionaries, sponsored by rulers and often imposed on subjugated pagan peoples, and monasticism became the supreme expression of European religious life.

'Europe' had been a geographical term since Graeco-Roman antiquity but the word acquired a cultural and political significance during Charlemagne's reign as king of the Franks (768–814). The scale of his victories gave Charlemagne a dominion over most of the territories which had once comprised the Western Roman empire, and in the year 800 he was crowned emperor by Pope Leo III. Charlemagne's heirs and successors however failed to maintain his expansionist momentum, and after the division of the former Carolingian empire (843) European kings found it difficult to raise the armies needed to enforce their authority. A century-long period of strain and danger followed with Magyar invasions from the east and Viking incursions from Scandinavia undermining Europe's recovery and self-confidence.

Hardened by these battles, European military and political leaders were able to regain the initiative by the late tenth century, and the papacy's decision to grant an imperial crown to the German king Otto I in 962 marks the start of the institution which would later be termed the Holy Roman Empire. Demographic growth, urban development, and a burgeoning sense of national identity – as well as the papacy's assertion of its own independent power – are the hallmarks of the central Middle Ages. From the 11th century onwards the chivalric code, which inculcated the virtues of valour, courtesy, honour and loyalty, achieved a widespread diffusion among the European élites. Chivalry's influence transcended the ethic's military origins, and its celebration of the cult of love, both human and divine, had a profound impact on social conduct, religious idealism and aesthetic inspiration.

The phrase '*medium aevum*' was coined during the early 17th century by French and English historians of jurisprudence, and its vernacular equivalents, '*moyen age*', 'Middle Ages' and 'medieval', were adopted subsequently. These authors also popularized the notion that 'feudalism' – another word they invented – was the universal form of social life in western Europe by the 11th century and that it lasted for at least another 300 years. The terms *feudum* (or 'fief') and *feodalitas* (services connected with the *feudum*) refer to a form of property holding which was especially common in France and England. But the way in which European societies changed in the post-Roman and medieval centuries inevitably assumed many different guises, and an uniform 'feudal system' did not exist at any stage in the history of medieval Europe. An assertion of lordship however did become widespread and its exercise showed how power at local, regional and national levels could be established by a mutual exchange of vows between superiors and inferiors. Obligations of service might then be incurred by those sometimes called 'vassals' and promises of protection would be made by the relevant lord.

During the 14th century Europeans had to cope with a series of both natural and man-made disasters: widespread famines, the Black Death of 1348 and subsequent years, as well as the mid-century collapse of Italian banks. Technological change meant that warfare became both more expensive financially and increasingly devastating in its human impact. Expansion and development halted in both the towns and the countryside, and Europe's population, which had stood at some 70 million in 1300, was almost halved. European resilience is nonetheless the key feature of this renewed time of trial with first the rural areas and then the urban centres being rapidly repopulated. The intellectual, political and social changes associated with an initially Italian renaissance evolved out of late medieval society, and are inconceivable outside that context. Personal enterprise, intellectual curiosity, and institutional responsiveness to change: these defining characteristics of European civilization were formed during the medieval centuries and it was that legacy from its past which enabled the culture to survive, evolve and flourish.

*Hywel Williams*

# THE OTTONIAN DYNASTY OF SAXON EMPERORS

## 919 — 1024

*The creation of the German people's first* reich *dominates the history of tenth-century Europe. Charlemagne, king of the Franks, revived the imperial title for the first time since the collapse of the Western Roman empire in the fifth century, and on Christmas Day 800 he was crowned emperor by the pope in Rome. However, his dynastic successors failed to maintain the empire's territorial unity. By c.900 the ancestral core of Charlemagne's empire had been split into a kingdom of the Eastern Franks, corresponding to much of modern Germany, and a kingdom of the Western Franks, whose boundaries anticipated those of France. The duchy of Saxony became the eastern kingdom's power base.*

The Saxons had been tenaciously pagan before Charlemagne conquered them in a series of fierce late-eighth-century military campaigns. Now a thoroughly Christianized territory, the duchy of Saxony was key to Germany's evolution into a power that embraced ancient Roman notions of empire and was the dominant partner in its alliance with the papacy. At the beginning of the tenth century Europe was still threatened from the north by the Vikings, and the danger of invasion from the east by the Magyars, a pagan and nomadic warrior race, posed major challenges until the 950s. However, the armies of the German *reich*, later to be termed the Holy Roman Empire, held the line against these threats and set the scene for the evolution of medieval European civilization.

In 919 Henry I, duke of Saxony and founder of the Ottonian dynasty, was elected 'king of the Germans' by an assembly of aristocrats meeting at Fritzlar. The Eastern Frankish duchies of Franconia, Swabia, Bavaria and Lotharingia soon acknowledged his kingship. Henry's heirs would rule as his lineal successors, and the practice of election to the throne, although retained, became a formality. The new king, dubbed 'the Fowler' because of his fondness for hunting wild birds, subdued the Danish Vikings, and in 924 he agreed a ten-year truce with the Magyars whom he then defeated at the Battle of Riade in 933. Henry's refusal to be consecrated a king was a major break with the traditions

RIGHT *A 1903 German mosaic of Otto I ('the Great'), who was crowned an emperor by the pope in 962.*

of 'sacral kingship'. But he was determined to exercise power on his own terms and to avoid any suggestion of indebtedness to the Church. However, Henry's son, Otto I ('the Great'), chose to be anointed and consecrated a king when he was crowned at Aachen's Palatine Chapel in 936. The bishops and abbots of the German kingdom became his vassals, and these royal appointees identified strongly with Otto's system of government and supported the consolidation of his command over an often fractious nobility. This German *reichskirche* or imperial church was also instrumental in the eastward expansion of the Ottonian dynasty. The sees established in Poland, Bohemia, Moravia and Hungary operated as outposts of the ecclesiastical centres at Mainz and Magdeburg, Salzburg and Passau, and the new bishoprics were pivotal in trying to impose German culture and enforce political assimilation on the conquered Slavic peoples. The scale of new building projects, together with the demands for military hardware, made this an expensive policy, but the discovery of silver in Saxony's Harz region during the early tenth century had enriched the Ottonian kings and helped to subsidize their imperial ventures.

## CAMPAIGNS IN THE SOUTH AND EAST

BELOW *A pen and watercolour manuscript illustration (c.1450) from the workshop of Diebold Lauber shows Emperor Otto I meeting Pope John XII.*

Otto's ambitions extended south as well as east. In 950 he launched a major campaign across the Alps in support of Queen Adelheid of Italy who was being threatened by the rebellion of Berengar, margrave of Ivrea in the peninsula's northwest. Success in battle led to Otto's recognition as 'king of the Lombards' by the Italian nobility. The decisive defeat he inflicted on the Magyars at the Battle of the Lechfeld on 10 August 955 entrenched his authority over the German aristocracy. The king's war machine gained another crushing victory on 16 October 955 when it defeated the Obodrites, a Slavic tribe established in the region of Mecklenburg on the Baltic coast. This gave the kingdom a 30-year period of peace on its eastern frontier, during which time a tight system of lordship was imposed on the Slavs by their German rulers.

Berengar remained ambitious and in *c.*960 he occupied the papal states of central Italy. Otto responded by marching his army into Rome to safeguard the position of the young pope, John XII, who, on 2 February 962, crowned the German king an emperor. The *Diplomata Ottonianum*, an imperial-papal agreement issued later that same month, gave Otto the right to confirm elections to the papacy. Pope John swiftly repented of this one-sided pact, and after making peace overtures to Berengar he was deposed in 963 by the Church council summoned by the emperor. For the remainder of his reign Otto was preoccupied with the Italian south, where a number of local princes retained their Lombard identity as descendants of the Germanic tribe that had invaded the region in the seventh century. Pandulf Ironhead, prince of Benevento and Capua, was one such ruler, and Otto enlisted him as his ally in the campaign to expel the Byzantines from the peninsula's south. Otto also engineered Pandulf's succession as prince of Salerno and granted him the duchy of Spoleto, a fiefdom (the territorial domain of a feudal lord) whose territories extended to the east of the papal states. A major anti-Byzantine power block was thereby created as the new German *reich* confronted the Greek empire.

## Maintaining Otto's dynasty

Otto's dynastic ambitions were endorsed when an assembly, meeting in Worms in 961, elected his son king of the Germans. The future Otto II was crowned joint-emperor with his father by the pope six years later and was thoroughly trained in the business of imperial war and government. His first major challenge came in 978 when Lothair, king of West Francia, launched an invasion and occupied Aachen. Otto retaliated in the autumn by leading his army over the frontier and inflicting heavy losses on the enemy. A peace agreement was arrived at in 980, and with his western boundaries secured Otto could plan an Italian campaign. He crossed the Alps with his army, and on Easter Day 981, accompanied by a retinue of courtiers and senior churchmen, Otto entered Rome. Here he held a magnificent court attended by nobles drawn from across the imperial territories. Otto's ambitions, however, lay further south.

## Defeated by the Arabs

The Arab pirates known as Saracens operated from bases on the north African coast, and they had been disrupting the Mediterranean sea lanes for over a century. An alliance with Arab-ruled Sicily was now enabling the Saracens to attack the southern Italian regions of Puglia and Calabria, and the German army advanced from Rome bent on confrontation. Pandulf Ironhead's heirs had fallen out with each other, but Otto managed to secure their recognition of his imperial authority and proceeded to annex Puglia – a region still controlled by the Byzantines. Military catastrophe followed. In July 982, at Stilo in Calabria, Otto's army was destroyed by the Arab army of Sicily whose emir, Abu al-Kasim, had declared a *jihad* or holy war against the Germans. The emperor managed to escape incognito on a Greek ship and return to Rome. At an imperial assembly held in Verona he secured recognition of his infant son as king of the Germans, and then started to plan a resumption of the southern campaign.

## THE OTTONIAN DYNASTY

**800** Charlemagne, king of the Franks and of the Lombards, is crowned emperor by Pope Leo III on Christmas Day.

**919** Henry I ('the Fowler'), duke of Saxony, is elected king of the Germans.

**933** King Henry I defeats the Magyars at the Battle of Riade.

**936** Otto I ('the Great'), founds Quedlinburg Abbey.

**962** Otto I is crowned emperor by Pope John XII.

**982** The army of Arab Sicily defeats Otto II's forces at the Battle of Stilo, Calabria. A rebellion of Slavic tribes settled between the Oder and Elbe endangers the German kingdom's eastern frontier.

**996** Otto III, German king and emperor, begins to rule in his own right.

**c.1000** Coronation of Stephen I, Hungary's first king, as a Christian monarch.

**1002** Duke Henry of Bavaria is elected king of the Germans and reigns as Henry II.

**1004** Henry II defeats Arduin, Margrave of Ivrea, who has proclaimed himself 'king of Italy'.

**1024** Henry II, the last Saxon emperor, dies.

Emboldened by the news of imperial defeat, the Slavic tribes settled between the Elbe and the Oder on Germany's eastern frontier now seized the chance to rebel. This massive and prolonged insurrection was a major setback for the empire, and its active eastward expansion would not be resumed until the 12th century. Otto learned of the rebellion just before his death in Rome in December 983 – and the event was to have long-term ramifications for his three-year-old heir, Otto III.

## OTTO III – AN ENLIGHTENED AND PRAGMATIC RULER

As soon as Otto III started to reign in 996 he demonstrated a deep conviction that Europe formed a unity and that the strength of his *reich* should therefore lie in its acknowledgement of diversity rather than in the imposition of a rigid uniformity. His keen sense of a common European culture was reflected in his veneration for Charlemagne's memory, and it also owed much to his Greek mother, Theophanu. The emperor made Rome his capital, and Pope Sylvester II, his former tutor the French intellectual Gerbert of Aurillac, became a reliable ally in the process of reforming the notoriously nepotistic late-tenth-century Church.

Otto grasped that his forebears' eastern ambitions were beyond the resources of his empire's German core. He also thought it strategically foolish, since the subjugated but hostile peoples might well turn to Byzantium for support. He therefore developed a federal policy for the eastern territories. The rulers of these lands were still expected to honour the imperial title, but they now enjoyed an internal autonomy within a looser structure than Otto I's tight model of subjugation. In Poland, therefore, Otto created an autonomous archbishopric at Gniezno as well as its three suffragan sees at Kolberg, Cracow and Breslau, and he also remitted the tribute payments previously made by Polish rulers to the emperors. These changes demonstrated to the Poles that they could remain part of the religious community of the Latin West without also having to become culturally German. Hungary's ruler, Stephen, was deeply influenced by this example and, encouraged by Otto, he opted for loyalty to the see of Rome when it came to the Christianization of his recently pagan country. Accordingly, he was crowned in about December 1000 as Stephen I, the first king of Hungary, with a crown sent him by the pope.

Otto III died in 1002 after contracting malaria in the marshes near Ravenna. Following his death various factions supported rival candidates for the succession. The year 1002 was marked by violent disputes among the imperial nobility, but the dynastic principle won the day as the best guarantor of order. Thus it was that Henry, duke of Bavaria, a direct descendant of Henry the Fowler, was elected to rule. Henry II had a thoroughly Ottonian view of the Church's role: he wished it to be powerful, and he

OTTONIAN
RULERS
919–1024

**HENRY I**
['the Fowler']
(876–936)
**r. 919–36**

**OTTO I**
['the Great']
(912–73)
**r. 936–73**

**OTTO II**
(955–83)
**r. 973–83**

**OTTO III**
(980–1002)
**r. 983–1002**

**HENRY II**
(973–1024)
**r. 1002–24**

expected it to use that might in support of the empire. Like his predecessors, Henry ruled through the bishops, which is why he opposed the monastic clergy's attempts to establish their own jurisdiction independent of the episcopate. Henry was a genuine Church reformer, but his initiatives also suited his own goals as a strong territorial ruler. The imposition of clerical celibacy, for example, meant that the powerful clergy had no chance to create their own family dynasties.

## FURTHER INSURGENCY IN ITALY

Henry was attracted to Italy for the same reasons as his predecessors: the prestige of an association with Roman antiquity, the power that came with the role of protector of the Church and the opportunity to fight the peninsula's dissident aristocrats. The latest of these rebels was Arduin who, like the equally troublesome Berengar half a century earlier, was margrave of Ivrea. Arduin had seized the opportunity presented by Otto III's death and, like his predecessor, proclaimed himself king of Italy. Henry's army marched into Italy in the spring of 1004 and crushed the margrave's forces at a battle fought near Verona. Henry then marched on to Pavia, where he was crowned king of the Lombards. He then proceeded to burn most of Pavia to the ground as punishment for its past support for Arduin.

It was necessary to embark on a second Italian campaign in 1013 as a result of Arduin's renewed military activities. In the following year Pope Benedict VIII, an imperial ally in the project of Church renewal, crowned Henry emperor. Henry's third, and most ambitious, Italian expedition was the result of a direct appeal from the pope, who feared that Lombard rulers in the south were flirting with Byzantium. Henry despatched three armies to the south in 1022 in order to assert his sovereignty over the whole of Italy. He also took personal charge of the siege of Troia, a fortress on Puglia's northern boundary.

The failure of the siege was a significant setback, but the submission of the rulers of Capua and Salerno demonstrated the empire's continuing ability to enforce its authority despite the daunting task of waging such long-distance wars. Henry died shortly afterwards in 1024 and, since he had no heirs, the line of Saxon emperors lapsed with him. The Ottonian century was over. The German empire's involvement with Italy would, however, be the central drama of European warfare and politics for the next three centuries.

ABOVE *An ink-on-vellum illustration from the* Liuthar Gospels *(c.1000) of Otto III enthroned.*

# THE OTTONIAN ARTISTIC LEGACY

*The Ottonian rulers' artistic patronage was directed towards projects that would illustrate and reinforce their imperial ideology. Religious foundations, such as the Abbey of Corvey in Westphalia and the monastery of Reichenau on Lake Constance, benefited from direct royal sponsorship, and the illuminated manuscripts produced by their scriptoria contain magnificent representations of the emperors being crowned by Christ.*

The style of Ottonian manuscripts built on the earlier Carolingian renaissance, an artistic and literary movement which owed its origins to Charlemagne's patronage. Ottonian art nevertheless contained its own distinctive motifs, often reflecting Byzantine influences.

Itinerancy was an integral part of Ottonian government, and the rulers had no fixed capital. Their power was exercised instead at a number of royal residences, episcopal cities and religious communities, and the journeys they made between these centres were public demonstrations of regal authority. Assemblies, legal proceedings and public ceremonials were held at these buildings while the kings were in residence and, often designed in the Romanesque style, their architecture reflected the Ottonian grandeur. This is particularly true of the great abbey founded at Quedlinburg by Otto the Great in 936 to honour his father's memory. The abbey was home to a community consisting of the unmarried daughters of the higher nobility, and it was here that the *Quedlinburg Annals* were compiled in the early 11th century. The *Annals* provide an account of the reigns of Otto III and Henry II, and the author may well have been a canoness of the community.

The poet and playwright Hroswitha (*c.*935–1002) was a major figure in the Ottonian renaissance, and she spent most of her life as a member of another religious community in Saxony, the Benedictine abbey at Gandersheim. She wrote a series of prose romances as well as six comedies based on the work of the Latin poet Terence. Even a writer as imaginative as Hroswitha could not escape the contemporary impact of Ottonian politics, though, as is shown by her verse eulogy of Otto I and his achievements.

*Quedlinburg Abbey, Germany, founded by Otto the Great in 936.*

# 987 — 1179

# THE RISE OF THE CAPETIANS

*The kingdom of the Western Franks was created by the Treaty of Verdun in 843, and members of the Carolingian dynasty reigned within that territory until the late tenth century. As anointed kings, their authority, like that of their Capetian successors, had a sacramental quality that was acknowledged by the princes who ruled in significant centres of power such as Normandy, Burgundy, Anjou, Poitou and Toulouse. Aquitaine, however, had ceased to be part of the West Frankish kingdom in the early tenth century, and Brittany was entirely independent. Capetian and Carolingian rulers conceded the nobility's right to run their own territories in return for loyalty and military assistance when needed.*

RIGHT *The* Grandes Chroniques de France, *a richly illuminated sequence of manuscripts that relate the history of the French monarchy, were compiled between 1274 and 1461. This detail from the* Chroniques, *dated c.1335/40, shows Hugh Capet at the council of St. Basle, held near Rheims in 991.*

Despite these agreements between kings and nobles, disputes concerning land and influence nonetheless recurred between the monarchy and the effectively independent dynasts. As a result, the kings' unfettered authority was confined to their personal fiefdom or 'demesne' in the Île-de-France, an area of the middle Seine centred on Paris and Bourges where the Capetians actually owned land. The primacy accorded these *reges Francorum* was therefore often merely ceremonial, and until the 13th century – when the title 'king of France' was first used – they struggled to assert themselves.

The Capetian monarchy eventually persuaded the nobility that solidarity with the Crown was in their own best interests, and a more cohesive governing élite emerged as a result. But the evolution of a widespread national identity was a very long-term development in medieval France, as in other parts of continental Europe. The loyalties and identities of the great mass of the population were local and particular rather than general and uniform. Linguistic profusion emphasized further the plurality of cultures which barely communicated with each other. If the north was the land of the *langue d'oil* it was the *langue d'oc* that predominated in the south, and out of these two broad linguistic groups there emerged several distinctive dialects, such as Norman and Burgundian, Provençal and Languedocien. 'Middle French' also existed by the 14th century, but this standardized language made few inroads in the south.

# HUGH – CLAIMANT TO THE THRONE

The Carolingian succession had been usurped on two occasions before the reign of Louis V, the last member of his family to rule in West Francia, with Odo of Paris and Robert I – both members of the Robertine dynasty – reigning as kings in 888–98 and 922–23 respectively. Hugh, the duke of the Franks, belonged to the same family, and his father Robert the Great had been guardian of Lothair IV's estates during the king's minority. Surnames had yet to be established as a general convention in tenth-century Europe, and Hugh 'Capet' owed his nickname to the headship or authority he enjoyed among the nobility who elected him to succeed Louis V in June 987. That prestige came to signify the start of a new phase in the history of kingship in West Francia, and the Capetian dynasty would go on to acclaim Hugh as its eponymous founder.

Hugh's claim to the throne was supported by his cousin Otto II. That family connection had deep roots, since the Capetians' Robertine ancestors had originally been members of the East Frankish nobility before establishing themselves in West Francia by the mid-ninth century. As crowned Roman emperors, the Ottonian dynasty could nominate West Francia's senior clergy, and these placemen enforced their patrons' policy by refusing to back the later Carolingian rulers of the western kingdom. Adalberon, the archbishop of Rheims, was one such nominee and his support for Hugh Capet had been crucial at the assembly of 987. Although Charles of Lorraine – King Lothair's younger brother – had a legitimate Carolingian claim to succeed the childless Louis V, it was not difficult to find reasons why he should be denied a crown. He had falsely accused Lothair's queen of infidelity with the bishop of Laon, and after being driven from the kingdom he paid homage to Otto II who made him duke of lower Lorraine in 977. In the autumn of 978 an invasion force led by Otto and Charles compelled Lothair to retreat to Paris where he was besieged until Hugh Capet's army stepped in and drove the invaders back across the frontier. Charles's ambitions did not cease on Hugh Capet's accession to the throne, however, and he managed to take both Rheims and Laon before he was seized in the spring of 991, after which he died in captivity.

Hugh's determination to secure a dynastic succession meant that Robert II ('the Pious') was elected king during his father's lifetime. But he had argued that the succession needed to be established because he was planning a campaign against the Arab forces that were threatening Borrel II, the count of Barcelona. Hugh may well have seen an opportunity here for an extension of his power, but the nobility refused to support him and the military offensive never materialized. Such an inability to enforce the royal will illustrates the real limits to Hugh's power, as well as explaining the king's anxious eagerness to get his son confirmed as his successor.

## An uneasy peace

In 1023 Robert II and the German emperor Henry II arrived at a landmark decision: they resolved not to pursue claims to each other's territories. Although an agreed boundary between the French kingdom and the German empire was now in place, this early phase of Capetian history remained one of dynastic insecurity. Possessed of so few lands of his own, Robert pursued his rights to any feudal territories that became vacant. However, the fact that these were invariably also contested by other claimants embroiled him in numerous military campaigns. He tried to invade Burgundy in 1003, but it took another 13 years before the Church recognized his title as the duchy's ruler. Furthermore, the civil wars waged against him by his own sons – Hugh Magnus, Henry and Robert – were prolonged and bitter struggles centred on inheritance rights. The dynastic style meant that Hugh Magnus was crowned a king in his father's lifetime, and from 1017 onwards he was co-ruler. But although earmarked for great things, he rebelled against Robert II and after his early death in 1025 the two surviving brothers continued with the campaign. When Henry succeeded to the throne, Robert maintained his dissidence until he was given the dukedom of Burgundy. In an age that was accustomed to violence Robert I of Burgundy remained notable for his uncontrollable behaviour. He set aside his wife Helie of Semur in *c.*1046 and then killed her father – having already arranged for her brother's murder.

The question of how to deal with the increasingly powerful duchy of Normandy preoccupied both Henry I and his two immediate successors. Henry had helped Duke William to assert his authority internally in 1047, when he was threatened by rebel vassals. However, William's marriage to Matilda, daughter of the count of Flanders, threatened the French Crown with a pincer-like alliance, and the two military campaigns that Henry launched in 1054 and 1057 sought to subjugate the duchy. These ended in an unsurprising failure, and Philip I reconciled himself to the reality of Norman power by making peace. The reign of Louis VI nevertheless saw a resumption of the Franco-Norman conflict and a dramatic improvement in the fortunes of French monarchy, along with a vigorous assertion of royal rights.

## The restoration of order in the Île-de-France

By the end of the 11th century large areas of the Capetian demesne in the Île-de-France were controlled by feudal lords who ignored their duties of vassalage and exercised an independent power by illegal and violent means. Although the military campaigns fought by Louis on his own lands lasted some quarter of a century, he had succeeded in reasserting his feudal rights by the 1130s, and orderly government was restored in the royal demesne. Louis's foreign policy was just as strenuous, and here he could take advantage of a split within the Norman élite when William Clito, the son of Robert

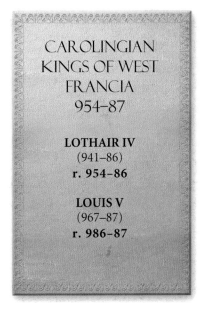

CAROLINGIAN KINGS OF WEST FRANCIA 954–87

**LOTHAIR IV**
(941–86)
**r. 954–86**

**LOUIS V**
(967–87)
**r. 986–87**

ABOVE *The Battle of Val-ès-Dunes, in which Henry I and Duke William quelled a Norman rebellion in 1047, is depicted in this section (c.1335/1340) from the* Grandes Chroniques de France *(1274–1461).*

Curthose, duke of Normandy, rebelled against his uncle Henry I and sought to replace him as ruler of both England and Normandy. In 1124 Louis's army and its allies won a great victory over the forces of Henry V – the German king and emperor who had been persuaded by Henry I that he should attempt an invasion of France. This martial success recalled Hugh Capet's prestige and earned Louis his acclamation as the second founder of his dynasty's authority.

An arranged marriage between Louis's infant son and Eleanor of Aquitaine meant that the French Crown was, for a while, reunited with the duchy of the southwest. That union nonetheless proved to be one of history's most significant *mésalliances* because, following her divorce, Eleanor married Henry, count of Anjou (who was also Normandy's duke, following his father Geoffrey's conquest of the duchy in 1144). Henry's accession to the throne of England as Henry II therefore created the vast power block of the Angevin empire. In theory, Henry held Normandy and Anjou as a vassal of the French monarchy and, since he had married Eleanor without seeking his suzerain's permission, Louis declared war on him. Subsequent defeats showed how much greater were the resources available to Henry, but if Louis could not compete in that particular theatre of war his pro-papal policies gave him a more positive role on the European stage. At the start of his reign he had rejected the papal nominee to the archbishopric of

Bourges, and Louis's territories had therefore been placed for a while under a papal interdict. His intervention in the great quarrel between Pope Alexander II and the German emperor Frederick I Barbarossa nonetheless showed the depth of Louis's attachment to the papal cause. Alexander had been elected pope by a majority of the College of Cardinals, but the minority who supported Cardinal Octavian broke away and elected him as Pope Victor IV. This anti-pope and his two successors enjoyed Barbarossa's support, and the years of Alexander III's exile in 1162–65 were spent in France where he enjoyed Louis's warm support. The alliance between the Church and the French Crown deepened as a result, and the strong identification of the French clergy with the monarchy gave Louis a chain of command that enabled his will to be imposed in areas far from the core royal demesne

## CHRONICLING A TIME OF CHANGE

The fact that both Louis VI and Louis VII survive in the documentary records as real personalities owes much to the pen of the Abbé Suger of Saint-Denis (c.1081–1151), who was a significant courtier by the late 1120s and the monarchy's chief adviser from the mid-1130s until his death. He wrote a history of Louis VII's reign as well as a detailed account of the governmental machinery, and these works in turn inspired the monks of Saint-Denis to embark on the chronicles that give a quasi-official account of the development of the French national monarchy during the 12th century. The challenges facing the kings remained enormous, and Louis VII's participation in the fiasco of the Second Crusade, which had to be abandoned in 1148, undermined the royal finances. But in other respects there was a real change of gear, with the city of Paris evolving both culturally and economically. The commercial quarter known as Les Halles started to operate on the right bank of the Seine during Louis VI's reign. The marshes on the left bank were drained, and this area became the heart of a celebrated academic *quartier*.

The problem of the succession had long tormented Louis VII in a manner entirely typical of his Capetian forebears. Eleanor had born him two daughters, as did his second wife Constance of Castile. It was his third wife, Adele of Champagne, who gave him the son and heir that he craved, however. In 1179, during the last year of his father's life, Philip II Augustus was crowned at Rheims in a ceremony whose precautionary nature would have been well understood by Hugh Capet.

THE EARLY
CAPETIAN
DYNASTY
987–1223

**HUGH CAPET**
(*c.*940–96)
**r. 987–96**

**ROBERT II**
['the Pious']
(972–1031)
**r. 996–1031**

**HENRY I**
(1008–60)
**r. 1031–60**

**PHILIP I**
(1052–1108)
**r. 1060–1108**

**LOUIS VI**
(1081–1137)
**r. 1108–37**

**LOUIS VII**
(1120–80)
**r. 1137–80**

**PHILIP II AUGUSTUS**
(1165–1223)
**r. 1180–1223**

# GOTHIC FRENCH
## ARCHITECTURE

*The abbey of Saint-Denis was a Merovingian foundation, and it was therefore already ancient when Suger decided that the Romanesque structure had to be rebuilt. Suger was the first of the ecclesiastical statesmen who rose to greatness in the service of the French Crown.*

During the five years following his election as abbot in 1122 Suger devoted most of his time to the administration of Saint-Denis, and the extensive account he wrote of the building project also places the abbey in its historical context. As a centre of learning, a royal necropolis and ceremonial setting, the abbey had reflected the policies and supported the interests of successive *reges Francorum*. If Saint-Denis was to remain relevant at the highest levels of government it needed to have a contemporary look, and for Suger that inevitably meant adopting the Gothic style. Suger was also a loyal servant to the monarchy and his work at Saint-Denis had aims similar to those of contemporary French kingship: in both cases the institution's past was being repackaged in order to secure its place in the future. By this time the principles of Gothic architecture typified by soaring spires, lofty rib vaults and pointed arches were being adopted by many of northern France's ecclesiastical foundations, and Saint-Denis would join the ranks of the Gothic masterpieces erected in Chartres, Laon, Bourges and Rheims. Gothic architecture's realization involved complex building plans, material wealth and a well-organized labour force, and the building projects reflected the self-belief of the ecclesiastical and courtly élite who were in overall charge. The fact that 12th-century summers were also proving to be unusually long and warm was an added bonus, and as a result the masons who laboured on site had more time to get the work done. The building of Notre Dame on the Île de la Cité from *c.*1163 onwards was a particularly spectacular example of the organizational capacity and self-confidence of the French monarchy. Maurice de Sully was the bishop who oversaw the work's initial phase and he also started the building of the Hôtel Dieu, a hospital that stood adjacent to Notre Dame.

*The Gothic clerestory of the Basilica of Saint-Denis, in Paris, founded by the Merovingian King, Dagobert I, in the seventh century, and burial place of successive French monarchs.*

# 1066 / 1135 | THE NORMANS IN ENGLAND

*The Norman conquest of the English people is an event without parallel in both the history of England and of medieval Europe as a whole. No more than 10,000 knights – perhaps even as few as 5000 of them – enforced a policy of military subjugation and wholesale expropriation of land in the former Anglo-Saxon kingdom during the generation that followed the Battle of Hastings in 1066, with the leaders of the native population being excluded from public office because of their ethnicity. Often brutal, the conquest of England by the Normans was also efficient and wide-ranging, changing forever the systems of government, social structure and culture.*

The Anglo-Saxon kingdom had been one of the glories of Europe's Christian civilization. When the Viking ancestors of the Normans were starting to penetrate the lower Seine valley in c.900, Anglo-Saxon culture was already ancient. Its leaders could count among their ancestors royal saints and martyrs who were venerated across the continent, and whose witness testified to the sacred nature of the authority that emanated from England's throne. Neighbouring powers admired the royal house of Wessex, England's reigning dynasty since the late ninth century, and marvelled at the efficiency of the tax-collecting bureaucracy that enriched English kings. Eleventh-century Europe supplied abundant examples of native populations subjected to the cruelty and violence of a conquering invader. But they were all pagans, whereas the Anglo-Saxons shared with the Normans the Christian faith. What happened in England during the second half of the 11th century was therefore unprecedented, since it took place within Christendom. Contemporaries noted this fact, and there were also papal protests. But all to no avail. How and why, therefore, did the Normans get away with it?

## THE ADAPTABLE NORMANS

It was the Franks who gave the *Nordmanni* their first opportunity by ceding them lands around the mouth of the Seine in c.911. From this base they extended their grip westward to 'Normandy', which soon became one of the most tightly controlled feudal

states in Europe. Conversion to Christianity and adoption of cavalry warfare did not remove the piratical restlessness that formed part of the Normans' Scandinavian inheritance. The Norman readiness to learn, adapt and assimilate gave them a swift command over conquered territories. Their evolution of the motte-and-bailey castle, a mound surrounded by a ditched enclosure, invariably marked the Normans' implacable territorial penetration. Their championing of religious orthodoxy was typically authoritarian, but their support for Benedictine monasticism, especially the foundations at Bec and Caen, turned Normandy into a pioneering centre of 11th-century scholarship.

ABOVE *A detail of the Bayeux Tapestry depicting Harold, king of England, being hit in the eye by an arrow at the Battle of Hastings in 1066.*

# THE INVASION'S ORIGINS

Norman interest in England dated back to 1002, when Ethelred II married Emma, the daughter of Normandy's Duke Richard. But contemporary Scandinavia had a longer tradition of pursuing ambitions in England. Alfred the Great, king of Wessex, had contained the Danish Viking raiders and then consolidated his authority as ruler right across the English south and west. A century later, however, the Danes resumed their offensive, and the Danish King Cnut became king of England after Ethelred's death in 1016. English, Norman and Scandinavian positioning ensued. Cnut's marriage to the widowed Emma solidified his power base, but their son Harthacnut died after a brief reign. Ethelred and Emma's son Edward had spent long years in exile after joining his maternal relatives in Normandy. His accession to the English throne in 1042 restored the line of Anglo-Saxon kings, albeit with a Norman slant, and Edward 'the Confessor' proved a good patron to the many Norman clergy, soldiers and officials who travelled with him from the duchy to the English court. This clique aroused the antagonism of Earl Godwine, England's pre-eminent aristocrat, who forced the king to dismiss his Norman advisers in 1053. When Edward died without issue at the beginning of 1066 the English aristocracy chose the earl's son and successor Harold Godwinson as king, and he was duly crowned.

The Scandinavian dimension to English kingship had one final card to play: Harthacnut was supposed to have promised Magnus I of Norway that if either died without issue the other would rule as king in both countries. Harald III Hardrada, king of Norway, therefore pursued a claim to the throne, and Harold of England's estranged brother Tostig Godwinson, the earl of Northumbria, supported him. Harold's army gained a great victory over the invading Norwegian army at the Battle of Stamford Bridge near York on 25 September 1066, in the course of which Tostig and Harald Hardrada were killed. Having marched south from Yorkshire to Sussex, the English army was already exhausted when it fought the battle that was joined at Hastings on 14 October and which ended in Harold's defeat and death. The English aristocracy immediately chose Edgar Atheling to succeed Harold, so William still had to fight his way to the Crown. He failed to take London at his first attempt from the east, after which he advanced on the capital from the northwest before eventually receiving the submission of the English aristocracy at Berkhamsted.

ABOVE *Ethelred II, the king dubbed 'unraed' or 'bad advice' by contemporaries, is shown holding a sword in the* Chronicle of Abingdon *(c.1220).*

## TAKING CONTROL OF TERRITORY

The coronation of William as England's new king took place at Westminster Abbey on 25 December 1066. It was the prelude to a series of campaigns of subjugation. In 1067 rebels in Kent attacked Dover Castle and a revolt spread in West Mercia. In 1068 William had to negotiate the surrender of Exeter, and there were further revolts both in Mercia and in Northumbria. Harold's sons were meanwhile raiding the West Country from their new bases in Ireland, and in 1069 a rebellion spread in Northumbria after the massacre of several hundred Norman soldiers garrisoned at Durham. William defeated the northern rebels in battle near York before pursuing the remnants into the city, many of whose inhabitants were then massacred. The arrival of a large Danish fleet off England's eastern coast in the late summer of 1069 inspired widespread English dissidence, and an allied Northumbrian-Danish army defeated the Norman garrison at York before establishing control over Northumbria. William stopped the Danish penetration into Lincolnshire, and after retaking York he bought off the Danes, who agreed to leave England by the spring of 1070. William's army then waged a relentless campaign of devastation across Northumbria in the winter of 1069–70 resulting in a death toll of around 150,000. The following spring saw the Conqueror established in Chester, from where he crushed remaining areas of Mercian resistance. Eastern England saw further resistance, since the Danes initially reneged on their assurances to leave. However, a further payment finally secured their departure. Deprived of Danish support the rebels – led by Hereward ('the Wake') in the Isle of Ely – were crushed in 1071.

Wherever they went, Norman knights wanted two things: land and titles. Those who were prominent in the English campaign were of higher birth than their compatriots who went to southern Italy, and their surnames often reflected the family fiefdoms they already held in Normandy. In an unusual move, William claimed personal possession of all English land, and this meant he could dispose of it as he saw fit. The territories of English nobles who had fought and died with Harold were redistributed among William's supporters. The pattern of confiscations explains the persistence of major anti-Norman revolts that led in turn to even more confiscations during 1067–71. Where a landholder died without issue, William and his barons claimed the right to choose the heir, who tended to be Norman, while widows and daughters who inherited property were often made to marry Norman husbands. William distributed his land-grants so that an individual's holdings were spread throughout the country. A noble who revolted would therefore find it difficult to defend all his territories simultaneously, and the system encouraged group solidarity by bringing the nobility into contact with each other rather than retreating into a regional power base. The loyalty of this élite group meant that William could rule England from Normandy by implementing the practice known as government 'by writ', and this was the system followed by his Norman successors on the throne. After 1072 the king returned to Normandy since his duchy faced serious external threats, and he visited England on just four further occasions.

## THE NORMANS IN ENGLAND

**1042** Edward ('the Confessor') is crowned king of England on returning from his exile in Normandy.

**1066** Following the launch of an invasion force led by Duke William of Normandy, Harold II (Harold Godwinson), last Anglo-Saxon king of England, is killed in battle at Hastings on 14 October. William is crowned king in Westminster Abbey on 25 December.

**1085** King William orders the nationwide compilation of English land holdings which becomes known as the Domesday Book.

**1089** Death of Archbishop Lanfranc of Canterbury, whose revenues are then seized for Crown use by William II (William Rufus).

**1100** Henry I succeeds to the English throne and issues the Charter of Liberties which confirms the nobility in its traditional freedoms.

**1105** Resumption of the armed struggle between Henry I and his brother Robert, duke of Normandy.

**1107** The Concordat of London: the papacy concedes substantial control over the Church in England to the English Crown.

**1135** Anarchy follows the death of Henry I.

# EFFICIENT NORMAN BUREAUCRACY

The Domesday Book, a compilation of land holdings ordered in 1085 by William, records that by this date the native English owned just five percent of their country's territory, and hardly any of them retained public office. The shires or shares were Anglo-Saxon administrative units, and they were run by the shire reeve, or sheriff, who was accountable to the highly effective central bureaucracy with its sophisticated archival system. Henry I established the treasury. Located in Westminster, it became the heart of government, although the institution evolved out of the central accounting office which the Anglo-Saxon monarchy had run in Winchester. Having seized the governmental structure, the Normans bent it to their own will by staffing it with their own people. A few Englishmen were appointed sheriffs, but after 1075 Normans monopolized the earldoms. There was a similar purge among the senior clergy: by 1096 there was not a single English bishop, and very few abbots were English. Loyal churchmen were crucial to England's Norman government and this form of episcopal rule represented an English application of William's methods in Normandy where, personally presiding over synods, he had secured a Church administration notably pliant and free of corruption.

# WILLIAM II AND ROBERT –
## QUARRELSOME BROTHERS

The Conqueror's decision to divide his inheritance between Robert, who became Normandy's duke, and William Rufus, who became England's William II in 1087, also divided opinion among the Anglo-Norman nobility. Those who also held lands in Normandy thought that there should be just one ruler for both areas to counter the risk of divided loyalties, especially since the two brothers were notoriously quarrelsome. The rebellion mounted by some of them against Rufus in 1088 aimed at placing Robert on the English throne. This was swiftly suppressed, however, and in 1091 the king invaded Normandy, forcing his brother to yield some of his lands. The two were subsequently reconciled, and when the duke needed money to go on crusade in 1096 he pledged the dukedom to his brother in exchange for a sum of 10,000 marks. This huge sum amounted to about a quarter of the entire annual revenue raised by the English Crown and was paid by William's imposition of a special tax. William then ruled as regent in Normandy during Robert's absence which lasted until September 1100, a month after the king's death.

William Rufus's relations with the Church were turbulent. The king quarrelled violently with Lanfranc, Archbishop of Canterbury, whose revenues were seized when he died in 1089 and appropriated for Crown use. Lanfranc's successor Anselm maintained his opposition, and on going into exile in 1097 he appealed to the pope for support. But Urban II was involved in a major dispute with the German emperor Henry IV and could ill afford to make another enemy. He therefore endorsed the status quo in England. William made a statement recognizing the pope's authority, and in return he was allowed to keep the revenues of the archbishopric of Canterbury since Anselm remained in exile.

## HENRY I – AN ASTUTE OPERATOR

As William the Conqueror's fourth son, Henry I was not expected to rule either in England or Normandy, and his scholarly education led to him being known as 'Beauclerc'. But he was an acute strategist. Taking advantage of the fact that his brother Robert was away on crusade, in 1100 he seized the royal treasury at Winchester shortly after burying William Rufus there. Since the baronage had colluded with him in sidelining Robert, the king gratified them by issuing the Charter of Liberties, a document that both affirmed aristocratic freedoms and corrected William Rufus's abuses of power. The charter also recorded the king's formal grant of the laws of Edward the Confessor, as amended by William the Conqueror, to the English people. Very little new legislation was in fact issued either by William or his sons, and the Conqueror – a great admirer of Edward's laws – had applied them as the basis of English common law. Formal restoration of these laws proved to be quite compatible with the entrenchment of Norman royal authority, especially through the use of Henry's establishment of the exchequer, an institution specifically designed to combat tax fraud and corruption.

ABOVE *Statue of Henry I of England (r. 1100–1135), Canterbury Cathedral, England.*

Henry's reign marked the high point of the Anglo-Norman dynasty's administrative machine. The Concordat of London (1107) represented a major papal concession to the English Crown's institutional control over the English Church, and Henry's reign witnessed an English assimilation of Norman authority. Unlike his father and brothers, Henry could speak English fluently. Marriage to his first wife linked him with the ancient nobility, since she was Edgar Atheling's niece. Nevertheless, Normandy remained important to him. Robert had first agreed to recognize his brother's right to rule in England, but hostilities then resumed. Although Robert was captured at the Battle of Tinchebrai (1106) and remained a prisoner for the last 28 years of his life, Henry's control of the duchy was not secure until the death in 1128 of Robert's son William Clito. Appropriating Normandy as a possession of the English Crown, Henry ruled the duchy through his title as England's king. Viceroys governed in his name there while he was in England, and when he was in Normandy the close-knit nobility administered his kingdom. These networks had been the very basis of Norman order in England, and though appearing so adamantine, they fractured after Henry's death. The English nobility rejected the claim of Henry's daughter Matilda and placed his nephew Stephen of Blois on the throne in 1135. Anarchy followed, and the Anglo-Norman order that had once seemed so entrenched looked set for dissolution.

# MEMORIALIZING
# EDWARD THE CONFESSOR

*The development of Edward the Confessor's posthumous reputation shows how subsequent royal regimes tried to assimilate the Anglo-Saxon past and sought to ensure its continuity with their own authority.*

An anonymous author in *c.*1067 completed a *Life of King Edward*, commissioned by his widow Edith. The second part of that work describes events that demonstrate the king's holiness and his miracle-inducing prowess. It was this section that was then worked up by Osbert de Clare, a Benedictine monk at Westminster Abbey, in his more explicitly hagiographical *Life* of Edward, which was finished by the late 1130s.

Belief in kings' ability to heal the sick by their touch was widespread in medieval Europe, and episodes that illustrate Edward's powers in that regard are included by de Clare in his *Life* of Edward. As prior, and then abbot, of Westminster, de Clare was a well-connected figure and he spent some time in Rome lobbying for Edward's canonization. Saints were divided into two categories by the medieval Church: martyrs who had died for the faith and confessors who had witnessed to it. The king was formally canonized by the papacy in 1161, and thereby acquired his soubriquet. Edward's remains were then placed in a shrine at Westminster Abbey in a ceremony that took place in 1163 with Aelred (1110–67), abbot of the Cistercian monastery at Rievaulx in Yorkshire, preaching the sermon. Aelred wrote his own version of Edward's life, and his many other works include a *Genealogy of the Kings of the English* which was partly intended to show that Henry II (r. 1154–89) was a true descendant of Anglo-Saxon kings. Henry was a vigorous promoter of Edward's reputation, and by the late 12th century the Confessor was widely recognized as England's patron saint.

Henry III (r. 1216–72) was devoted to the cult of the Confessor, and he decided to honour his predecessor by replacing the original Romanesque structure of Westminster Abbey raised by Edward in the late 1040s with the Gothic building that survives today. He also ordered the construction of a magnificent shrine to replace the earlier one, and the Confessor's body was brought to its new place of rest in a solemn procession on 13 October 1269. Edward III (r. 1327–77), a very martial figure, decided that Edward should be replaced as England's patron saint by George, an obscure soldier saint of the third century who has been linked to the then Greek-speaking eastern region of Asia Minor. But the Confessor was central to the elevated role that Richard II (r. 1377–99) claimed for English kingship and which is illustrated in the Wilton Diptych, commissioned to accompany the king on his travels. On the left the Confessor is joined by John the Baptist and Edmund, king and martyr, as they present the kneeling Richard to the Virgin and the infant Christ who, encircled by angels, are portrayed on the diptytch's right panel. By the side of the Saviour and Virgin stands an angel holding a pennant bearing the Cross of St George. The sense of the scene suggests that the king has presented England into the Virgin's care and protection, and the presence by Edward the Confessor's side of Edmund, the king of East Anglia killed by the invading Danes in 868, is highly suggestive. Edmund was much venerated by the Anglo-Norman aristocracy, and that popularity was used to support the post-Conquest regime's claim that it was offering continuity with the Anglo-Saxon past. On the back of the diptytch a heraldic shield incorporates two coats of arms side by side: that of the kings of England, and that of the Confessor – which was devised for him after his time, since armorial bearings were only invented in the mid-12th century. By such means the Confessor lived on.

*The Wilton Diptych.*

# The birth of the European city-state

## 1073 — c.1300

*From the 11th century onwards urban centres concentrated in central and northern Italy, as well as in parts of France and southwest Germany, were starting to grow both in size and institutional importance. The markets and craft guilds located in these towns and cities were at the heart of Western Europe's economic development, and the new prosperity was reflected in rising population levels. An equally novel movement was evident among citizens who wished to assert greater control over their own destinies: like-minded individuals organized themselves into 'communes', groupings sustained by oaths of mutual defence.*

The 11th century saw the advent of communes in both rural and urban settings. For example, adjacent villages in northern France combined to form communes that guaranteed the security of local roads, and the later Swiss Confederation owed its origin to the communes established in the alpine valleys. But it was the ancient towns built by the Romans that provided the commune with its most characteristic setting with walled fortifications protecting the population from the world outside. The communes helped to give physical security to townspeople and their goods, and also helped safeguard the livelihoods of travellers who were frequently threatened with attacks by bandits – as well as by the assaults of dominant nobles who held themselves to be above the law. A desire for revenge therefore led the communes to launch retaliatory attacks on their enemies, but it was the more political and economic focus of their activity that encouraged greater urban independence.

### TAMING THE ARISTOCRACY

The charters granted to towns by monarchs gave them the right to hold markets and to run their own civic and financial administration without being subjected to interference by local lords. European kings and emperors who wished to elevate their central authority therefore found the towns to be useful allies in a common cause: the attempt at taming the territorial nobility. England's powerful 12th-century monarchy was able

Within the image: DIE STAT NÖRDLINGEN MDXLIX

Gros Sorheim · Clofter · Decking · Enckingn · Lierheim · Heroltingn · Zißwing · Smeiling Hach · Klein Sorheim · Balgheim · Hirnheim Ho · Möting · New pfar · Vnder Reimling · Ober Reimling · S:Emerans Piar · Rehmlinger thor · Carcer · Rabniteni · Ertel thorn · Die Breiw · Berg thur · Carmelite · fingn · Tungertvor · Barnut: · Theatru · Pratũ imperiale · Des Richß wife · Septerno · Mitnacht

to impose its authority without relying on such local alliances, however, and the impact of the communal movement in England was therefore restricted to the work of the guilds that regulated craftsmen and merchants. France's Capetian monarchs came to enjoy a comparable institutional success. But the lack of an equivalent centre of power in Germany and Italy meant that conurbations in these areas became increasingly autonomous. As a result, many towns devised their own, often tightly regulated, internal systems of government.

ABOVE *A map, dated 1549, showing the Bavarian town of Nördlingen whose encircling medieval wall remains in place today.*

## THE GROWTH OF GERMAN TOWNS

The German towns of ancient Roman foundation were mostly in the Rhine and Danube river valleys, and many of these were episcopal sees. During the tenth century successive German emperors had delegated juridical and administrative powers to the bishops who therefore appointed officers in the towns' government. The great walls originally raised to surround these centres of population had in many cases survived, and this explains why the German term *burgh* or fortification was used to describe settlements

that were so clearly divided from the surrounding countryside. Legal offences were more severely punished if they had been committed within this privileged area, and its inhabitants, including those who had fled to the *burgh* from rural areas, could only be prosecuted in the town's own courts. Such arrangements emphasized the ancient towns' special status, and the same provisions would also apply to the new towns established by the bishops and nobility on the lands they owned in the centre of Germany.

Vibrant markets in both these types of German towns, as well as the possibility of practising their skills as craftsmen, encouraged the migration of serfs who often left the rural areas without seeking their lord's permission. Urban courts came to accept the principle that a serf who had stayed for a year and a day within his chosen town was henceforth a free man. Population flows from the countryside increased accordingly, and the attempts by some bishops to continue treating these arrivals as serfs led the emperor Henry V to declare, in his charters for Speyer and Worms, that serfdom should cease in all towns. There was, therefore, a real enough basis to the common

German saying *Stadtluft macht frei* ('city air makes one free'). Thus encouraged at the very highest level of imperial government, the German towns acquired the institutions of self-government, including the *Rat* or town council. Headed by the *Burgermeister* or mayor, they started to create their own legislation and to raise money by imposing an excise duty. Groups of town merchants also began to issue the legislation that governed their trading activities.

## CURBING CLERICAL POWER

Bishops often took a dim view of these developments, and in the 13th century they began lobbying the imperial court to issue decrees limiting the powers of the *Rat*. These attempts at restoring the episcopal initiative proved futile, and the establishment of craft guilds had long since entrenched the cause of town independence among the wider urban population. Craftsmen such as bakers, butchers and shoemakers who brought their produce to markets had been subjected to quality control by town authorities since Carolingian times, and the 'masters' were the individuals who represented their fellow craftsmen at such inspections from the ninth century onwards. These practitioners subsequently claimed the right to elect their master as well as to play a role in framing the by-laws regulating the production and sale of their wares. These successful attempts at self-regulation encountered further opposition from bishops keen on maintaining their own authority. Nevertheless, the craft guilds' societies – sometimes called the *bruderschaft* or fraternity, and which were devoted to social, philanthropic and religious activity – were keenly supported by the Church. Episcopal opposition to trading self-regulation waned accordingly, and the craft guilds that spread from their German origins to neighbouring lands became a distinctive feature of Western European urban existence.

The fact that the bishops owed their original authority in the German towns to an imperial delegation of power proved useful if it became necessary to defend urban autonomy. In 1073, for example, the citizens of Worms rebelled successfully against their bishop in order to provide a place of refuge for the emperor Henry IV at a time when he faced a German princely revolt. Bishops could therefore be reminded on occasions that they were in fact mere representatives of the imperial authority rather than lords exercising power in their own name. The *Vogt* was an official who presided over each town's chief court of law as the senior legal officer appointed by the bishop, but he received the *ban* or power of executing justice directly from the king or emperor. And during the period when the emperor held a diet or imperial council in a particular town, he and his circle of officials resumed control of all the powers that had once been delegated to the locality by his imperial predecessor. The independence of the 'imperial free cities'

### THE BIRTH OF THE CITY-STATE

**1073** The city of Worms affirms its independence by providing the emperor Henry IV with refuge at a time when German princes are rebelling against imperial authority.

**1155** Arnold of Brescia is burnt to death having sought to revive ancient Roman republican institutions while leading the commune of Rome in the late 1140s.

**1162** Following Frederick I Barbarossa's attack on the city of Milan a revolt directed against the emperor spreads to other north Italian towns, that combine to form (*c.*1167) the military alliance known as the Lombard League.

**1176** The Lombard League inflicts a defeat on Barbarossa's forces at the Battle of Legnano.

**1248** The emperor Frederick II is defeated at the Battle of Parma.

**1250** A popular rebellion in Florence expels the republic's nobility from power.

**1294** Election of Benedetto Caetani as Pope Boniface VIII. The pro-papal Guelph party divides subsequently into a 'Black' and a 'White' faction. Black Guelphs support Boniface's interpretation of papal authority. White Guelphs advocate the extension of constitutional rights in Florence.

of medieval Germany, such as Basel, Speyer, Regensburg, Worms and Cologne, was based on these early developments, and their numbers were greatly augmented when the Staufer dynasty established towns on its own demesne land in the 12th and early 13th centuries. Independence nonetheless proved to be quite compatible with oligarchy. A small number of rich families dominated the towns' councils, which included the craftsmen whose guilds sought to exclude competition by adopting protectionist measures.

## ITALIAN CITY-STATES' STRUGGLE FOR AUTONOMY

From the 11th to the 13th centuries northern Italy was Europe's most densely populated region as well as the richest. It was also home to a myriad of vigorously independent city-states, each of which would eventually succumb to a system of political control exercised by a single powerful individual (the *Signoria*) despite the maintenance of republican constitutional forms. Italian political turbulence took its cue from the nobility who, in contrast to their German equivalents, established their headquarters in the towns that consequently witnessed intense conflicts between the *capitani* or greater nobility, the *valvassori* or lesser nobility, and the *popolo* or mass of the population who included affluent merchants.

Lombardy's prosperous and well-fortified towns were in the front line of the struggle to maintain Italian city-state independence against the expansionist ambitions of German emperors. Geography also explains their central economic role. The Po valley connected the trading networks of the Middle East with Western Europe, which was well served by the itinerant Lombard merchants – many of whom also acted as bankers to the Holy See. Temporal authority exercised by bishops was an early casualty of the city-states' assertiveness, but the papacy was nonetheless a willing ally in the joint struggle against the threat from the German north. That danger did not stop these states from competing against each other initially for regional predominance, with the alliance headed by Milan clashing with the group of towns led by Cremona and Como. Frederick I Barbarossa sought to take advantage of this division while pursuing what he took to be his imperial rights in north Italy, but his military onslaught on the city of Milan in 1162 led to a general uprising that united the region in a common hostility. The Lombard League, which included most northern Italian cities, inflicted a decisive defeat on Barbarossa's army at the Battle of Legnano in 1176. Frederick II was subjected to similar humiliation when he insisted on the unconditional surrender of Milan and its allies; his imperial army was routed by the Lombard League at the Battle of Parma in 1248. These defeats were significant economically as well as strategically; military power financed by commercial wealth had proved superior to an army raised by land-based feudal kingship.

The constitutions of the independent Italian city-states at the height of their influence in the 13th century harked back to the peninsula's earlier history of Roman republicanism, with the commune's three components being represented by elected consuls who also presided over the law courts. Sovereignty was vested in a *consilium generale* or popular assembly composed of male citizens who, elected on a franchise restricted by mostly property qualifications, debated issues and selected officials. Service in the local militia was a near universal obligation, and the majority of the male population were therefore involved in public life to some degree. Many of these republics also administered a territory of dependent towns, but most remained small in scale. Florence, with its population of some 100,000 in 1300 was certainly large by contemporary standards; the figure of 15,000 inhabitants for Padua at that time was nearer the average.

Although their constitutions looked republican, the reality was that power at the highest levels within the Italian city-states was almost invariably exercised by a small number of influential individuals. This grouping was itself subject to factional squabbles, but these went some way to being resolved by the appointment of a *podesta* or chief magistrate who came from outside the city and who therefore stood above the locality's quarrelling élite. This official was usually a nobleman and his elevation, as in the case of the Visconti in Milan, the Gonzaga at Mantua, and the Carrara of Padua, led to one-man rule. If this was the characteristic pattern from the late 13th century onwards in the north of Italy, the towns of Tuscany, including Florence, managed to retain not just their communes and consuls but also some of the reality of republican liberty until well into the 14th century. Such republican survivals also preserved the conflicts that had become endemic to these city-state arrangements, and as the commune came under the control of the rich, so the lower orders among the *popolo* started to establish their own organizations. A popular rebellion of 1250 in Florence saw the *popolo* electing their own leader as well as 12 other representatives, and the republic's nobility were expelled from power in the first of a series of revolutions and counter-revolutions that continued for well over a century.

ABOVE *Simone Martini's contemporary portrayal of Guidoriccio da Fogliano, in Siena's Palazzo Publico, shows the Sienese conquest of the castles of Montemassi and Sassoforte in 1328.*

# The Venetian system of government

Venice's steady evolution as an independent state ruled by a close-knit group of patricians gave it remarkable stability. Executive power, the right to summon an assembly (the *concio*), and the appointment of tribunes and justices: all were vested in the *doge* or duke in the early eighth century shortly after the republic asserted its independence of the Byzantine empire. Other Italian city-states might experiment with republican politics, but Venice's ruling class steadily restricted the rights of its subjects.

ABOVE *A presentation is made to the* doge *of Venice in this 1534 painting by Paris Bordone (1495–1570).*

The *concio* was only rarely summoned from the late 12th century onwards. Instead it was replaced by a great council of some 450 members chosen by delegates elected by the city's six wards. This was the body that appointed state officials, and each of the wards also produced a member for the six-man executive council. Eleven aristocrats who were themselves chosen by the nobility elected the *doge* for life, and the fact that no *doge* could elect his successor accentuated the Venetian government's oligarchic nature. In 1296 membership of the great council was restricted to the descendants of a small number of aristocrats. The failure of Bajamonte Tiepolo's 1310 conspiracy to depose the ruling *doge* led to the establishment of the notoriously secretive *Consiglio dei Dieci* or Council of Ten, the executive that really ran Venice from that time onwards.

Unlike other Italian city-states, Venice had not suffered from the intrusions of a rural aristocracy who brought to the towns and cities in which they settled the very substantial baggage of their own well-established patterns of feuding, rivalry and bloodshed. The business of Venice was business. Its aristocrats were not members of a feudal nobility but successful merchants who shared a common interest in commerce and in the maintenance of a stable political regime that allowed them to become even richer. That formidable solidarity created an enduring élite and, since Venice's earliest origins were barely seventh century, the city had no ancient republican history that might be evoked in protest at the irreversible diminution of liberty.

Rome, on the other hand, was the very fountainhead of the republican tradition, but it was the alliance of aristocratic influence with papal politics that predominated in the city's domestic politics. The commune of Rome, under the leadership of the monk Arnold of Brescia, sought to revive the ancient republic in the late 1140s. Cola di Rienzo attempted a similar feat in 1347 by expelling the aristocracy from the city and proclaiming himself a tribune. But these were short-lived experiments that ended in failure. It was tiaras and not tribunes that mattered in medieval Rome.

# Guelphs and Ghibellines

*Aristocratic factionalism, popular rebellions and the relationship between Italian and German culture all combined to ensure the long-term use of the terms 'Guelph' and 'Ghibelline'.* Welf, *the family name of Bavaria's dukes, and* Waiblingen, *the Staufer family's castle in Swabia, may have been used as rallying cries during the Battle of Weinsberg (1140) fought during the German civil war that broke out when these two great dynasties competed for the imperial title.*

The Italian campaigns of Frederick I Barbarossa (r. 1152-90) a generation later saw the two terms crossing the Alps and assuming an Italianate form. Barbarossa was a Staufer and his followers, who embraced the cause of the empire, became known as the Ghibellini. Defenders of the Italian cities' independence adopted the term Guelph as a label describing an anti-Staufer, and hence anti-imperial, position. The papacy's association with the cities in opposing the Staufen meant that Guelph became a label denoting those who supported the papal cause in general. The words subsequently became part of the internal Italian political struggle and were used as party labels with different cities competing against each other in the late 12th and throughout the 13th century.

Geography and strategy, rather than consistent ideology, determined whether a city should be 'Guelph' or 'Ghibelline'. Either label could be used so long as it helped to define and defend a city's pursuit of its independence. A city in the north, where the empire was a real threat, tended to be Guelph. But a central Italian city threatened by an expansion of papal territorial power was more likely to call itself Ghibelline. Size as well as regional position determined affiliations. Florence was far enough from Rome to call itself Guelph, and the much smaller Siena – threatened by the expansion of its neighbour – was therefore Ghibelline.

The removal of the Staufer dynasty from the imperial throne in the mid-13th century ended one particular external threat, but Italy's Guelph-Ghibelline struggle continued. Different occupational groups, guilds and areas within the cities were now using the labels to describe and justify their factionalism, and these vicious conflicts supplemented the traditional intercity struggle. Florence was now riven between the two parties, and it was here that the Guelphs themselves split in reaction to the election in 1294 of Benedetto Caetani as Pope Boniface VIII. Black Guelphs still supported the papacy, but the White Guelphs, who included Dante Alighieri, opposed Boniface's particularly aggressive exposition of the papacy's temporal power. Dante was exiled when the Black Guelphs seized power in Florence in 1302, and his eventual disillusion with the entire political scene supplies the immediate background to his composition *The Divine Comedy.*

*A map illustration of the town of Weinsberg in 1578.*

# 1016 — 1184 | THE NORMANS IN SICILY

*At the beginning of the 11th century Norman mercenaries had begun to reach the southern Italian mainland – a region where the Greek empire was facing rebellions from local Lombard leaders. Conflicts between Lombard princes, as well as the ultimately successful struggle to eject the Greeks from the south, gave the Norman knights their opportunity. In recognition of their military service they were granted fiefdoms that became the basis of their own independent power and led to the establishment of a Norman kingdom that included the island of Sicily as well as the southern Italian peninsula.*

RIGHT *A mosaic depicts the coronation of Roger II by Christ, in the church of St. Mary of the Admiral, commonly know as 'La Martonora', Palermo, Sicily. King of Sicily from 1130, he was the second son of Count Roger I of Sicily (1031–1101).*

Before the Norman intervention, Puglia and Calabria, located respectively at the 'heel' and 'toe' of the Italian peninsula, constituted a Byzantine province. They were separated, however, by the southern half of the independent Lombard principality of Salerno. To the north of these territories lay two other Lombard principalities, Benevento and Capua, as well as the duchy of Amalfi, an area along the western coast that was effectively independent despite owing allegiance to Byzantium. The eastern port of Bari was the Greek province's capital, and the rebellion that started here in 1016 was the first example of military action by a joint Lombard-Norman force. The Greeks retaliated by building the military fortress of Troia at the Apennine Pass in order to guard access to the Puglian plain. This fortification greatly alarmed the papacy which, as the representative of Latin Christianity, had its own cultural and religious reasons for wishing to expel the Greeks from Italy. The earliest Norman mercenaries to arrive in Italy may indeed have enjoyed some papal support as a result. Troia symbolized a resurgent Byzantium, and some Lombard princes had submitted to the Greeks following the counter-offensive. Pope Benedict therefore appealed to the German emperor to send an army to the south, and although the campaign of 1022 failed to take Troia, Henry II was able to reassert imperial authority over his Lombard vassals.

Subsequent military disputes between the Lombards gave employment to opportunistic Norman knights whose sole consistent aim was to prevent the dominance of any single Lombard prince. The year 1030 saw the creation of the first Norman principality in

ΡΟΓΕΡΙΟC ΡΗΞ    ΙC    ΧC

southern Italy when Sergius IV, duke of Naples and a nominal vassal of the Greeks, granted the county of Aversa as a fiefdom to his ally Ranulf Drengot. This concession was a tremendous coup for the Normans, and the county became a convenient rendezvous for the arriving mercenaries. A further honour awaited Ranulf in 1037 when the emperor Conrad II recognized his title and, consequently, the countship of Aversa was held directly from the emperor. In the following year Ranulf invaded Capua, and as a result his territory became part of the Capuan principality.

## THE RISE OF THE HAUTEVILLES

By this stage, however, another Norman clan, the Hauteville family, were having an impact on the south of Italy. Guaimar IV, ruler of Salerno, had employed some of its members in the campaign of 1038–40 waged by the Greek army and his own Lombard force against Arab-ruled Sicily, and William de Hauteville gained his nickname of 'Iron Arm' during that struggle. On the mainland, however, it was the fight against the Greeks that mattered, and a Norman force gained a major victory over the Byzantine army at the Battle of Monte Maggiore, fought near Cannae on 16 March 1041. Guaimar remained a key Norman ally but the mercenaries were also now coalescing around William Iron Arm, and in September 1042 he was elected their leader. The deal that was subsequently struck suited all parties. William de Hauteville and his circle proclaimed Guaimar as 'duke of Apulia and Calabria', while they in turn received lands in the region surrounding Melfi that were divided into 12 baronies and held as fiefs.

The Hauteville brothers, William, Drogo and Humphrey, were therefore now territorial nobles rather than mere mercenaries. Two Norman dynasties had been established in the south, and the de Hautevilles, like the Drengots, became direct vassals of the Holy Roman Emperor. The brothers pursued the southern campaigns against Byzantium, and their victories in Calabria also empowered their half-brother, Robert 'Guiscard' ('the resourceful'), who was destined to take his family's fortunes to new heights. The papacy, alarmed by the rise of Norman power, sponsored a coalition force that included equally disenchanted Lombard leaders, and it was this army that confronted the united Normans at Civitate on 18 June 1053. Robert Guiscard's strategic brilliance and personal bravery played a key role in a Norman victory, and papal realism dictated an eventual rapprochement. In 1057, on succeeding Humphrey as count of Apulia, Robert Guiscard abandoned his loyalty to the empire and became a vassal of the pope, who in return granted him the title of duke.

Richard Drengot had succeeded to the countship of Aversa in 1049, and continued his relative's policy of aggression against neighbouring Lombard territories. He conquered both Gaeta and Capua and then pushed at the Salerno principality's northern borders. As prince of Capua, Richard pursued alternately aggressive and peaceful policies in relation to the papacy whose lands he bordered to the north, but his ineffective successors became dependent on Hauteville patronage by the late 11th century. Benevento to the east of Capua succumbed to the Hautevilles by stages following the victory at Civitate. It then became a base for the clan's penetration of contiguous papal territories that continued until 1080, when the Hautevilles undertook to respect papal territory.

## STRUGGLING FOR CONTROL ON THE ITALIAN MAINLAND

The Salerno principality had enjoyed a long period of splendour and riches under the Lombards. Its subjugation by Robert Guiscard in 1077, along with the conquest of neighbouring Amalfi, gave the Normans their biggest victory so far. The city of Salerno was southern Italy's greatest city and it became a focal point for the exercise of their authority. However, control of Amalfi proved elusive, with revolts and local dissidence only dying out after the duchy's final subjugation by the Normans in 1131.

In the late 1050s, shortly after Robert Guiscard's accession, Puglia seemed securely Norman but the Greeks retained control of much of Calabria, a region where cultural Hellenism ran deep. By 1060 Robert, together with his youngest brother Roger, had taken most of the Calabrian Greek cities, and they agreed to share power in the region. But Byzantium refused to give up without a fight, and the end of the year saw the arrival in Puglia of a large Greek army that then besieged Melfi. In 1061 the two Norman leaders were able to expel this Byzantine force, but the Greek army based at Bari posed a major challenge despite repeated Norman attacks during the late 1060s. Bari was the last outpost of Greek power in Western Europe, and following its seizure in 1071 Norman ambitions seemed uncontainable.

## SICILY – JEWEL IN THE NORMAN CROWN

The island of Sicily's mixed population of Greek Christians, Arabs and Jews were ruled by Arab conquerors who, however, were quarrelling with each other in the mid-11th century. Once again, the Normans took advantage of dissension among a ruling élite. Roger and Robert crossed the straits of Messina in May 1061, with Robert Guiscard having been invested with the (very theoretical) title of 'duke of Sicily' when he became a papal vassal. After conquering and fortifying Messina,

### THE NORMANS IN SICILY

**1016** Outbreak of a Lombard-Norman rebellion in Bari, capital of the Greek empire's province in southern Italy.

**1030** The county of Aversa becomes the first Norman-held principality in southern Italy.

**1041** A Norman army defeats the Byzantine force at the Battle of Monte Maggiore.

**1061** Robert Guiscard and his brother Roger expel a Greek military expedition that had been besieging Melfi, Puglia.

**1071** Bari, the last Western European outpost of Greek power, falls to the Normans.

**1072** Palermo falls to Robert Guiscard, whose brother Roger is then granted the title 'count of Sicily'.

**1077** Robert Guiscard de Hauteville, duke of Apulia, conquers the Lombard principality of Salerno.

**1112** Roger II starts to rule as count of Sicily. He invades Puglia (1126) following the death of its Norman duke, establishes his authority in southern Italy, and is crowned king (1130).

**1184** Constance, the posthumously born daughter of Roger II, marries Henry VI, son and heir to Emperor Frederick I Barbarossa.

their swift progress through eastern Sicily was eased by an alliance with one of the local emirs. But the Norman army was defeated at Enna, the formidable fortress at the island's centre, and evacuation followed. Subsequent campaigns witnessed a deepening of the Norman presence on the island, and in 1072 both the city of Palermo and its military citadel fell to the army commanded by Robert Guiscard. Roger became count of Sicily under his brother's overall suzerainty and was to rule most of the island with the exception of Palermo and half of Messina, where Robert retained authority. Arab occupation nonetheless remained widespread, and Roger's subsequent successes over the local emirs at Trapani in 1077 and at Taormina in 1079 had to be supplemented by a systematic campaign of conquest that started in 1085. Syracuse only capitulated in the spring of 1086 after a year-long siege, and Sicily could not be said to be securely Norman until the fall of Noto in the island's southeast in 1091.

While Roger was consolidating Norman Sicily, his brother had been pursuing his ambitions across the Adriatic in the Greek-controlled Balkans. Robert Guiscard's army left Brindisi in May 1081, and the battle fought in October at Dyrrhachium against the Greek army led by the emperor Alexius ended in one of the greatest of all Norman victories. The prospect of a Norman being enthroned in Constantinople now seemed realistic, but at this crucial juncture Robert returned to Rome to support Pope Gregory VII, who was being besieged by the German emperor Henry IV. Robert's son Mark Bohemond conquered Thessaly but failed to maintain authority over the Norman conquests of 1081–82. Robert himself died in 1084 while attempting to restore Norman control in Corfu and Cephalonia, and Bohemond returned to Italy where he and his half-brother Roger Borsa were disputing the succession to their father. The island of Sicily was the jewel in what became the Norman's Mediterranean crown, and Count Roger's son, who shared his name, succeeded to the title in boyhood before assuming the reins of

BELOW *The 12th-century Norman Castello di Venere in Erice, Sicily, is built on a sheer cliff face, an ideal situation for a defensive fortification.*

government in 1112. Roger II then sidelined his Guiscard cousins who were facing baronial rebellions in their south Italian domains. Having given them military support, he received in return control of their Sicilian territories. Roger had inherited Calabrian territories from his father, and in a dramatic move he invaded Puglia in 1126 following the death of its Norman duke. Southern Italy was now his, and Roger subsequently gained the authority unique to a king. In 1130 there was a disputed papal election and Roger supported the rebel pope Anacletus II, whose emissary duly crowned him that year in Palermo. After Anacletus died in 1138 Roger captured the rival pope Innocent II, who then obliged him by confirming the kingly title in 1139.

The papacy's Sicilian association had been unusually close ever since Urban II appointed Roger I an apostolic legate in 1098. This gave the count the right to appoint bishops and collect church revenues in the island but, far from being a concession of its authority, the papacy saw it as a mere expedient. Arab emirs had ruled the island for centuries, and even under Roger II western Sicily's population was heavily Arabic. The Church therefore could not enforce Latin Christianity on its own, and the Norman rulers oversaw the new episcopal administration established at Palermo, Syracuse and Agrigento. Nonetheless, the papacy insisted that kings of Sicily were its vassals and that the office of apostolic legate, claimed by Roger II as his father's successor, could not be inherited. Still, Roger now had his crown, and popes agreed that Roger was 'king of Sicily, of the duchy of Apulia, and the principality of Capua'. In 1131 he established military control over Amalfi which, although part of Norman Puglia since 1073, had tried to retain some autonomy. In 1139 the duchy of Naples was incorporated within Roger's kingdom, which by now was a major European power.

## IMPOSING BUREAUCRATIC POWER

Roger II's strategies had one consistent aim: that his kingdom should be run as a single and independent territorial unit. He might delegate some powers to feudal lords, but military service was expected in return. Furthermore, since Roger controlled the rights of inheritance to fiefs, he could bar vassals he deemed unsuitable. Only the king's courts, rather than those of abbots and counts, could try capital cases. Justiciars – judges appointed by the Crown – travelled into the remote southern Italian countryside to dispense Roger's justice. Baronial power remained significant on most of the mainland, but things were different on the island of Sicily and in Calabria. Since most of the island consisted of royal demesne land under direct government control, the king was also its landlord. A Norman bureaucracy controlled the towns' administration, the activities of their merchants and the organization of supplies. The monarchy also had extensive rights over salt production, while iron and steel manufacture was an exclusive regalian right. This gave Roger an unusually concentrated degree of economic power regulated by a civil service built on Norman foundations and supplemented by Greek and Arab influences.

The emperor Justinian's heritage was a major intellectual resource for Roger, since his jurists showed how rebellion against a divinely instituted ruler was a form of sacrilege. The emperor's law codes – the basis of Roman law – were circulated widely in 11th-century southern Italy, and they heavily influenced Roger's own code promulgated at the Assizes of Ariano in 1140. Notions of lordship, by now common in Western Europe, could also be pressed into service. In 1129 Roger assembled his barons at Melfi in central southern Italy and proclaimed a land peace at this *parliamentum* or gathering of nobles. This was a very Norman baronial endorsement of a feudal overlord. And the mixture of influences deployed to confirm Roger's rule did not end there. If he seemed like a Greek *basileus* or king to his Greek subjects, his Arab ones looked on him as the latest emir set over them.

Sicily's agricultural fertility and buoyant trade produced the revenues that enabled Roger to reign over the Mediterranean's most sophisticated courtly milieu. His monarchy also bribed on a grand scale – especially in Lombardy where Sicily needed the local towns to maintain their resistance to the encroaching German emperors. If Lombardy fell, it was thought that Sicily would be next. The marriage in 1184 of Roger's posthumous daughter Constance to Henry VI, son and heir to the German emperor Frederick I

# A POLICY OF LATINIZATION

*Sicily's unusually polyglot nature meant that Roger's government had to issue its documents in Greek, Latin and Arabic if the king's will was to be understood. The cultural variety of his kingdom was further reflected in its ruler's harem, Saracen bodyguard and Arab chef. Muslim poets benefited from royal patronage, and Sicily was an important 12th-century centre for the translation of Greek texts into Latin. Roger's chief intellectual interest lay in science, and he commissioned the north African Muslim al-Idrisi to produce the* Kitab Rujar (Book of Roger), *which aimed to describe the known world's natural resources.*

Royal policy was, nonetheless, directed towards making Sicily culturally more Latin at the expense of its earlier Arab and Greek components, and Roger's aims were hardly multicultural. The king's smattering of Arabic helped him to negotiate trade agreements with the Fatimid rulers of Egypt, and he promoted some Muslims at his court. That patronage was, however, Roger's method of keeping the local Greek and Norman nobility in their place, and Muslims promoted to the highest levels in his service were expected to convert to the Latin church. Palermo's Palatine Chapel shows the Sicilian cultural mix: a Latin church design, a typically Arabic stalactite roof, and Byzantine mosaics that portray Roger as a new David returned to rule on Earth. He claimed

*This disc is the preface to Muhammad al-Idrisi's world atlas, the* Tabula Rogeriana, *which was produced in 1154.*

to rule as God's own deputy within the Sicilian kingdom, and when attending major church services Roger was both dressed as a king and robed as a priest. On these high festivals he wore a tunic and dalmatic made of Sicilian silk. The king's mantle, just like his silk shoes and stockings, was deep red – a colour evoking the purple worn by the emperors of ancient Rome and Byzantium. The royal tombs he commissioned made the same insistent point, since they were made of porphyry, the purple marble used by Roman emperors. Roger's calculated fusion of temporal might with spiritual authority was intended to inspire awe, and the zest with which he developed the iconography of power showed a typically Norman blend of wiliness and aggression.

Barbarossa, changed the political and military landscape of the central Mediterranean. Sicily and the empire were reconciled by a personal union between the dynasty of Sicilian Normans and that of the Staufen, although Sicily's Crown retained its independence within the empire. The marriage produced the emperor Frederick II, who inherited the abilities of both his grandfathers as well as their defining ambitions: Barbarossa's southward thrust into Italy and Roger's exalted notion of a supreme kinship.

# 1071 — 1109 | THE FIRST CRUSADE

*In March 1095 ambassadors from the Greek emperor Alexius I Commenus delivered a message to Pope Urban II, who was presiding at the Church council convened in Piacenza. The Byzantine empire had lost most of Anatolia to the Seljuk Turks following the Greeks' defeat in the Battle of Manzikert (26 August 1071), and Alexius wanted Western military aid in order to regain his lands. His emissaries had also been instructed to remind the pope and council that Jerusalem was Muslim-controlled, and that Western pilgrims' access to the Holy City was being frustrated as a result. This call to arms was to lead to the series of fierce struggles between Christian and Muslim forces known as the crusades.*

When the Greek emperor Alexius requested military aid to help expel the Muslims from Jerusalem, his timing could not have been better. Seljuk princes were quarrelling among themselves, and the Turks' advance had stalled. The papacy's confrontation with the German empire was proof of its new self-confidence, and relations between the Greek and Latin Churches were once again relatively amicable. The East-West split had become a formal schism in 1054, and the Greeks were resolute in denying primacy to the Roman see over their patriarchates at Constantinople, Nicaea, Antioch and Jerusalem. Following his election to the papacy Urban was, however, keen to end the divide. He had lifted the sentence of excommunication imposed on Alexius by Gregory VII and was also sympathetic to the plight of Greek Christians subjected to persecution by the Turks.

## HOLY WAR

The pope's formal and public response to Alexius's missive came in November 1095 at the synod held in Clermont in the Auvergne. Urban had spent the intervening months in his native France drumming up support for intervention in Palestine and Syria. His discussions with Adhemar, the bishop of Le Puy, as well as with Raymond IV of Toulouse, prepared the ground for his announcement at Clermont, and their influential support gave a powerful leadership in southern France to the crusading cause. Urban's impassioned speech of 27 November proclaimed the vision of an armed pilgrimage

whose adherents would fight for the liberation of the holy places. His statement guaranteeing that the pilgrims' sins would be remitted if they died fighting for so sacred a cause gave an original, and highly appealing, twist to this declaration of war. From late 1095 onwards the message was spread by the clergy not only in the rest of France but also in Italy and Germany. Most who 'took the cross' were poor and pious peasants, and their vow committed them to a pilgrimage that would only end on arrival at Jerusalem's

ABOVE *Pope Urban II presides over the Council of Clermont in 1095, as shown in this manuscript of* Livres des Passages d'Outre-mer, *c.1490.*

THE FIRST CRUSADE    49

Church of the Holy Sepulchre. During 1096 a group of knights and nobles emerged to lead and organize the vast and French dominated army of devout peasants that had been created so suddenly.

This, then, was the crusade that would lead to the establishment of the kingdom of Jerusalem, the principality of Antioch, and the counties of Tripoli and of Edessa. These crusader states would help to relieve Byzantium of the pressure it had been under in the late 11th century, while the Greeks re-established control of much of Western Asia Minor. However, the victorious Latins refused to hand back to the Greeks territories in Palestine and Syria that had been in Byzantine control before the Arab armies' seventh-century conquests in the region. Western European rulers would direct eight further crusades towards the Middle East in the next two centuries, but none enjoyed the success that came to the first of these ventures – a campaign whose mass appeal surprised even its own leadership.

ABOVE *15th-century woodcut engraving of Godfrey of Bouillon arriving in Jerusalem on horseback in 1099.*

Following the Battle of Manzikert, the Greek empire was mostly confined to the Balkans and a narrow strip of land in northwest Anatolia. But the Seljuk Turks failed to maintain a co-ordinated impetus, and in the 1090s there were separate, and often quarrelsome, principalities located in Anatolia, Aleppo and Damascus. Further south the Seljuks confronted a major enemy in the Fatimids, an Arab dynasty that had ruled Egypt since the late tenth century and which had subsequently expanded into parts of Palestine. The Fatimids' regime seems to have been a tolerant one so far as Christian areas within Palestine were concerned. However, their Shiite Muslim faith divided them from the Seljuks – who were followers of Sunni Islam – and the military conflict between the two powers caused massive disruption to the Christians of the Palestinian region. Jerusalem was Fatimid controlled until the early 1070s, and the dynasty regained the city from the Turks in 1098, just before the crusaders' arrival. It was the Turkish occupation of Anatolia and the Syrian south that formed the immediate background to the First Crusade. Accounts of the suffering inflicted on the regions' Christians reached Western Europe and gained a wide circulation by the 1090s. But the Seljuk occupation of Palestine from *c.*1073 onwards had a similarly destructive impact on Christian lives and property.

## CRUSADER ARISTOCRATIC FAMILY CONNECTIONS

In the early 1080s Bohemond, prince of Taranto and the son of Robert Guiscard, had directed his fellow Normans' campaigning against Byzantine lands in southern Italy. He was joined on the crusade by his nephew, Tancred. Although Bohemond had carved out a small principality for himself in the Italian south, he hoped to take over a larger one while on crusade. Godfrey of Bouillon also joined the crusade, despite having been a supporter of the emperor Henry IV in the imperial struggle against the papacy. He was joined in the venture by his brother, Baldwin of Boulogne. The other major leaders joining the crusade included: Hugh of Vermandois, who was the younger brother of King Philip I of France; King William II of England's younger brother Robert of Normandy; Count Robert II of Flanders; and the Count of Blois, Stephen II, who was married to William the Conqueror's daughter.

## THE 'PEOPLE'S CRUSADE'

The crusader forces were due to congregate in Constantinople in mid-August 1096. But the enthusiasm engendered by Urban's call to arms led many peasants to form their own crusading organizations. Peter the Hermit, a priest from near Amiens, was the most celebrated of the many populist preachers who travelled through France advocating a crusade. In the spring of 1096, assisted by a few knights, he was leading thousands of illiterate peasants towards the east when some of their number massacred Jews in the Rhine valley – an area that was the scene of much anti-Semitic violence in 1095–96. In fact, Peter's unofficial 'People's Crusade' posed a threat to public order, and it provoked counter-attacks by the armies of both the Hungarians and the Greeks as the rabble advanced towards Constantinople. An alarmed Alexius ferried Peter's army across the Bosphorus as quickly as possible, and most of the force was slaughtered by the Turks at the Battle of Civitate in October.

## NICAEA AND ANTIOCH – DECISIVE SIEGES

Alexius was also keen to be rid of the official crusading army, which was camped outside his capital's walls in the winter of 1096–97. Hungry crusaders were already pillaging in the outskirts of Constantinople. Alexius had no interest in joining them, but he did expect the leaders of these Latins to swear fealty to him in return for food and military supplies. Raymond of Toulouse would only go as far as promising not to damage the Greek empire's interests. Eventually, however, all the other crusade leaders agreed to the oath, and in the opening months of 1097 the entire expedition, accompanied by two Greek generals, was transported to Asia Minor.

### THE FIRST CRUSADE

**1071** Following the defeat of the Byzantine army at Manzikert, most of Anatolia is controlled by the Seljuk Turks.

**1095** At a synod held in Clermont, Auvergne, Pope Urban II launches a campaign for the liberation of the 'holy places' in Syria and Palestine.

**1097** A crusading army is transported from Constantinople to the shores of Asia Minor: Nicaea's Turkish garrison surrenders (19 June), and by October the crusaders are besieging Antioch.

**1098** Establishment of the county of Edessa, the first crusader state. Antioch falls (June).

**1099** The crusading army arrives at the walls of Jerusalem (early June) and besieges the city. Jerusalem falls (15 July). Godfrey of Bouillon is elected to rule the city, and establishes the Principality of Galilee and the county of Jaffa as territorial components within what will become known as the 'Latin kingdom of Jerusalem'.

**1100** Baldwin, count of Edessa, succeeds his brother Godfrey and is crowned king of Jerusalem.

**1103** Raymond of Toulouse launches a military offensive in the Lebanon against the emir of Tripoli. His son Bertrand continues the campaign after Raymond's death (1106) and, following the emir's surrender (1109), a county of Tripoli is established.

The ancient Christian city of Nicaea, captured 20 years earlier by the Seljuk Turks, was now the capital of their Anatolian principality, the Sultanate of Rum. It was subjected to a month-long siege and Alexius, encamped some distance away, supplied the crusaders with military reinforcements. The Greek general Manuel Boutoumites received the surrender of Nicaea's Turkish garrison on 19 June. Boutoumites was named *dux* or duke of Nicaea, and the city once more became part of Byzantium's empire.

The crusading army, now divided into a Norman component led by Bohemond and a French division led by Raymond, advanced across the Anatolian plain. On 1 July, at Dorylaeum, the reunited army gained its first victory in battle over the Seljuk Turks, but further progress was slow. The local population were mostly Christian and therefore friendly, but lack of supplies still meant that the crusaders had to resort to pillaging and looting. Leadership quarrels were also emerging, and Baldwin of Boulogne separated from his colleagues. The kingdom of Cilicia (in modern southeast coastal Turkey) was a recent foundation established by Armenians fleeing from the Seljuk invasion, and this Christian state would be a strong ally of European crusaders. To its east lay Edessa – another region populated by Armenians but ruled by Thoros, a local nobleman alienated from his subjects by his Greek Orthodox religion. Thoros was first persuaded to adopt Baldwin as his heir and was then assassinated – possibly by his protégé, who duly succeeded him as ruler in March 1098 and then took the title of count.

The first of the crusader states had therefore been established, but by now the main body of the crusading force was facing the immense challenge of Antioch – a city that had been heavily fortified by the Byzantines for centuries and whose walls were guarded by the Turks after its occupation in 1085. During the eight-month siege that started in October 1097 the crusaders defeated two major expeditionary forces sent by the princes of Damascus and Aleppo to relieve the city's defenders. When Antioch fell in June 1098 a bloody massacre of its inhabitants followed. Internal rivalries within the Seljuk army that arrived shortly afterwards to besiege the city led to another major Christian victory.

The crusade's military commanders continued to quarrel, however, and Adhemar's death in August deprived the expedition of a significant spiritual leader and shrewdly political counsellor. Bohemond now contended that Alexius had deserted the crusade and that the oaths sworn to the Greek emperor were therefore invalid. Raymond of Toulouse was among those who objected to Bohemond's territorial claim to the defeated city, and the crusade came to a halt in the remaining months of 1098. Both pilgrims and knights became increasingly resentful at the delay, and it became critical for the dispute to be resolved. The resolution came early in 1099; as the expedition resumed its march to the south and towards Jerusalem, Bohemond was left behind in possession of Antioch as its prince.

It was a ragged, fractious and hungry army – reduced perhaps to a quarter of its original strength – that arrived outside Jerusalem in early June. A prolonged siege was therefore out of the question, and the Fatimid occupiers easily repulsed the crusaders' initial full frontal assault. The arrival of a party of Genoese sailors in mid-June transformed the situation, however, since their engineering skill and timber supplies enabled siege towers to be built.

*ABOVE An illustrated poem 'Estoire d'Outremer' by William of Tyre (c.1130– c.1185) depicting the Siege of Antioch, which began in October 1097.*

## THE BATTLE FOR JERUSALEM

On 13 July 1099 the final assault began, although even then the organization of troops reflected differing group loyalties. Raymond's southern French troops were massed by the south gate, while Godfrey of Bouillon and Tancred were among the commanders gathered at the north wall. The final push of 15 July was, however, a co-ordinated exercise, and the crusaders breached both the northern and the southern defences. Atrocious scenes followed, with Muslims and Jews being put to the sword. Jerusalem's population of Greek Christians had already been expelled from the city at the start of the siege, otherwise they, too, would probably have been massacred. A large number of Muslims had fled to take refuge in the Al-Aqsa mosque located on the Temple Mount.

Tancred initially offered them his protection when calling a halt to the slaughter on 15 July, but then had them killed the following day. Jerusalem's synagogue was burnt to the ground by the crusaders, and Jews who had sought safety inside the building were killed.

Jerusalem would be organized as a kingdom. But was it seemly that the city where Christ the King had worn his unique crown of thorns should be ruled by a prince whose title would also be that of king? Raymond of Toulouse and Godfrey of Bouillon, the two leading candidates for Jerusalem's leadership, both had reservations on this point. (Both also recognized the political expediency of advertising so pious a reluctance.) When the crusaders' council met at the Church of the Holy Sepulchre on 22 July its members elected Godfrey to be the secular leader of Jerusalem, and he would rule without holding a kingly title. In a fit of anger Raymond led his men from the city. On 12 August, at the coastal site of Ascalon, Godfrey's authority and the kingdom's security were confirmed when the forces of Christian Jerusalem defeated the coalition force led by Fatimid Egyptian commanders. The enmity between Raymond and Godfrey stopped the crusaders from capturing the city of Ascalon itself, but Jaffa, Tiberias and Haifa were among Godfrey's subsequent conquests during his brief period as ruler. Furthermore, his creation of the Principality of Galilee and the county of Jaffa laid the foundations of a system of vassalage within the kingdom's enlarged boundaries. Following his death in July 1100 Godfrey was succeeded by his brother Baldwin of Edessa, who had no qualms about being crowned king.

The great majority of the First Crusade's partisans who made it to Jerusalem were back home by 1100, leaving no more than a few hundred knights behind in the new kingdom. Many crusaders had returned home before Jerusalem's capture, however, and they were keen to regain their honour by fulfilling the vow made when they took the Cross. Many of them, including Stephen of Blois and Hugh of Vermandois, therefore joined the further expedition that was launched in 1101. Most members of this subsidiary crusade, including Hugh, were slaughtered by Seljuk Turks while crossing Anatolia, and it was a mere remnant that arrived in Jerusalem by Easter 1102.

Raymond of Toulouse's ambition to rule his own crusader state led him to launch an offensive in the Lebanon against the emir of Tripoli in 1103. Following Raymond's death in 1106 his son Bertrand continued the campaign and, following the emir's surrender in 1109, he became ruler of the county of Tripoli – the last of the crusader states to be founded in the Levant. Latin princes therefore controlled the entire eastern Mediterranean coast by that stage, and the greatly weakened Seljuk Turks no longer bore down on the Greeks as heavily as had been the case in the 1080s. Islamic civilization, however, regarded the crusader states with a sense of shame mixed with anger. The question now was how best to beat the infidel on the doorstep.

# NEW CULTURAL OPPORTUNITIES

*Although the crusading story is dominated by war, it also marked the beginning of a new phase in the history of the cultural relationship between Latins, Greeks and Muslims. La Chanson de Roland (The Song of Roland) was circulated in manuscript form in 12th-century France, and these copies incorporate references to Outremer, the crusaders' name for Palestine.*

But there was an earlier oral tradition behind the *Song*, and the celebration of Roland as a self-sacrificial Christian hero is a literary anticipation of the crusading ideology. Settlers in the crusader state brought Western attitudes with them while also being affected by an international milieu. Crusaders who stayed, and their descendants, often learned Greek and Arabic. Intermarriage with Muslims who had converted was exceptional but more frequent in the case of Greek, Syriac and Armenian Christians. Information about Outremer circulated in the West, and William of Tyre (*c.*1130–86), archbishop of that see and before then chancellor of Jerusalem, produced a magnificent account of 12th-century Outremer in his *Historia rerum in partibus transmarinis gestarum* (*History of Deeds Done Beyond the Sea*). Born and raised in Jerusalem, and then educated at Paris and Bologna, William wrote as a Latin Christian, but his account of both Greeks and Muslims shows a nuanced appreciation of cultures very different from his own. East-West trading contacts, aided by the presence of many Italian merchants, acquired a new vitality as a result of the crusader states' foundation. Northern European woollen textiles appeared for the first time in the Middle East, and Palestine – which had been a commercial centre for

*An illuminated detail from the* Grandes Chroniques de France, *depicting an episode in* La Chanson de Roland.

centuries – acquired new European markets. Sugar, lemons and melons, cotton, muslin and damask, powder, glass mirrors, and even the rosary – all made the journey from East to West and ensured that the crusades created a new appetite for luxury as well as spreading a taste for war.

# THE INVESTITURE CONTEST

## 1024 — 1125

*The late 11th century saw a new and explosive issue arise in European politics: whether it should be kings or popes that had the right to appoint the senior clergy. Up until then* sacerdotium *and* imperium *(spiritual power and temporal power) had barely been distinguishable from each other. The empire presided over by German princes had been a particularly strong papal ally. In turn, successive popes endorsed the imperial campaign to convert and colonize the pagan populations to the east, and the senior clergy of the German Church – who were frequently noblemen and invariably appointed by the princes – played a key role in administering the* reich *or empire.*

Family connections and the politics of patronage had created a close-knit imperial governing circle by the late 11th century, but now the stability of this élite was first threatened and then undermined by the papacy's assertion of its own independent power and rights. The contest over the right to 'invest' or appoint senior clergy raised momentous questions about the nature of power, the basis of obedience and the legitimacy of government itself. Although its impact was greatest within the empire, the investiture struggle also acquired a pan-European dimension. It formed a major chapter in the development of public opinion, with both sides deploying speeches, sermons and texts in order to gain popular support. The papacy's stance was startlingly novel, and its opponents had to counter it with explicit statements defining the basis of regal power.

The wide-ranging assertion of papal authority instigated by Pope Gregory the Great (590–604) was the inspiration for reformers who now reacted against the papacy's recent stance. Aristocratic factions in Rome and Italy had turned the papal office into their plaything in the tenth century, and the 'Gregorian' reform movement's pronounced idealism proposed a different path. The reformers asserted that it was God's will that all mankind should be embraced within one Christian structure, and since the Church was the divine instrument charged with implementing such a vision, its authority was supreme over all forms of secular power. Providence allowed kings and princes to have

RIGHT *A copperplate painting of Pope Gregory VII from Salerno Cathedral, Italy, which he consecrated in 1085 and where he is also buried.*

their *imperium*, but they were subject to the papacy that, as the central and governing Church institution, existed on higher spiritual and moral planes. Successive legislative initiatives from the mid-11th century onwards sought to implement this lofty vision and succeeded in creating a new body of canon law.

## Hildebrand – eloquent champion of the Church

The intellectual vigour and brisk administrative style of Hildebrand, the son of a blacksmith, brought a meritocratic edge to the papal confrontation with Europe's lay princes. Hildebrand bore the imprint of the great abbey at Cluny, the Benedictine foundation that spearheaded monasticism's revival in Western Europe. His earlier career as a papal administrator, which included a period serving as legate in Paris, showed the same reformist zeal he would later display as Pope Gregory VII (1073–85). When the Roman aristocracy reverted to their old ways and elected their own candidate as pope, it was Hildebrand who led the papal army to victory on the island of Corsica where the unfortunate Benedict X had taken refuge. His eloquence made him the natural spokesman for the Gregorian movement's distinctive causes – including clerical celibacy, which was seen as a way of nurturing collective self-confidence and entrenching the distinction between ecclesiastical and secular government. Church centralization meant that contentious cases had to be referred to Rome, and this irritated the many bishops who campaigned against this curtailment of their influence. By 1059 Hildebrand was serving as archdeacon in the city of Rome where he became a popular figure among the local population. The papacy of Alexander II saw a widespread implementation of the reform movement's objectives, including restricting the right of papal election to the College of Cardinals. This denied the emperor his previous right to nominate a candidate – a measure that was central to the restoration of the Church's independence. Hildebrand's own accession to the papacy owed much to the support expressed for his candidacy on the streets of Rome, where a series of popular acclamations preceded his election by the cardinals on 22 April 1073.

Simony involved the buying of Church offices, and Gregory was as devoted to its eradication as European monarchs were to its preservation. It was a good source of revenue and, for the imperial territories in particular, simony helped to ease the appointment of rulers' relatives and supporters as bishops and abbots. In 1074 Gregory's first council condemned simony in general and confirmed that celibacy should now be the rule for all clergy. A second council held in the following year stated that only the pope could appoint churchmen to their offices or move them from see to see. The German territories would be the testing ground for the implementation of these policies, and the newly elected emperor Henry IV was already having difficulty asserting his authority.

# HENRY – A WEAKENED MONARCH

Henry's childhood and youth had been turbulent, and the king's headstrong temperament compounded his problems in the 1080s. Crowned king of the Germans as an infant in 1054, he succeeded to his father's throne on Henry III's sudden death three years later. The regency of his mother, the dowager empress Agnes, weakened her son's position by assigning Bavaria, Swabia and Carinthia to nobles who were intent on reducing the infant king's authority. Moreover, papal policy was already intent on interfering in the election of German bishops. In 1062 Henry was kidnapped by a group of noble conspirators led by Arno II, the archbishop of Cologne, who then took over the reins of power and supervised the young king's education. Henry asserted his independence of that tutelage when he came of age, however, and he was enthroned at the age of 15 in 1065. In 1068 he attempted to divorce his wife Bertha but had to yield in the face of papal opposition. This only strengthened his suspicion of the papacy as an institution. At the same time Henry was facing major challenges to his rule. He confronted Slavic incursions, which included a major siege of Hamburg, and he had to quell revolts led by Rudolf of Swabia and

Berthold of Carinthia. His conflict with Otto of Nordheim, duke of Bavaria, occupied Henry for years. Otto had been involved in the earlier kidnapping of the young king and, following accusations of further plotting, in 1070 Henry declared the duke to be deposed and took the opportunity to plunder Otto's estates in Saxony. Otto had enough support, however, to sustain a rebellion in Thuringia as well as in Saxony until his submission in 1071. Henry was an unpopular figure among the Saxon population at large, since he had ordered the restoration of all Crown lands in the region and had built a series of fortifications there in an attempt to cow the local population. From 1073 until 1088 Henry was forced to deal with major insurrections among both the Saxons and the Thuringians.

Pope Gregory was therefore confronting a weakened monarch, and the Church Councils' decisions meant, in effect, that the German Crown was threatened with the removal of the rights to about half of all its lands. Since Henry also ruled as king of Italy, there were major implications for the dispersal of power in the peninsula. Henry was right to see the papal policy as an attempt at delegitimizing him as king, and the authority of the German Crown would have collapsed if the bishops had removed their

*ABOVE In this illustration from the* Life *of Matilda of Tuscany, written by her courtier Donizo of Canossa and completed by 1115, the excommunicated Henry IV is on his knees. He is begging Matilda and Abbot Hugh of Cluny to intervene on his behalf in the conflict with Pope Gregory VII.*

allegiance. The king, however, carried on nominating his candidates to German and Italian sees. Furthermore, he declared the new conciliar and papal decrees to be illegal. After Gregory excommunicated several members of the court in 1075 and threatened Henry with the same punishment, the king retaliated and held his own synod of the German Church.

Gregory's abduction on Christmas Day 1075 by Cencio I Frangipane – a member of the local nobility – together with his subsequent imprisonment, introduced a new level of violence to the dispute. Moreover, the pope, who was later released by local Romans, accused Henry of involvement in his abduction. On 9 June of that year Henry gained a crucial victory over the Saxon rebels at the Battle of Langensalza, and now he was ready for a major fight with the papacy. At a synod of bishops and princes held in Worms on 24 January 1076 Henry took the extraordinary step of declaring Gregory's deposition. On 22 February the pope retaliated by excommunicating Henry and all the German bishops involved in the synod. Henry was now encountering opposition to his policy among some very alarmed German aristocrats. In October 1076 a diet of German princes meeting at Tribur gave Henry a year to repent and to get the excommunication lifted. Otherwise they would declare the throne to be empty. Henry therefore relocated to north Italy, where some of the clergy of Lombardy were among his supporters, and shortly after Christmas 1076 he arrived in Pavia. Gregory at the same time was travelling to Augsburg for a prearranged meeting with the emperor. On learning of Henry's arrival on Italian soil Gregory, fearing a military attack, took refuge in the castle of Canossa in Reggio-Emilia owned by his great supporter Matilda, the margrave of Tuscany.

## HENRY'S ACT OF PENANCE

In order to lift the excommunication placed upon him Henry needed to perform an act of penance. His continued competence as a ruler was now in doubt, but his decision to perform as a penitent in Canossa rather than wait for Gregory's arrival in Augsburg showed immense flair. Henry was going through the motions while at the same time consolidating his power in a region of northern Italy sympathetic to him. He also had with him the army he had raised in order to oppose the pro-papal Tribur agreement. From 25th to 27th January 1077 the German king stood outside the gates of Canossa's castle in penitential mode, asking to be admitted and begging that the sentence of his excommunication be rescinded. His wish to be admitted was granted, and the sentence of excommunication was duly lifted on certain conditions – which Henry violated soon afterwards. Elements of the German aristocratic opposition now seized their moment. Judging Henry to be fatally weakened, in March 1077 the nobility of Saxony, Thuringia and

Bavaria elected Rudolf of Rheinfelden to be king of the Germans. Rudolf declared his obedience to the papacy and promised to respect the rights of individual German princes. Henry would eventually suppress the revolt in 1080, and in March of that year the pope renewed the sentence of his excommunication. Popular sentiment and German national feelings were now going Henry's way and, after Rudolf's death from injuries sustained at the Battle of Elster near Leipzig on 14 October 1080, support for the rebellion faded away. Henry, moreover, now had a very powerful supporter in Frederick I von Staufen, whom he had appointed to be the new duke of Swabia.

## MONARCHY VERSUS PAPACY

The synod of the higher German clergy convened by Henry at Bamberg in June 1080 declared Gregory deposed as pope, and elected the archbishop of Ravenna in his stead. An emboldened Henry returned to Italy, where he built up his support network by granting privileges to many cities in the north. War then broke out with Matilda's army in Tuscany, and in the course of 1081–82 Henry's forces attacked Rome in three separate offensives. By the end of 1082 the Roman populace had made their own peace treaty: it stated that Gregory and Henry's quarrel should be resolved by a special synod and, if that failed, another pope would need to be elected. At this point the pope took refuge in the Castel San' Angelo and Henry, aided by reinforcements from the Byzantine army, took the city in March 1084. The Romans then made their own declaration of Gregory's deposition and Ravenna's archbishop, now confirmed by them in office as Clement III, crowned Henry as Holy Roman Emperor on 31 March 1084.

Gregory seemed encircled but he was rescued by the intervention of Robert Guiscard who saw an opportunity to attack his Greek enemies in Rome. Guiscard's army forced Henry to withdraw from Rome and Gregory was freed. The pope died the following year in Salerno, still urging the whole of Christendom to campaign against the German king-emperor. Gregory's great cause did not die with him. In March 1088 Otto of Ostia was elected to the papacy by legitimate means, and as Victor II he pursued thoroughly Gregorian policies. He excommunicated Henry, who had now returned to Germany, as well as the antipope Clement, and set about creating a formidable anti-imperial coalition consisting of the Normans, the

BELOW *Canossa Castle, in northern Italy, where Pope Gregory VII received Henry IV in 1077.*

Rus of Kiev and the cities of the Lombard north of Italy. Henry's retaliatory expedition marched across the Alps and was defeated in 1092 by the allied Lombard communes, who took advantage of the ambitions of Henry's son Conrad and crowned him king of Italy at Monza in 1093. Henry was therefore forced to retreat to his German lands where by now his power was securely consolidated, and he therefore designated his younger son, the future Henry V, to be his heir in place of the rebel Conrad.

Pope Paschal II, elected in 1099, pursued his predecessors' policies and upheld Henry's excommunication, although the emperor's promise to go on crusade showed a readiness to conciliate. However, compromise became impossible once his son Henry rebelled in 1104, stating that he could owe no allegiance to an excommunicated father and emperor. Saxony and Thuringia, those chronic centres of rebellion, revolted against Henry. At a diet held in Mainz in December 1104 he was forced to resign his crown and was imprisoned, but Henry escaped from captivity and a final drama now unfolded. He joined the army formed in 1106 to oppose Henry V and Pope Paschal, and led that force to its victory on 2 March before dying a few days afterwards. Henry V would choose one more antipope, despite his support for the Gregorian position, but in 1122 at the Concordat of Worms he renounced his rights of investiture and was therefore admitted back to the Roman communion. The agreement meant that Henry could now be recognized by the papacy as a legitimate emperor, but the longer-term effects of the contest were catastrophic. Although the Staufen emperors revived the imperial ambition to consolidate Germany's territories, unification would not be finally achieved until 1871.

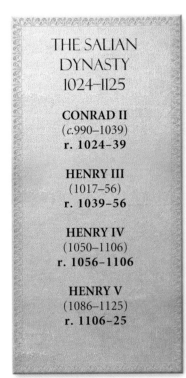

## THE SALIAN DYNASTY 1024–1125

**CONRAD II**
(*c.*990–1039)
**r. 1024–39**

**HENRY III**
(1017–56)
**r. 1039–56**

**HENRY IV**
(1050–1106)
**r. 1056–1106**

**HENRY V**
(1086–1125)
**r. 1106–25**

## WIDER EUROPEAN IMPLICATIONS

The universality of the claims made by Gregory for the Holy See's authority had their own implications for the English and French monarchies. Those abbots and bishops appointed by William the Conqueror, and by his successor Henry I, were loyal to the Crown and resistant to papal control on the terms set out by Gregory and his circle. There were heated exchanges between papal courts and English courts, but Gregory's concentration on the German dimension limited his ability to act against Henry I, and the terms of the Concordat of London (1107) favoured the English monarchy. Henry gave up his right to invest bishops and abbots, and he therefore no longer appointed them. But he also required that they should swear homage to him in recognition of their status as feudal vassals with regard to the land that they held as bishops. So far as these territories were concerned, England's bishops were treated no differently from the secular lords who went through the same ceremony of *commendatio* or acknowledgement of loyalty. In practice, therefore, the investiture contest greatly strengthened the position of English monarchs, and their chanceries became increasingly staffed by secular scholars who could be rewarded with bishoprics and abbeys.

Philip I of France was equally high-handed in relation to the Church, and his devotion to simony meant that the threat of excommunication hung over him in the mid-1070s. Here again, though, it was the gravity of the situation in Germany that saved Philip from papal condemnation. The Normans in Italy were perhaps the most perfidious of all Gregory's allies. Previous popes had made substantial concessions to them and had hoped thereby to limit the Normans' advance into central Italy as well as to gain some military protection. Robert Guiscard abandoned Gregory's cause at the moment of Henry IV's advance towards Rome, and when the city was captured the outraged local population despatched Gregory, Robert's ally, to his exile in Salerno.

The investiture controversy's effects were both destructive and creative, with spiritual power and lay authority becoming more sharply defined than in the past. Gregory transformed papal government: the curia became the central administrative machine running an international organization, and the papal legist emerged to become a key figure in the history of the medieval papacy. Gregory's trans-European awareness meant that he was inevitably concerned about the fate of the Greek Church, and the deepening split between Latin West and Greek East troubled him greatly. His alarm about the fate of Greek Christians who were coming under Arab and Turkish attack in Palestine and Syria led him to conceive of a military expedition aimed at retaking the Church of the Holy Sepulchre in Jerusalem. He is therefore one of the intellectual ancestors of the crusading ideal. Germany was broken by the contest and lapsed into a collection of small states. As the power of the monarchy dwindled so the rights of local lords grew, with the result that more peasants were turned into serfs. Local taxes and levies bore heavily on the population, while the Crown's revenues dwindled. Justice became localized as well, since local courts reflected the regional power patterns and could evade regal control. This German model was replicated in northern Italy since here, too, the imperial and royal power dwindled away and was replaced by local lordship. The scene was set for the Staufer dynasty, the family that attempted to resolve these difficulties by subsuming them within a truly imperial and dynastic dimension.

# GOSLAR AND THE SALIAN DYNASTY

*The Romanesque structure of the imperial palace at Goslar in Saxony was built in the 1040s for Henry III and is an enduring monument to Salian dynastic ambition.*

Goslar became a major centre of government under Conrad II, and its wealth, derived from local mineral resources, was central to his family's political ambitions. The silver deposits of the Harz Mountains lay nearby, and Goslar itself is situated at the foot of the Rammelsberg Mountain, where mining operations yielded one of Europe's major supplies of copper ore during the Middle Ages. Local riches turned Goslar into a 'Rome of the north' with 47 churches, private chapels and monasteries being established there from the 11th century onwards. The representative diets of the Holy Roman Empire were frequently convened in the city, and although no less than 62 imperial palaces are recorded as having existed, it was the *kaiserpfalz* or imperial palace at Goslar that was Henry III's favoured summer residence. He died there, and a sarcophagus within the building contains his heart.

The Salian dynasty first rose to greatness as dukes of Franconia, with the family's power base sited in the cities of the Rhineland in the duchy's west. Their dynastic name recalled the Salians, who were a dominant tribal grouping among the Franks. The family could also claim an impeccably imperial bloodline: Conrad II's father, Count Henry of Speyer, was the grandson of Liutgarde, a daughter of Otto the Great. Conrad was elected king of Germany in 1024 and then crowned emperor by Pope John XIX three years later. He was, however, the last to bear the title 'duke of Franconia', and after Conrad died the great cities of Rhenish Franconia – Mainz, Worms and Speyer – were ruled by their local prince-bishops as mini-states within the empire.

Conrad and his successors looked north and to Goslar partly because of the prospect of bullion. Cash might liberate them from dependence on

the aristocracy and help them to assert German kingship's independent authority.

Conrad also recovered many expropriated lands, especially those given to monasteries and bishops, which he then returned to the royal demesne (lands personally owned by the Crown). These estates were then run on the Crown's behalf by the *ministeriales*, a class of knight-administrators who worked as the king's agents. Bullion supplies and demesne revenue gave the kings resources other than their own lands when it came to rewarding their adherents. And when looking to the east of Saxony, the Salians saw other political opportunities for independent assertion: new Crown territories might be established in the colonized lands.

Conrad's son Henry III was personally pious and much influenced by the Church reform movement advocated by the monastery at Cluny in Burgundy. He also thought he had the right to impose such a reform on the Church, and he used his powers of patronage to appoint serious-minded reformers. But it was exactly that degree of imperial power

over the Church that the reform movement came to regard as an outrage in the generation that followed. Confronted by three rival claimants to the papacy, Henry convened the synod which met at Sutri near Rome in December 1046, and which followed his wishes by electing Suidberg, bishop of Bamberg, to the papal office as Clement II. Clement was enthroned on Christmas Day, and on the same day he crowned his patron emperor. Henry would use his influence to elect three more reforming German popes, but he was the last emperor able to dominate the Church, and his high-handedness alienated him from the German clergy. Godfrey II, duke of Upper Lorraine, led serial rebellions against the emperor, who also faced aristocratic dissent in Saxony and southern Germany. In 1054–55 the nobility in Bavaria and Carinthia tried to depose Henry, and his legacy included the power struggles of the German nobility that surrounded Henry IV in his boyhood.

*The 11th-century imperial palace at Goslar.*

# 1152 ── 1266 | THE STAUFER DYNASTY

*The Staufer family derived its name from the castle in Swabia, Germany, which was the dynasty's original power base. Frederick von Staufen, appointed duke of Swabia by Henry IV in 1079, was a key imperial supporter. However, Henry V, the last of the Salian emperors, left no male heirs, and the struggle to succeed him – waged between Lothair, duke of Saxony, and Frederick II of Swabia – simply highlighted the lack of focus in the German national identity. By the end of his reign Henry V had in effect conceded victory to the papacy in the long-running investiture contest, and the campaign to provide national leadership had all but ended. That deficiency was also to be a Staufen opportunity.*

RIGHT *Frederick I ('Barbarossa') with his two sons, Henry VI, Holy Roman emperor, and Frederick V, duke of Swabia (from the* Welfenchronik *produced by the Benedictine monks of Weingarten Abbey, the Welf family monastery in southern Germany, during the 1180s).*

By 1125, when the reign of Henry V was over, Lothair was 50 years of age, childless and guileless. He was thus the ideal candidate for those who wanted merely a figurehead king of the Germans. His wife's family, the Welfs of Bavaria, supported Lothair's regnal ambitions, and in a contested election he defeated Frederick to become king in 1125. The German nobility's decision was nonetheless controversial, since it ignored the rights of dynastic succession. Frederick's mother, Agnes, was Henry IV's daughter, and Henry V had therefore been his uncle. Frederick and his brother Conrad, duke of Franconia, thus inherited as family members the territories personally owned by Henry V and his Salian ancestors. However, they also claimed the Crown lands gained by the Salians as emperors. This amounted to a declaration of war, and in the ensuing conflict most of the German imperial cities backed the brothers. Lothair's imperial coronation by Pope Innocent II in 1133, although a token of subservience to the papacy, nonetheless solidified his authority, and the Staufen conceded defeat in the following year.

Recognition of Staufen leadership came after Lothair's death in 1137, when Conrad was elected to succeed him. Factionalism nonetheless persisted and the Welf leader Henry the Proud, duke of Bavaria and of Saxony, contested Conrad's election. As Lothair's son-in-law, Henry had inherited the Saxon duchy. He was immensely rich, and therefore well placed to start a civil war. Conrad's decision to deprive Henry of

his duchies proved unpopular in both Bavaria and Saxony, and that divisiveness led to the first prolonged period (1137–42) of Welf-Ghibelline armed conflict. In 1152 Conrad lay on his deathbed. His son was only six years old and his brother Frederick had died five years previously. Conrad was never crowned emperor, but he recognized in his brother's son, Swabia's new duke Frederick, those qualities of military prowess, personal charm and ambitious idealism that might drive the family on to imperial greatness. It was the north Italians he tried to conquer who would dub this particular Frederick 'Barbarossa', and Conrad's nomination of his nephew heralded a century of Staufen struggle for European predominance.

## FREDERICK I – A KING WITH CHARISMA AND GUILE

Frederick I Barbarossa devoted himself to the cause of restoring the imperial power both in Germany and north Italy. The tenth-century dynasty of Ottonian emperors provided him with an inspiration in this regard, and so did Charlemagne's memory. He was crowned king of the Germans in Aachen in 1152 and returned there in 1165 to attend the great service marking Charlemagne's canonization – a recognition that Barbarossa, with his appreciation of symbolism, had promoted personally. His imposing physical presence, crowned by flaming red hair, contributed to his charisma, as did his keen practical intelligence and courtly grace. Symbols and gestures were also needed, because he had few other cards to play outside the Staufen power base in Swabia and Franconia. However, the inventiveness with which he impressed himself on the German public's imagination meant that his leadership acquired a mythic quality, even in his own lifetime. He was crowned king of Italy in Pavia in 1154, and an initially obliging papacy gave him an emperor's crown in 1155. Those were largely nominal roles, but his lineage gave Barbarossa a more tangible asset since his mother Judith belonged to the Bavarian ducal house. This great representative of the Ghibelline interest was therefore also a Welf, and that fact encouraged the hope of reconciliation between the two factions. This, though, was to underestimate the tenacity of Henry the Lion, the Welf leader who had inherited the duchy of Saxony from his father, Henry the Proud, following its restoration to the family by King Conrad in 1142. Henry the Lion was Barbarossa's equal in grasping the importance of symbolic gesture and, unlike his rival, he had the means to express his vision of German glory through artistic patronage. Henry was Barbarossa's supporter initially, and the duchy of Bavaria was therefore returned to his dynasty in 1156. His foundation of Munich, together with Henry's embellishment of Brunswick, his capital in Saxony, marked the duke's command of a Saxon-Bavarian power block stretching from the North Sea to the Alps. Marriage to Matilda, daughter of England's Henry II, was further confirmation of Henry the Lion's standing as one of Europe's greatest princes.

Barbarossa's decision to return Bavaria to Welf control was part of his initial policy of compromise with regard to the fractious German princes. Henry II Jasomirgott, the ousted duke of Bavaria who was also margrave of Austria, was compensated with the title of duke of Austria. Initially, Barbarossa's papal policy was similarly realistic, since he wanted an ally in the struggle to restore German imperial influence in north Italy. In 1160, however, he was excommunicated by Pope Alexander III, who had decided that such ambitions undermined the papacy's own position as an Italian territorial power. In retaliation, Barbarossa backed the claims of dissident clergy who rejected the legitimacy of the official papal leadership, and it was therefore the antipope Paschal III who canonized Charlemagne at the emperor's request.

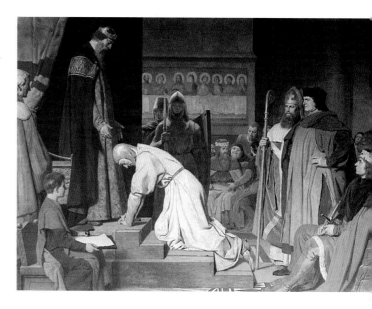

## DEATH IN THE HOLY LAND

Henry the Lion did not share Barbarossa's conviction that true German glory required an Italian dimension. Moreover, he had his own, anti-Slavic, campaigns to fight on the northeast frontier. His decision not to join the emperor's military expedition against the city of Rome in 1166 contributed to its defeat, and the pattern was repeated in Barbarossa's fifth Italian expedition, launched in 1174. Barbarossa was again denied Henry's support, and he was decisively defeated by the combined forces of Lombard north Italy at the Battle of Legnano on 29 May 1176. As a result the emperor had to moderate his Italian ambitions, and the subsequent peace deal arrived at in Venice required his recognition of the Papal States' sovereign independence. Barbarossa's title as king of Italy remained merely nominal, therefore, but in Germany he was able to punish Henry the Lion for disloyalty to the imperial cause. Roman law was one of the great rediscoveries of 12th-century Europe, and Barbarossa relied on its distinctive methodology – interpreted by a new cadre of professional lawyers – to override traditional German law and give new substance to the imperial authority. In 1180 the case against Henry was brought before an imperial court of law, and use of the Roman system ensured that the duke was deprived of his lands and declared an outlaw. A subsequent military invasion of Saxony by Barbarossa's army led to Henry's exile in England, although he was allowed to return in 1184. The emperor's death during the Third Crusade contributed to the evolution of the Barbarossa legend. Having reconciled himself to the papacy, Barbarossa took the Cross at Mainz in 1188 but was drowned in the Saleph River, in Armenia, on 10 June 1190 as his army approached Antioch. Attempts at preserving the body in vinegar failed: Barbarossa's flesh was buried in Antioch, his bones ended up in Tyre cathedral, while his heart and vital organs were interred in Tarsus.

## ITALIAN MANOEUVRES

The Norman kingdom of Sicily had been a papal ally in the anti-Staufen Italian opposition. William II (1155–89) was keen to make peace, however, since he wished to concentrate his forces on a campaign against the Greek empire. The Treaty of Venice (1177) therefore stipulated that William's aunt Constance, daughter of Roger II, would marry Barbarossa's son, the future emperor Henry VI. That same year William married Joan, the daughter of England's Henry II, and he can hardly have imagined that the eventual marriage of his aunt at the age of 32, in 1186, would lead to the end of Norman rule in Sicily. Constance was an elderly bride by the standards of the age, but she was nevertheless William's legitimate heir and his death without issue in 1189 had momentous consequences. Henry VI and Constance were crowned emperor and empress in 1191 by Pope Celestine III, and by then both were intent on pursuing their Sicilian claim.

Southern Italy's Norman nobles, appalled at the prospect of German rule, had chosen Tancred, a grandson of Roger II, to be their king, and the final rebellion of Henry the Lion meant that Henry VI needed to remain in Germany at the start of his reign. By 1194, however, the German situation was under control, and a deal with the north Italian cities allowed Henry's army to cross their territories on the way to the southern kingdom. He was also by now suddenly and enormously rich, thanks to the payment of a ransom in order to secure the release from captivity of his prisoner, Richard I of England ('the Lionheart'). Plantagenet support for Tancred and for Henry the Lion played their part in the emperor's hostility, and Richard had quarrelled with Leopold, duke of Austria, during the Third Crusade. Richard's seizure by Leopold while travelling back to England gave the emperor a chance to renew his coffers by demanding, and getting, a ransom of 150,000 marks.

## THE WORLD'S ASTONISHMENT

Tancred died in February 1194, and the divided Norman nobility was no match for the imperial army that took Palermo on 20 November. On Christmas Day Henry VI was crowned king of Sicily, which he would rule as joint monarch with Constance. The papacy's worst fear had been realized: a German imperial hegemony on both its northern and southern frontiers. It had been a year of wonders, including the birth on Boxing Day of an heir to Constance and Henry. When her labour began the queen was travelling through central Italy to join her husband in Palermo, and she stopped at the town of Jesi, in the march of Ancona, in order to give birth. She was now 40 years of age and, in order to allay any doubts about the authenticity of the event, she gave birth in public, surrounded by courtiers and local witnesses within the tented pavilion raised for the occasion in Jesi's central square. The child was then taken to Assisi, where he was baptized and christened Frederick.

The sense of wonder that surrounded Frederick at birth clung to him as he grew to manhood, and stayed with him throughout his life. Contemporaries would dub him *stupor mundi*, 'the world's astonishment'; because of his questing intellect, restless personality and unconventional ways. In the eyes of the papacy, which excommunicated him repeatedly, he was an anti-Christ figure, a religious sceptic who refused to go on crusade. But so far as the Staufen were concerned, Frederick II (1194–1250) was the best thing since Barbarossa.

Henry VI wanted his title to be hereditary, and he therefore secured Frederick's election as king of the Germans when the infant was just two years old. But the emperor's death a year later led his brother, Philip of Swabia, and Henry the Lion's son, Otto of Brunswick, to make their own claims to the German throne. Constance meanwhile kept her son in Sicily where he was crowned king in 1198, the year of her death. She renounced on his behalf any claim to the German throne and sent Henry VI's retinue back to Germany. Frederick spent most of his life in Sicily's cosmopolitan ambience, but the claims of his Staufen lineage were not so easily denied, and rebels against Otto of Brunswick, who had become the German king and emperor, elected him to be the rival king of the Germans on three occasions. An election was one thing, but making it effective was another. Even after the third election in 1215, it was another five years before Pope Honorius III crowned Frederick emperor in Rome. His numerous concessions to the German princes left them firmly in the saddle, and in 1232 Frederick allowed them the right of veto over imperial legislative initiatives. The ideal of a German national monarchy waned accordingly, but Frederick's devolution of his rights to the German princes included an accommodation with the Welf dynasty, and by the mid-1230s Germany's Welf-Ghibelline conflict was over. From 1220 to 1236 Frederick was either in Sicily or on crusade, and after a final visit to Germany in 1236–37, he never went there again.

It was his Sicilian kingdom that inspired Frederick as ruler, and the Constitutions of Melfi (1231) remain a landmark in the constitutional development of written, as opposed to customary, law. That Italian dimension, along with Frederick's crusading exploits, brought him into prolonged and embittered confrontation with the papacy. Frederick's failure to join the Fifth Crusade contributed to its defeat in 1221, and he was excommunicated in 1227 after illness delayed his participation in the Sixth Crusade. By now Frederick was, at least nominally, king of Jerusalem following his marriage to Yolande, the heiress to the Latin kingdom and whose father John of Brienne transferred the title to his son-in-law. Frederick joined the crusade in 1228 at a time that inconvenienced the papacy, and a second excommunication followed. He operated independently while on crusade and, taking advantage of a Syrian-Egyptian divide within the region's Ayyubid rulers, the emperor negotiated the return of the

ABOVE *A statue of Frederick II in Pfullendorf, Germany, which he made a free imperial city in 1220. The statue, sculpted by Peter Klink, was erected in 2006.*

city of Jerusalem, lost to the kingdom since 1187. On 18 March 1229 Frederick, still an excommunicate, crowned himself king in Jerusalem. However, the tensions between his own agents and the kingdom's nobility erupted in open warfare, and Ayyubid authority over the city was re-established in 1244.

Frederick's German concessions meant that he could concentrate on north Italian campaigning, and in 1237 he won a decisive victory over the Lombard League at the Battle of Cortenuova. However, his demand that Milan be surrendered unconditionally only strengthened the resistance of the north Italian communes. A frightened papacy renewed Frederick's excommunication in 1239, and he responded by annexing large areas of the Papal States. The election of Sinibaldo Fieschi to the papacy as Innocent IV (1243–54) brought to the fore an incendiary personality who loathed the Staufen adventurism. In the summer of 1245 the pope declared Frederick deposed as emperor. He also plotted, unsuccessfully, against him in Germany by backing Heinrich, landgrave of Thuringia, as an alternative king.

## The end of the Staufer dynasty

Fredrick met his nemesis at Parma following the city's rebellion in the summer of 1247 against the imperial government that had been imposed on it. Frederick's army settled into a lengthy siege, but after its defeat at the Battle of Parma (18 February 1248), rebellion spread to the rest of north Italy. The emperor lost control of the areas of the Papal States he had annexed, only to regain them by the beginning of 1250. But the capture and imprisonment of his son Enzio, imperial vicar general for north Italy, by the victorious Bolognese following the Battle of Fosalta (26 May 1249) was a debilitating blow.

Frederick was by now ailing, and following his death on 13 December 1250 at the castle of Fiorentino in Puglia his son Conrad succeeded him as king and ruler of both Sicily and Germany. He was unable, however, to assert military control in Sicily. After Conrad died of malaria in 1254 it was his half-brother, Manfred, the true inheritor of their father's physical and intellectual energy, who exercised power there as regent on behalf of the dead king's infant son Conradin. In 1258 Manfred took advantage of a false rumour that Conradin had died, and quickly crowned himself. He then refused to give up the crown, and embarked on a series of highly successful anti-papal campaigns in northern and central Italy. The papacy turned to Charles, count of Anjou, as its protector against this latest Staufen enemy, whom it inevitably excommunicated. Invested with the kingdom of Sicily by the papacy in 1263, Charles defeated and killed Manfred at the Battle of Benevento on 26 February 1266. The Staufen had lost their kingdom in the sun, and the dynastic line was extinguished when Conradin was beheaded as a traitor following his capture by French forces near Naples.

# PARZIVAL

*The Bavarian knight and poet Wolfram von Eschenbach (c.1170–c.1220), author of* Parzival, *was not the first great artist to be attracted by the story. Chrétien de Troyes, author of the unfinished* Perceval, le Conte du Graal *(Perceval, the Story of the Grail), was also inspired by the tale. He dedicated the romance to his patron Philip, count of Flanders, and his account of the Arthurian hero has a stylistic and thematic connection with* Peredur, *one of the medieval Welsh prose tales collectively known as the* Mabinogi.

The true origin of Parzival's story is unknown, but the variety of its treatments shows how literary material reflected local circumstances within a cosmopolitan ambience. Von Eschenbach's poem, arguably the greatest of the German medieval epics, is infused by the knightly ethic with its portrayal of the need for compassionate love when searching for a healing wisdom. Parzival's grief-stricken mother, Herzeloyde, has consciously brought him up to be ignorant of chivalric knighthood following the death in battle of the boy's father Gahmuret. Itinerant knights, however, inform the youth of the glories of Arthur's court at Camelot, and Parzival departs for the island of Britain. His despairing mother, however, dresses him in a fool's clothes in the hope that his appearance will exclude him from courtly life and the dangerous attractions of knighthood.

Parzival's strange appearance makes him an object of curiosity at Camelot, and he is instructed in the need for knightly self-control. An even higher calling is reserved for him, however, and he arrives at the castle of the Grail where he meets the mysterious Anfortas, the wounded 'Fisher King'.

*Parzival (right) is shown in this manuscript (1443–46) of Wolfram von Eschenbach's poem.*

Anfortas is the keeper of the Grail, but his wound means that he can do little other than fish, and his suffering mirrors that of his kingdom, which seems doomed to sterility. Many knights have tried to heal him, but only an individual with exceptional spiritual self-understanding can relieve Anfortas's suffering. That penitent knight turns out to be Parzival, who therefore holds the key to the regeneration of the kingdom itself. Liberated from earlier ignorance and self-centredness, Parzival learns that Anfortas is, in fact, his mother's brother, and he himself becomes in time the Grail king.

Von Eschenbach's highly charged account of knighthood's challenges and tribulations gives a mythological dimension to the German empire of the Staufen. His primary emphasis is on the need for a spiritual self-understanding, but the theme of a regenerated kingdom that has recovered from its wounds and divisions has obvious affinities with the German empire's political and military struggles in the age of the Staufen princes.

# 1154 — 1216 | THE ANGEVIN EMPIRE

*Stephen of Blois (c.1096–1154), raised to the throne by nobles hostile to the succession of Henry I's daughter Matilda, was the last member of the Anglo-Norman dynasty to wear the English Crown. His regnal claim, following Henry I's death in 1135, was reasonably justified: his mother, Adela, was William the Conqueror's daughter, and Stephen had been partly raised at the English court. But for the reasons why England's Norman aristocracy objected to Matilda, Henry's sole direct heir and his chosen successor, we must look beyond her sex. She was also married to Geoffrey of Anjou whose lands, including Touraine and Maine, bordered Normandy – and the count was the latest in a line of Angevin rulers who had territorial designs on the duchy, which was a possession of the English Crown.*

Matilda's first marriage – to Henry V, the Holy Roman emperor – had given her the courtesy title of empress. Although not crowned as such by the pope, she was keen on the title and continued to use it after Henry's death in 1125. Matilda was not someone whose rights could be trifled with, all the more so since her second husband, Geoffrey – handsome, vigorous and militarily talented – was extremely eager to conjoin her claims with his own ambition. As soon as Henry I died Matilda crossed the border into Normandy to claim her inheritance, but although she had some local supporters the duchy's wary nobility declared for Stephen. Matilda and Geoffrey remained undaunted, and the empress's invasion of England in 1139 marked a new stage in the succession crisis. Stephen was briefly deposed in April 1141, but although Matilda ruled in London for a few months her refusal to cut taxes made her unpopular locally, and by the end of the year the king had regained his throne.

In Normandy meanwhile Matilda's cause was prospering, and Geoffrey's campaigns in 1142–43 secured all the fiefdoms west and south of the Seine. He then took Rouen in 1144 and proclaimed Matilda and himself as Normandy's rulers. The duke and duchess ruled their territory jointly until 1149 when it was ceded to their son, the future Henry II of England. Louis VII who, as king of France, was the vassal lord of Normandy's dukes,

RIGHT *Geoffrey of Anjou is shown bearing a sword and shield on his tomb at Le Mans Cathedral, France.*

ENSET VO PRINCEPS PRC DONVM TVRBA IFVCATVR
...MRS PACE...VICENTE DATVR

authorized this arrangement. Henry succeeded his father as count of Anjou following Geoffrey's death in 1151. At Poitiers on 18 May of the following year he married Eleanor of Aquitaine, who ruled that duchy in her own right and whose marriage to Louis VII of France had been annulled just two months previously. Although restored to his throne, Stephen's position in England remained precarious. Henry arrived in England with an army in January 1153 and, after the sudden death in August of Stephen's son and heir Eustace, the king agreed to a compromise: the succession rights of his surviving son William would be set aside, and Matilda's son was recognized as Stephen's heir. From the end of 1153 onwards Henry – already count of both Anjou and Maine as well as duke of both Aquitaine and Normandy – was therefore also in effective control of England. Following Stephen's death in October 1154 this multititled dynast was crowned king of England in Westminster Abbey on 19 December.

## Maintaining the Angevin territories

The new king's father, Geoffrey, had called himself 'Plantagenet', after the broom flower (*Planta genista*) he had adopted as his personal emblem. During the 15th century the term came to be used to describe the dynasty of English kings descended from Matilda and Geoffrey, and whose rule ended with the accession of the Tudor Henry VII in 1485. In the case of Henry II, and his sons Richard I and John I, the phrase 'Angevin empire' was coined in the 19th century to describe their collection of territories that, covering the whole of western France, extended from the northern English border to the Pyrenees. Twelfth-century contemporaries did not use that term, however, and the assemblage of so many different titles owed everything to the luck of the gene pool, the accident of dynastic succession and good fortune in the chancy business of warfare. A ruler capable of maintaining his authority across such a diverse territory needed to be not just clever and tough but also lucky – as John I's loss of Normandy, Anjou and most of Aquitaine would demonstrate.

Henry II was educated in the law and is a major figure in the evolution of England's precedent-based common law system. The rights of the Crown he inherited in England were well defined and supported by an administration which, given a strong-minded monarch, could give a direct expression to the royal will. Unsurprisingly, Normandy was the regime's closest parallel for efficient authority on mainland Europe. Civil breakdown during the anarchic period of Stephen's reign had led to widespread usurpation of property, and the provisions of Henry's measure, the Assize of Clarendon (1166), specified how 12 knights could determine legitimate rights and order redress to be made. This arrangement built on earlier provisions in Anglo-Saxon law and would become known as the jury system. Henry's appointment of 'justices' (judges) who travelled the country hearing cases elevated the Crown's authority while limiting the obstructive powers of self-interested local nobles.

Revenue was the key to the enforcement of authority, and Henry's rigorous application of the tax called *scutage*, which allowed vassals to buy out their obligation of military service, enabled him to employ the mercenaries who played a major role in his army. It was Henry's determination that the secular law of the king's justice should predominate over Church law that brought him into conflict with Thomas Becket, the archbishop of Canterbury who had formerly been the king's ostentatiously loyal lord chancellor. Church courts had been a continuing source of authority during the recent years of disorder in England, and they had extended their area of competence during that period. The Constitutions of Clarendon (1164) represented Henry's attempt at restricting their powers and limiting the scale of immunities enjoyed by the clergy. A provision that clergy who had been convicted by the Church courts should then

ABOVE The Martyrdom of Thomas Becket, *a panel from Master Francke's St. Thomas Altarpiece, commissioned in 1424.*

**1128** Matilda of England, widow of emperor Henry V and daughter of Henry I of England, marries Geoffrey Plantagenet of Anjou who succeeds (1129) his father as count.

**1135** Henry I of England dies and is succeeded by his nephew, Stephen of Blois. Matilda contests the succession.

**1144** Geoffrey and Matilda become duke and duchess of Normandy following a military campaign. They cede the duchy to their son Henry (1149), who is crowned king of England as Henry II (1154).

**1170** Murder of Thomas Becket.

**1173–74** Henry II's sons Henry, Richard and John unite in armed rebellion against their father's rule in England.

**1188** Richard ('the Lionheart') betrays his father and does homage to Philip II of France: the two allies invade Anjou (1189) and defeat Henry II's army.

**1189** Henry II dies and is succeeded by Richard.

**1199** Death of Richard I, who is succeeded by his brother John.

**1204** A French military offensive drives the English out of Normandy, Anjou and most of Aquitaine.

**1215** Supported by a French army, the English baronage launches a military offensive against John, who dies (1216) while fleeing from rebel forces.

be handed over to secular jurisdiction and prosecuted in the king's courts was especially contentious. From late 1164 to 1170 Becket was in exile in France, and his theatrical campaign against the monarch's policies continued until knights belonging to the king's retinue killed him in his cathedral at Canterbury on 29 December. The murder undermined Henry's authority, and the agreement he arrived at with the papacy two years later conceded the central point that clergy had a right of appeal to Rome.

## THE STRUGGLES OF HENRY II

Henry II embarked on a series of wars aimed at establishing vassal states that would operate as buffer zones on his territories' frontiers. Welsh princes were unco-operative in this regard, and the two most significant of them – Rhys ap Gruffudd, who ruled the kingdom of Deheubarth in the southwest, and Owain Gwynedd, who ruled in the north – joined forces to defeat Henry's army at the Battle of Crogen, fought in the country's northeast in the summer of 1165. But Henry learned from his mistakes. Since a projected invasion of Ireland was going to be launched from the coast of Deheubarth, the king entered into a form of alliance with Rhys: the prince's authority over the rest of Wales was recognized, and Rhys became a vassal of England's king.

Henry met with greater success in Ireland, a country whose provincial kings had been battling each other for the dignity of high king and where Norman institutions, including a very patchy form of feudalism, began to spread as a result of military intervention by the English Crown. In 1167 Henry recognized Dermot of Leinster and allowed him to recruit English and Welsh mercenaries in his struggle for supremacy. The successes enjoyed by the newly arrived knights in establishing their own power bases in the island discomfited Henry, who wanted to imprint his own regal stamp on a fast-evolving situation. He therefore led personally the major military expedition that landed at Waterford in October 1171, following which most of the island's native princes caved in and paid homage. The institution of a lordship of Ireland – a fiefdom in the king's gift – was a cornerstone of family policy, and Henry had originally intended his younger brother William, Count of Poitou, to be the beneficiary of a conquest of Ireland. The count died young, however, and Henry's son John was made lord of Ireland by the king in 1185. John's visit to the island in that year, though brief, established his unpopularity, and in subsequent decades Norman authority in Ireland dwindled to cover the area of the Pale that surrounded Dublin.

In 1173-74 Scotland's King William I ('the Lion') launched two invasions of Northumberland – a territory seized for Scotland by David I during

Stephen's reign but regained for the English Crown in 1157. After being captured at the end of 1174 William had to swear fealty to Henry, and the establishment of English garrisons in Edinburgh and along the border meant that southern Scotland was under the control of the English. This situation lasted until 1189, when Richard I ceded authority in the region to William in return for the money he needed to take part in the Third Crusade.

Normandy was Henry's core territory on the European mainland, and his tactics along its borders were similar to the ones he adopted in Ireland and on the English frontiers within Britain. Brittany was in the middle of a succession dispute in the 1150s after Duke Conan III's disinheritance of his son Hoel, and Henry initially supported the reigning duke, Conan IV, who was Hoel's nephew. In 1166 he arranged the betrothal of his seven-year-old son Geoffrey to the duke's daughter, and he then forced Conan's abdication. Henry thus became, in effect, the ruler of Brittany, though it was never his fiefdom. In the face of serial rebellions by the Breton nobility, he installed loyal aristocrats who built up his authority within the duchy.

The marriage to Eleanor made Henry duke of Aquitaine – a title he held as the successor to her first husband, Louis VII. By the same token he became duke of Gascony, a territory to the southwest that had been part of Aquitaine since the early tenth century, but whose awkward terrain required careful management. The county of Toulouse lay to Aquitaine's southeast and was a vast area whose many fortified towns impeded the progress of the army launched by Henry from Poitiers in 1159. He returned with another army in 1161 and then left his local allies, who included King Alfonso II of Aragon, to continue the struggle on his behalf. In 1173 Count Raymond V eventually yielded and decided to pay homage to Henry, though the vassalage was not enforced very rigorously.

## RELATIONSHIPS WITH THE FRENCH

Henry's tortuous relations with the French Crown were a constant theme of his career. King Louis was constantly trying to subvert Henry's position: he had been a supporter of King Stephen of England, and he gave comfort, as well as refuge, to Thomas Becket during the archbishop's exile. His own position was, however, precarious. Not only did Louis lack Henry's material resources, but until the birth of the future Philip II in 1165 he also lacked a male heir. Five years earlier, Louis had succumbed to English pressure and agreed to the marriage of his daughter Margaret to Henry's second son, the younger Henry, when she was two and he was five. Philip's birth removed the prospect of a united English-French Crown, however. In retaliation, Henry made a claim to the Auvergne and Bourges, where he conducted major military campaigns in 1167 and 1170 respectively. Once crowned king, however, it was Philip who would be Henry's nemesis, by taking advantage of his sons' disloyalty.

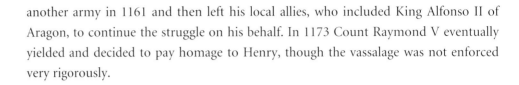

Henry II was a consistently expansionist ruler but also a dynastically minded one. He therefore allowed his sons to have their own titles: Henry the Younger was crowned king in 1170; Richard became duke of Aquitaine in 1172; Geoffrey became duke of Brittany in 1181; and in 1185 John was attempting to exert his authority as lord of Ireland. Henry the Younger's request that he be allowed to rule part of his father's territories was denied by Henry. But his son could count on the support of both Richard and Geoffrey, and the three combined to attack their father in the civil war of 1173–74. Eleanor, by now estranged from her husband, took Henry the Younger's side and was for a while imprisoned as a result. The rebel also had the support of his father-

LEFT *An equestrian statue of Richard I ('the Lionheart') stands outside the UK Houses of Parliament.*

in-law, Louis VII of France. Henry survived that challenge, only to be confronted by the implacable Richard, whose rule in Aquitaine turned out to be a particularly rough form of military administration.

Just before his death in 1183 Henry the Younger had joined a local Aquitainian revolt against Richard, who then rejected his father's demand that he should yield the duchy to John. Geoffrey of Brittany had joined his brother Henry in attacking Richard in Aquitaine, and would do the same in combination with John, although they were no match for the Lionheart, whose military prowess crushed their forces with ease. Geoffrey's animosity towards his father led him at the same time to plot with Philip II of France. Although Geoffrey's death in 1186 removed an important prospective ally, Philip soon found another one: in 1188 Richard paid homage to him for all the lands that Henry II held in France as a vassal of the French Crown. In the summer of the following year the two allies invaded Anjou, the heartland of the Plantagenet dynasty, and overran both Maine and Tours. Henry was defeated in battle and died in 1189 in the knowledge that John, too, had joined the alliance against him.

## JOHN – COLLAPSE OF A KING

The loss of Normandy and of Anjou to the armies of Philip II occurred in 1204 during John's reign as king, and a triumphant Capetian dynasty forced the retreat of English forces within Aquitaine to the region of Gascony, which remained loyal. Despite his reputation as a calamitous king, many of John's achievements recall his father's preoccupations. He quarrelled with the papacy and refused its nomination of Stephen Langton as archbishop of Canterbury, although he eventually submitted after an eight-year struggle in 1213. Just as Henry had done, John involved himself closely with the workings of the justice system, and he was an efficient administrator as well as a keen raiser of revenue. But the loss of his dynasty's continental possessions at the start of his reign affected the exercise of John's authority in England, and the English baronage voiced their resentment at being taxed as they would never have done during Henry II's reign. The list of demands contained in the *Magna Carta* presented to John at Runnymede on 15 June 1215 represented a rejection of his father's style of strong and centralizing kingship. Having signed under duress, the king obtained the pope's permission to break his word, and he was defeated in the two-year civil war that followed – waged in part by a French army invited in by the English baronage in order to support their cause. John's reign had seen the entire dissolution of his father's assemblage of territories, and his own failures had also dealt a blow to the style of kingly authority exercised by Henry II. Both in England and in France, the future lay with the cause of national monarchies whose dynasties exercised their power within established frontiers – rather than across areas as geographically separate, politically disparate and culturally diverse as the territories of the 'Angevin empire'.

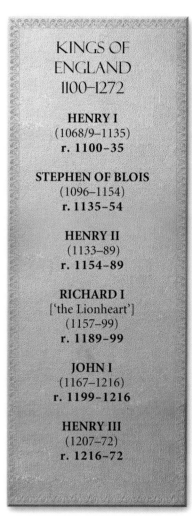

**KINGS OF ENGLAND 1100–1272**

**HENRY I**
(1068/9–1135)
**r. 1100–35**

**STEPHEN OF BLOIS**
(1096–1154)
**r. 1135–54**

**HENRY II**
(1133–89)
**r. 1154–89**

**RICHARD I**
['the Lionheart']
(1157–99)
**r. 1189–99**

**JOHN I**
(1167–1216)
**r. 1199–1216**

**HENRY III**
(1207–72)
**r. 1216–72**

# ROBIN HOOD

*The story of the outlaw Robin Hood, who evades the established order by escaping to the forest where he lives with his band of 'merry' men, is an enduring part of English folklore. Robin's escapades are first recorded in literary form in ballads whose earliest manuscripts date from the 15th century, and which are set in the England of one or two centuries earlier.*

Robin springs to life in this literature as an anti-clericalist, a skilled archer, and an opponent of the sheriff of Nottingham. The notion that Robin was a supporter of Richard the Lionheart and that he was driven out of society during the misrule of Richard's brother John while the king was on the Third Crusade, is a 16th-century addition to the fable. Robin's portrayal as the earl of Huntingdon, an aristocrat down on his luck, is similarly post-medieval; in the original 15th-century verses he is described consistently as a yeoman. The ballads form part of a wider cultural tribute to Robin the English hero. May Day celebrations in late medieval England frequently involved revellers dressing up as Robin and his companions, and plays about his exploits were often performed during these springtime festivities. It was through these dramas that the figure of Maid Marion was added to the Robin Hood literature.

No historical figure has been identified as the original Robin Hood, and the ballads that portray him are works of literature, not of biography. Hood's social views do nonetheless cast a sharp light on some medieval English attitudes. Although the balladeers describe a Robin who is on the side of the down-trodden, there are in fact no examples in this early literature of his 'giving to the poor', and the peasantry is mostly significant by its absence from the Hood ballads. The forms of courtesy observed by Robin's followers when they kneel before him in acknowledgement of his authority follow medieval notions of precedence and honour. The fact that they carry swords, not staffs, indicates that they are, like Robin, yeomen, and the literature presents them as the backbone of the nation. Robin's qualities of courtesy, politeness and piety are seen as the consensual virtues that enable a society or kingdom to hang together.

These contrast with his enemies' mean-spirited materialism and selfishness.

There was a ready appetite for the Hood ballads among the tiny minority of England's population that was literate and, therefore, influential, and the legend was particularly popular in gentry households. It may well be, therefore, that the medieval literary tradition that invented Robin Hood reflects the governing order's idealization of the English virtues and of the personal values that will promote a sound and just social order.

Robin has always been a protean figure, and each period has invented the character it wants. Promotion to the aristocracy in the 16th and 17th centuries made him an establishment figure, one whose romantic exile ended with the restoration of a benign ruler. The Victorians were attracted by Robin's philanthropy, and they turned him into a leader of freedom-loving Saxons who are pitted against feudal Norman barons. Warner Bros' *The Adventures of Robin Hood* (1938) gave a Hollywood sheen to the English tale, with the hero and his band being presented as cheerful exponents of a 'can-do' attitude to life's challenges.

Robin's physical beauty is an important feature of the Hood tradition. Recent commentary has speculated on whether there may be a covertly gay dimension to the appeal of the legend. The original corpus of Hood literature, together with its subsequent interpretations, celebrates the intensity of male comradeship and shows how the rejection of convention can lead to the discovery of true identity. Maid Marion's femininity, and passivity, relegated her to the margins in the world of Hood.

*A coloured woodcut of c.1600 depicting Robin Hood, the hero of late medieval English ballads.*

# THE 12TH-CENTURY RENAISSANCE

## 1080 — 1218

*From the late 11th century onwards, European culture witnessed a revival of the arts and letters so profound and wide-ranging that it may be compared to the Renaissance that spread from later medieval Italy to the rest of the continent. Romanesque art achieved its fullest development during this period, and Gothic architecture began to evolve. Poetry – both lyric and epic – began to be written in the vernacular, and the Latin language was used innovatively to describe advances in philosophy and theology. Universities were founded across Europe at centres such as Salerno, Paris and Montpellier, Bologna and Salamanca, Oxford and Cambridge. These were the places that pioneered the rediscovery of ancient authors like Euclid, Ptolemy and Aristotle, as well as the revival of Roman law.*

The 12th-century revival was a cosmopolitan movement. Italian centres of learning were particularly important for the advances in Roman and canon law, in medical science and in the new translations from ancient Greek. France's clerical and lay intelligentsia were especially active in philosophical speculation and verse composition. England and Germany followed these French cultural patterns, and Spain linked the European milieu with Islamic culture. The Carolingian period of ninth-century cultural advance had been real enough, but it was centred on the court and on the schools attached to monasteries and cathedrals – and many of these establishments had suffered from the tenth-century anarchy unleashed by Vikings, Saracens and Magyars. A more expansive awakening of the mind and spirit was now being witnessed, and its leading lights sought not just to preserve the legacy of the past but also to revive its content and make that knowledge relevant to their own times.

*RIGHT The rose window of Chartres Cathedral, a building which has become synonymous with the revival of the arts and scholarship in 12th-century Europe.*

Universities were not the only centres of this enlightenment. New cathedrals such as Chartres, Rheims, Orléans, Canterbury and Toledo played their part, too. The royal bureaucratic machine was also important: learned clerks employed by rulers like Henry II of England and Frederick II in Sicily worked at courts that rivalled the great monasteries, such as Bec in France and Monte Cassino in Italy, as centres of learning.

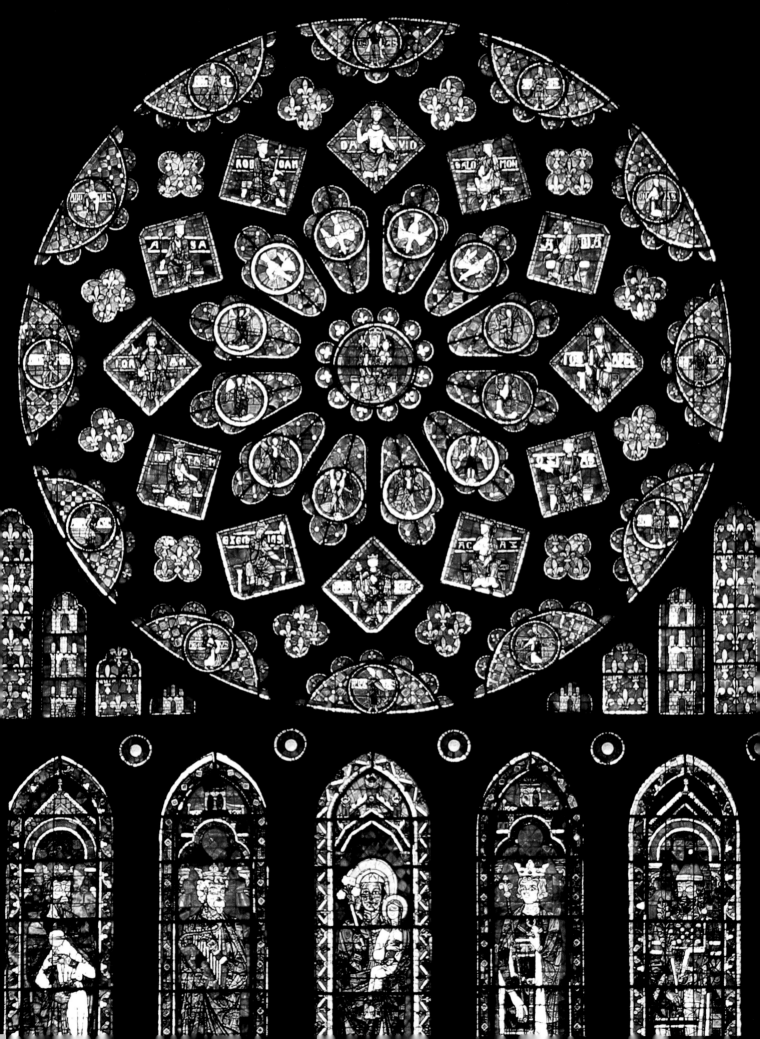

These were the places where libraries could be found, although collections of manuscripts were still mostly very small. The 340 or so volumes owned by the abbey at Corbie in Picardy and the 546 titles owned by Durham Cathedral marked them out as exceptional places in the year 1200.

## THE IMPORTANCE OF THE WRITTEN WORD

All books were of parchment, since papyrus had passed out of general use in the earlier medieval period and paper had not yet been introduced to the West. Carolingian art excelled in illuminated manuscripts but this tradition had been lost in Europe by the 11th century, and the 12th-century manuscripts whose beautiful initials are painted in red, green and gold represent a sublime recovery. Such books naturally included many copies of the Bible, as well as church service books such as missals and lectionaries. They also included the definitive volumes of Fathers of the early Church such as Augustine, Jerome, Ambrose and Gregory the Great. But the libraries also contained more recent works. Commentaries written by Abelard and Anselm mattered greatly, as did those of authors who communicated the learning of the past, such as Boethius, Martianus Capella, Isidore of Seville and Bede. Their textbooks on logic, rhetoric, arithmetic, music and etymology became the standard authorities. Archives became more important as administration evolved, and the documentation gathered by the monarchs of England and Sicily rivalled the extensive papal sources in their sophistication.

ABOVE *In this detail from the* Très Riches Heures du Duc de Berry *(15th century) a monk is shown working as a copyist in a scriptorium.*

The 12th-century Church had an ambiguous attitude towards Latin literature. It taught the language – its medium of communication – while condemning the pagan milieu that was the context for the writings of authors such as Cicero, Virgil and Ovid. Nonetheless, the literary style of the past furnished many writers with models of composition. This was especially true of John of Salisbury (*c.*1120–80) whose wide-ranging powers of quotation and graceful literary style were learned when he was a student at the school of Chartres, the most eminent of the 12th-century cathedral schools. Virgil was read and admired at Chartres as well as at many other such schools, for example, Orléans, and he was almost universally seen as the supreme poet and stylistic model. His themes could be allegorized as anticipations of Christian truths, and as a celebrant of ancient Rome's empire Virgil was especially pertinent to the Staufer dynasty's revival of the imperial tradition. But Ovid's love poetry and his *Metamorphoses* also inspired many, and his verses were copied even in the Benedictine monastery at Cluny. Among prose writers Cicero was revered as the chief representative of rhetoric, a subject placed on the medieval curriculum as one of the seven 'liberal arts', and Pliny the Elder's *Natural History* could be plundered for bizarre tales.

Latin was also a living language for contemporary artists, scholars, priests and lawyers, and the standards of grammar and vocabulary were greatly improved. The standard textbook was the *Institutiones* of Priscian of Caesarea, composed in the early sixth century and comprising 16 books. It was being copied vigorously, but there were shorter manuals, too, and the age also produced numerous dictionaries and encyclopaedias. Adam du Petit-Pont, a master at Paris in the early 12th century, wrote a descriptive vocabulary in which he put words into sentences that explained their meaning. That genre supplies valuable information about the fabric of daily 12th-century lives. While studying grammar could illuminate the imaginative and literary workings of language, rhetoric fared less well as a subject. Forensic oratory had disappeared with the passing of the Roman political and judicial system, and rhetoric only survived as a model for writing letters.

## The resurgence of satire and drama

There was an appreciative public audience for poetry composed in Latin. In religious verse especially there was a move away from the language's older forms and towards the new intensity of rhymed verse. The most famous of the period's Latin poets were the Goliards, a group of mostly clerical students and authors in France, Germany, Italy and England whose texts in praise of wine, women and song often satirized the official Church hierarchy, and especially the Roman curia. Their collective *Carmina Burana* combine secular impulses with religious inspiration, and the notion of an Order of Goliards, which was a burlesque on the Orders of monks, shows the popularity of parody at this time. Drama had disappeared with the closing of the last Roman theatres, but the Christian liturgy resonated with dramatic power, and it inspired the medieval miracle plays that recreated scenes from the Passion. Other miracle plays described the lives of saints, and these were performed at associated shrines and cult centres. Students at the monastic and cathedral schools played an important role in the development of these plays and their widespread diffusion.

## Changing laws

The 12th century saw the arrival of the lawyer at the heart of government, and that meant the Church no longer enjoyed a monopoly on learning. Rulers everywhere needed this new class of educated laymen as counsellors and administrators, and an immense intellectual effort went into the revival of Roman law and the advance of jurisprudence in general. The ancient materials were preserved in the *Corpus Juris Civilis* as codified in the sixth century by the emperor Justinian. This consisted of the *Code* or collection of the emperor's legislation; the *Digest* that summarized the conclusions of Roman jurists; the *Institutes*, a textbook used in

## THE 12TH-CENTURY RENAISSANCE

**1080s** The Italian jurist Irnerius establishes, at Bologna, a new school of law whose scholars will produce commentaries on Roman law.

**1088** The University of Bologna is founded.

**1109** Death of the Italian philosopher Anselm, archbishop of Canterbury since 1093.

**1121** Peter Abelard's philosophical views are condemned as heretical by Church authorities.

*c.***1159** John of Salisbury, secretary to Archbishop Theobald of Canterbury, writes *Policraticus*, a work of political philosophy describing monarchs' rights and duties.

**1160s** The University of Paris has an institutional identity.

**1209** Official date of the foundation of the University of Cambridge, England – possibly due to scholars deciding to leave the University of Oxford.

**1218** Spain's first university is established at Salamanca.

**1289** Montpellier University is founded by amalgamating earlier centres of study, such as the school of law founded in the 1160s.

teaching law; and the *Novels*, or later legislation of the emperor Justinian. It was jurists teaching at the University of Bologna in the early 12th century, and especially Irnerius (*c.*1055–*c.*1130), who set about producing interpretations of these great texts. They and their successors, termed the 'glossators', purified the original texts and brought out their contemporary relevance. The *Digest* gained a special importance as a model of juristic method which was then applied to the law of the Church and to the feudal customs of Europe.

Economic expansion in the Mediterranean and northern Italy created new patterns of trade and commerce. Urban centres were therefore drawn to the revived Roman law since it could reflect contemporary realities more readily than the established early medieval codes that were, as in the case of the Lombards' system, rural based. Governments developing a comprehensive territorial bureaucracy were also attracted by a system of laws based on general validity rather than local custom. Roman law also benefited from, and contributed to, the revival of imperialism under successive German emperors who sought to strengthen the Roman tradition and ideology. Frederick Barbarossa was an astute user of its teachings, and he enjoyed the support of the Law School of Bologna when he asserted his rights as a ruler over the towns of Lombardy.

Italian universities diffused the Roman law to France and Spain. Montpellier was well placed to do this since Provence, once a Roman province, retained many features of the classical legal system. The English Crown declared against Roman law, but many of the country's churchmen used Roman legal principles when arguing canon law (so called because it was based on the collections of rules or canons produced by Church councils). Canon law argued for the legal system of a universal Church, and its universality therefore blended well with Roman jurisprudence. Its sources were various, and so in *c.*1140 the monk Gratian of Bologna produced the immensely influential collection of canon law known as the *Decretum*, which systematized and reconciled these authorities. Canon law became a fully independent system and, since it had also absorbed the principles of Roman jurisprudence, it also served as a vehicle for the transmission of the Roman law. Even England therefore observed the influence of this continental system so far as the Church was concerned. Here, however, it was the common law – a system based on custom and precedent – that was the cornerstone of the king's law.

## ARAB INFLUENCES IN SCIENCE AND CULTURE

European learning was stimulated by the arrival in the West of the texts describing ancient Greek philosophy and science. Since there had been so few translations into Latin of these works, the chief conduit here was those scholars of Byzantium who had translated the Greek texts into Syriac, Hebrew and Arabic. Many of these translations travelled east to the Persian court, and they also existed in the Byzantine provinces that fell to seventh- and eighth-century Arab invaders. Those conquests gave a new impetus to translation, since many of the Islamic caliphs were enthusiastic patrons of learning. Arabic translations were therefore made direct from the Greek, as in the case of Ptolemy's *Almagest* (*The Great Compilation*) in 827, as well as from Syriac and Hebrew. The focus was on works in medicine, mathematics, astronomy, astrology and alchemy, with the Arab translators adding their own observations and discoveries to the ancient texts.

Until the 12th century there had been little intellectual contact between the Latin West and Arab culture. The multicultural kingdom of Sicily – administered by Arab rulers in the tenth and 11th centuries – saw real cultural synergy, and the Sicilian court employed many Arab doctors and astrologers even after the island's conquest by the Normans. But it was in Spain, with its long history of Islamic occupation from the eighth century onwards, that most of the important work was done. Translation from the Arabic versions of the ancient Greek texts took place in the major cities of the peninsula, and that work became especially active in the 12th century with new attention being paid to astronomy and mathematics. From Spain came Euclid and his algebra, as well as the philosophy and science of Aristotle and his Arabic commentators, in forms that changed subsequent European thought. Euclid's

*Elements* appeared in a Latin translation from the Arabic in the early 12th century, with his *Data* and *Optics* following a generation later. The arrival of Aristotle's *Physics*, along with his *Meteorology* and *De Caelo* (*On the Heavens*), transformed Europeans' understanding of the natural world. European medicine was revolutionized by the full recovery of the ancient Greeks' literature on the subject, especially so in the case of works by Galen and Hippocrates, and translations from the works of Arab doctors also gained a wide currency.

Some Arabic words were left untranslated, which is why the terms algebra, zero and cipher survive in mathematics, along with almanac, zenith and nadir in astronomy. The translations inspired some independent scientific observation in the West, as can be seen in the work of Albertus Magnus. But their more widespread impact was curricular; the arrival of ancient wisdom in accessible form stimulated arithmetic, geometry, astronomy and music – the subjects comprising the *quadrivium* or the mathematical part of the seven liberal arts that were the basis of medieval education.

# The Aristotelian revival

Ancient Greek science was abstract and deductive rather than experimental, and as such it was seen as a branch of philosophy. This suited the classification of knowledge in 12th-century Europe, and the veneration of Aristotle as the supreme philosopher was a profound feature of the period's recovery of classical Greek thought. Plato's more discursive and literary style had little influence compared with the compact and systematic method of Aristotle, with his many textbooks and manuals fashioned from lecture notes. The universal nature of Aristotle's genius is the background to the development in the 13th century of the system of Thomas Aquinas. By the end of the 12th century, Aristotelian logic had been absorbed into European thought, and the philosopher's *Metaphysics* was translated in *c.*1200, followed by *Ethics* and *Politics*. Aristotle was therefore assimilated within the Christian consensus, though this required a softening of some of his more un-Christian beliefs, such as the teaching that the universe was eternal. With Aristotle, however, there also arrived Averroes (1126–98), his greatest Arab commentator. Averroes highlighted doctrines such as the eternity of matter and the unity of the intellect and, since these teachings denied individual immortality, their impact would stimulate heresy and dissent in medieval Europe.

Anselm and Abelard were the chief philosophers of the age, and both pre-date the real impact of Aristotle in the West. Anselm (1033–1109) sought to prove the necessary existence of God, and his use of dialectic showed how faith should also be enquiring. Abelard (1079–1142) was a teacher of dazzling originality, and one who was not averse to being the centre of a Parisian personality cult. The orthodoxy of his day defended universals – or general categories – as necessary before the mind could proceed to grasp particulars. Abelard's dissent on this subject led to his condemnation for heresy in 1121 and 1141. His pungent treatise *Sic et Non* (*Yes and No*) was a pioneering work in the development of the dialectical style, since it took evidence from the past on various topics and arranged them as a series of propositions. Abelard's emphasis on the contradictions tended to undermine orthodoxy. The method itself though proved immensely influential in the 13th-century development of the scholastic system, and university teaching of the *trivium* (a division within the seven liberal arts) was therefore slanted towards logic at the expense of its other components: grammar and rhetoric. Theology remained the highest form of knowledge, and when philosophy trespassed on its terrain it was to be condemned – as Abelard had been. Some followers of Averroes in the Latin West tried to advance a doctrine of double truth, with philosophy and theology both being true, but only within their own respective domains. But the Church forbad that escape route out of contradiction. That interdiction is the background to the establishment of a series of inquisitions, or formal investigations into heretical teachings, that began in the 1180s, and whose penalties of death by burning showed that some 12th-century speculation could be dangerous as well as audacious.

# HISTORICAL WRITING

*History was one of the growth subjects of the 12th century, and a fresh sense of critical enquiry is evident in the vogue for biographies and memoirs that supplemented the annals and chronicles of saints' lives which were the traditional medieval way into the past.*

The *Ten Books of Histories*, written by Gregory of Tours (*c*.538–94), were still being used to provide information concerning the Franks' early traditions and the process of their Christianization as the Gaul of late antiquity mutated into early medieval France. But the hagiographical element in Gregory's work sets it apart from those 12th-century historians and their immediate successors who, while no less devout than Gregory, could nonetheless distinguish between fables and reasonably ascertained fact. This was a great period for the compilation of encyclopedias. *Speculum Maius* (*The Greater Mirror*), written by the Dominican friar Vincent of Beauvais (*c*.1190–*c*.1264), is divided into three books that deal respectively with the natural sciences, contemporary forms of applied knowledge such as surgery, agriculture and political science, and world history.

The Englishman Orderic Vitalis (1075–*c*.1142) a monk of the rich and influential foundation at Saint Evroul in Normandy, wrote an *Ecclesiastical History* which, although starting with the birth of Christ, is chiefly remarkable as a work of contemporary history that describes Western European political developments in the late 11th and early 12th centuries. Orderic's background led him to take a special interest in the workings of the Anglo-Norman state, and the frequent visitors to Saint Evroul from England, as well as from southern Italy where the monastery had established many daughter foundations, supplied him with the information that lends an international dimension to his work. The Cistercian monk Otto of Freising (*c*.1114–58) authored a *Chronicle* that offers a superb general history in a philosophic vein, and his *Gesta Friderici imperatoris (Deeds of Emperor Frederick)* describes the history of Germany during the investiture contest as the background to Frederick I Barbarossa's election as King of Germany in 1152. Otto discusses the first years of Barbarossa's reign in some detail, and although he was related through his mother to the emperor, who commissioned him to write the book and supplied a preface, the *Gesta* offers a strikingly objective historical narrative. William of Malmesbury (*c*.1080–1143) was a monk of the local Benedictine foundation in Wiltshire, and his *Gesta Regum Anglorum (Deeds of the Kings of England)* is a research-based and sophisticated account of the monarchy's development from the mid-fifth century up to the author's own time. A comparable sense of how institutions develop and change is present in the history of the abbey of Saint-Denis near Paris written by Abbé Suger (*c*.1081–1151), who shows great skill in relating the foundation's past to the wider context of early French history.

*A statue of Gregory of Tours, sculpted by Jean Marcellin in the early 1850s, stands in the Cour Napoléon of the Louvre Museum, Paris.*

# THE TRIUMPH OF THE CAPETIANS

## 1180 — 1328

*The later period of Capetian rule, from the reign of Philip II Augustus (1180–1223) to the reign of Charles IV (1322–28), saw the French monarchy established as the greatest power in Europe. A regular sequence of male heirs to the throne guaranteed the dynastic succession, and no other family of French aristocrats challenged the Capetian right to rule. The vast territorial acquisitions of the 13th century meant that substantial fiefdoms could be granted to the king's younger sons, and that system of 'apanage' softened the blow of primogeniture while promoting the ruling family's solidarity. A generally close relationship with the papacy was an important element in the Capetians' international renown. But the kings were also sustained by their reputation for sacral power. The activity known as 'touching for the king's evil' was based on the belief that sufferers of the skin disease scrofula could be cured by a touch of the king's hand. The healing ceremony was a mass phenomenon and testified to the intimate association between the king and his people.*

From the late 12th century onwards royal administration acquired some of its typical institutions such as the *conseil du roi* or *curia regis*, the council that advised the king on policy and administration. With the consolidation of a French state there came a new appetite for adventure. The later Capetians' restoration and rearrangement of the tombs of the Merovingian and Carolingian kings at Saint-Denis in Paris showed more than just a respect for the past. This was also a symbolic gesture placing the Capetians in a tradition of monarchical ambition that wished to extend Francia's boundaries.

RIGHT *The* Grandes Chroniques de France *(1274–1461) illustrate a scene in which Philip II Augustus is in conversation with a bishop.*

The fact that Philip II Augustus broke with Capetian precedent by not having to designate his son, Louis VIII, as king during his own lifetime shows the degree of security he brought to the French Crown. Philip can be seen as the French national monarchy's effective founder and his local architectural legacy can still be seen in Paris, a city he encircled in a massive defensive wall enclosing a new civic area of some 600

acres (250 hectares). In 1202 he ordered building to start on the major stronghold called the Louvre, and it was a royal initiative that ensured the paving of the major streets of Paris. Philip also ordered the construction of two large stone buildings at the market of *Les Halles* on the Right Bank. The city's increasing levels of safety, hygiene and embellishment were paid for by taxes imposed on royal vassals. Philip proved to be adept at augmenting his revenue, and in the Order of Knights Templar – whom he used as his bankers – he had a reliable ally. Much of the money also came from Parisian Jews, who were abominably treated by the king. In 1180 Philip ordered that Jews who had previously enjoyed royal protection should be imprisoned and then forced to buy their freedom by surrendering all their gold and silver. A subsequent decree of 1182 that wiped out debts owed to the city's Jews was unsurprisingly popular among debtors. Philip's expulsion of the Jews from France in that same decree was only partially implemented, however, and those who did leave eventually returned and settled in the area of the Marais.

## RECOVERING ENGLISH TERRITORIES

Philip's campaigning, both diplomatic and military, was dominated by one consistent goal: the removal from French soil of the English Crown's territorial rights. He started a series of disputes against Henry II of England, who was also count of Anjou as well as duke both of Normandy and of Aquitaine, and in doing so he was able to exploit Henry's fraught relations with his rebellious sons. Richard the Lionheart chose to pay homage to Philip in November 1188, and their joint military campaign in Anjou during the summer of the following year forced the English king to renew his homage to Philip just before his death. Relations between Richard, now king of England, and Philip became strained during the Third Crusade, however, and after his precipitate departure from the expedition Philip started to plot to ensure the return of the territory known as the Vexin to the French Crown. The Vexin adjoined the duchy of Normandy and had been granted to Richard when he became engaged to Philip's sister, Alice. Although Richard broke that engagement in 1191, Philip had initially allowed him to keep the territory in order to maintain the Third Crusade's coalition. He now wanted it back and persuaded Prince John, Richard's brother, to join him in waging war against the Lionheart.

In 1193 Philip invaded first the Vexin and then Normandy, where he made substantial territorial gains. Richard was at this time still a prisoner of the German emperor Henry VI, following his capture while travelling back from the crusade. But his release from captivity at the beginning of 1194 heralded the start of a major English campaign to regain control of all Normandy – which had been largely achieved by the end of 1198. However, Richard's death the following year,

and the accession of his brother John, led to a sharp reversal of English fortunes. Under the terms of the Treaty of Le Goulet (1200), the English ceded control of large parts of Normandy and John had to acknowledge that the counts of Boulogne and Flanders were vassals of the French, rather than the English, Crown. The treaty's provisions emphasized that John only held his remaining French territories as Philip's vassal, and his failure to obey a summons to attend the French king led to a further outbreak of war in 1202. By 1204 the French army had seized the last English territories in Normandy as well as most of Aquitaine and the countship of Anjou. As a disloyal vassal, John was then formally dispossessed by Philip of all the French lands he had held under the suzerainty of the French Crown.

Philip's exploitation of a weakened England also played its part in his European continental policy. The German emperor Otto IV, of the Welf dynasty, was King John's nephew and an English ally, but both monarchs had fallen foul of the papacy. John was refusing to accept a papal nomination to the see of Canterbury, and Otto was trying to dispossess Frederick II of his Sicilian kingdom. The papacy, however, regarded kings of Sicily as its vassals, and Otto's campaign therefore impinged on papal rights. Philip's intervention in German affairs saw him backing rebellious nobles who were supporting Frederick's cause, while John inevitably supported Otto.

At first, Philip envisaged capitalizing on the Anglo-papal quarrel in order to justify a French invasion of England. John was portrayed in French propaganda as an enemy of the Church, and the invasion was therefore being canvassed as a principled campaign in support of papal authority. This plan came unstuck when John capitulated and accepted the right of papal investiture. An agreed formula declared that the kingdom of England was a papal fiefdom ruled by John as the pope's vassal, and a French attack on it would therefore also have been an outrage committed against the papacy. However, the fact that Ferdinand, count of Flanders, was the only one of Philip's feudal barons

ABOVE *A dramatic reconstruction of Philip II Augustus's victory at Bouvines (July 1214) by the French artist Horace Vernet (1789–1863).*

to oppose the invasion plan – and had done so moreover at a time when John was still an excommunicate – gave the French king the pretext for another war. The ruler of Flanders, having breached his feudal obligation of obedience, could be punished legitimately. The armies of John of England and the German emperor Otto supported Ferdinand in the ensuing conflict (1213–14).

The major victory won by Philip's army at Bouvines on 27 July 1214 set the seal on Western Europe's new power alignments. The humiliated English Crown seemed to have no prospect of ever regaining its French territories, and in this weakened condition the monarchy was forced to accept the demands for baronial representation as drawn up in the *Magna Carta* in 1215. The German nobility deposed the shamed Otto and replaced him with Frederick II. And French monarchy gained in authority as an institution strongly identified with the cause of the nation.

## LOUIS IX – CRUSADER AND PERSECUTOR

The crusading activities of Louis IX during his reign (r. 1226–70) showed the French monarchy's international authority as well as the king's intimate association with the Church. He was captured by the Egyptian army in 1250 during the Seventh Crusade, and the four years Louis spent in the Middle East following his release saw him rebuilding the crusader settlements' defences and engaging in diplomatic negotiations with the neighbouring Islamic governments of Syria and Egypt. Fearful of the crusader states' exposure to the military threat posed by Baybars, the Mamluk ruler of Egypt and Syria, Louis launched an Eighth Crusade. It was that expedition which claimed his life after he was taken ill at Tunis in 1270. The magnificence of the Sainte-Chapelle, commissioned by the king to be his private chapel and consecrated in 1248, makes St Louis an important figure in the evolution of French aesthetic taste. And the building's position within the royal palace that stood on the Île de la Cité was also designed to show how French monarchy was replacing the crisis-afflicted Holy Roman Empire as the institutional leader of Christian Europe.

## REVENUE-RAISING SCHEMES

Louis's own model of a Christian monarch embraced anti-semitism as a matter of course, and some 12,000 manuscript copies of the Talmud were burnt on royal command in 1243. Jews engaged in usury were expelled from France on the proclamation of the Seventh Crusade, with the sale of their confiscated properties being used to subsidize the expedition's costs. Increasing revenue by turning against the Jews was something of a Capetian tradition; Philip IV ('Le Bel'), who reigned from 1285 to 1314, appropriated their outstanding loans after ordering the expulsion of all Jews from France in 1306. Philip's determination to maximize royal revenue was partly a result of the costs of war. He went to war against Flanders, and although the peace of 1305 recognized Flemish

LEFT *A statue of Louis IX in Paris's Sainte-Chapelle, a building commissioned by the King and which served as his private chapel.*

independence, the prosperous cities of Lille and Douai, enriched by the cloth trade, had to be ceded to France. He also campaigned in Aquitaine where, in 1294–98 and 1300–03, Edward I of England was forced to defend the region of Guienne, which was the only part of their once expansive dukedom that the English still controlled.

Technological advances were certainly increasing the costs of war, but the drive to raise more money also reflected Philip's conviction that the French national monarchy should be an efficient bureaucracy with an exclusive authority over its subjects. His establishment in 1307 of a new court of law, the *Parlement* of Paris, was part of that programme since its jurisdiction covered the whole kingdom. Philip's subjects could use the *Parlement* to appeal against the lower courts' decisions, a right which diminished the nobility's rights of jurisdiction locally.

Philip's drive for uniformity resulted in his imposition of taxation on the French clergy. That measure, while showing the increasingly important role of civil lawyers in the governmental machine, also led to a quarrel with Pope Boniface VIII (1294–1303). The wealth and independence of the Knights Templar made them Philip's next victims. Heavily indebted to the knights, Philip took advantage of their unpopularity and in

1307 ordered the arrest of those members of the Order who were operating in France. The papacy had now reverted to its usual pro-French position, and later that same year Clement V obliged Philip by issuing a papal bull instructing European monarchs to arrest all Templars and confiscate their assets. Following a series of trials on trumped-up charges, dozens of the knights arrested on Philip's command were burnt at the stake in Paris in 1310, and the papacy officially dissolved the Order in 1312.

Three sons born to Philip IV sat on the French throne during the last years of Capetian kingship. The reign of Louis X (1314–16) saw alliances of regional nobles reacting against the fiscal demands initiated by Philip, and Louis's decision of 1315 to grant freedom to French serfs was prompted by the need to plug the consequent gap in royal revenue. Serfs owned directly by the king had to pay him for their freedom, and those owned by the king's subjects had to pay a sum shared equally between Louis and the former owners. Serfs who could not, or would not, buy their freedom had their goods confiscated, with the proceeds going to the Crown. The revenue-producing capacity of Jewish commerce prompted another major change in government policy: in 1315 Jews were allowed to return to France for an initial 12-year period under specific conditions that excluded them from practising usury.

Some of the Crown's money was spent keeping military and commercial pressure on Flanders, whose independence and great wealth irked its feudal suzerain, the French monarchy. Philip V (1316–22) succeeded to the throne when John I, Louis X's posthumously born son, died after a reign lasting five days, and it was Philip who attempted a diplomatic solution of the Flemish question. Count Robert III agreed that his grandson Louis would inherit, and since the young prince was being brought up at Philip's court the agreement seemed to guarantee a reliably pro-French future for Flanders. Louis I (1322–46), however, lacked a local power base, and French forces had to intervene in his support following the Flemish revolt (1323–26) against the count's rule.

## Asserting Capetian dominance

Philip V's accession had been controversial initially, but those nobles who supported the rights of Louis X's daughter, Joan, were trumped by Philip's swift coronation at Rheims in 1316. Thereafter, he relied on the famous Salic law, and its denial of a female right of regal succession, to bolster his authority. Philip's establishment of the *cour des comptes*, charged with governmental audit and prompt revenue payment, proved to be a lasting feature of French administration. Both Philip and his brother, who succeeded him as Charles IV (1322–28), nonetheless faced English challenges in the southwest. Guienne might be the only sliver of French land left to English kings, but it was a near-autonomous province. Edward II refused to pay homage to Louis X, only reluctantly paid homage to Philip V and then renewed his refusal in regard to Charles IV.

# 'TENNIS BALLS, MY LIEGE'

*The insulting 'treasure' that France's Dauphin sent to Henry V in Shakespeare's play had long since played its part in French sport. Louis X (1314–16) was an enthusiastic player of* jeu de paume *or 'game of the palm' from which modern tennis is derived, and his innovation of an indoor court supplemented the game's outdoor version.*

In both cases the aim was to serve and hit the ball with gloved hands, though barehanded versions of the game were also played at an earlier stage. The server's cry of '*tenez*', or 'look out', may be the origin of the word 'tennis'. Its indoor form, when played with the racket (a post-medieval innovation), would later be called 'real' to distinguish it from the lawn-based version that became popular in the 19th century. *Jeu de paume*, when played indoors, involved the hitting of the ball within an entirely enclosed space, while the original outdoor version involved a court consisting of just a front wall and two side walls. The game Louis played, however, was already historic, and earlier versions of it were being played in France by at least the 12th

Le Jeu de Paume, *an anonymous 18th-century engraving of the precursor to modern tennis.*

century. The Spanish game of *pelota* and the Italian *palla*, also handball games played within a court, are of similar antiquity. The English fives, a game played without a racket, belongs to the same family of sports. Louis's innovation was widely imitated in royal and aristocratic palaces across Western Europe, and the playing of *jeu de paume* in specially built indoor courts showed the emergent influence of the French as arbiters of fashion and social style. The pneumonia, or possibly pleurisy, that killed the young king has been attributed to the large amount of chilled wine he quaffed to cool himself down after a particularly vigorous game of *jeu de paume*.

Anglo-French resentments came to a head in the military conflict of 1324 which is named after the village of Saint-Sardos in Guienne. It was here, just within the English-controlled side of the border, that a French subject had raised a *bastide* or small fortified town. Local landowners who feared it might attract their workers away from the land burnt the *bastide* to the ground; in doing this, they had enjoyed the tacit support of the local English administration. Charles IV therefore declared that the English had forfeited the duchy of Aquitaine, and his forces encountered little resistance during their six-week campaign as they swept through Gascony. Charles IV, last of the Capetian kings, had made his point, and the English were allowed to retain their exiguous territorial presence in the southwest with the exception of the border region of Agenais, which became French controlled. Right to the last, therefore, Capetian kingship could exult in its triumphs, and England's courtiers, nobles and soldiers were left pondering the question of how best to avenge so bitter a defeat.

# 1144 — 1192 | THE THIRD CRUSADE

*By the late 12th century the predominant power in the Islamic Middle East was the Ayyubid dynasty, whose founder Saladin (Salah ad-Din, c.1138–93) was of Kurdish descent. Following the deposition of Egypt's Fatimid caliphate Saladin became first the country's vizier (1169) and then its sultan. In 1174 he imposed his rule over Damascus, and in subsequent years his authority extended to Aleppo (1176) and then Mosul (1183). Saladin's construction of an Egyptian-Syrian power block meant that Muslim territories administered by a single ruler now surrounded the Latin kingdom of Jerusalem.*

In the early 12th century Jerusalem's Latin rulers had enjoyed substantial success in consolidating and extending their kingdom. Baldwin I's reign (1100–18) saw the capture of Acre (1104), Beirut (1110) and Sidon (1111). With its command of the Palestinian coast secured, Jerusalem's suzerainty was acknowledged by the crusader states to the north at Tripoli, Antioch and Baldwin's own county of Edessa. The first military Orders of monastic knights, the Templars and the Hospitallers, were established in Jerusalem during the reign of the king's relative and successor Baldwin II (1118–31), who maintained a series of offensives against Fatimid Egypt and the Seljuk Turks. The Council of Nablus, composed of the higher clergy and leaders of the aristocratic laity, issued in 1120 the canons that comprised the kingdom's earliest written laws, and although Baldwin II was held captive by Aleppo's emir in 1123–24 the king subsequently led his army to victory over the Seljuk Turks at the Battle of Azaz (11 June 1125). A regency government ran the Latin kingdom during Baldwin's captivity, and the extensive trading rights granted to Venice's merchants in the agreement of 1124 guaranteed significant Venetian military support in the campaign of that year which secured Jerusalem's capture of Tyre.

*RIGHT Crusaders fight a bloody battle during the Crusades in this detail from 'Passages fait Outremer' (Overseas Voyages), by Sébastien Mamerot, c.1475.*

The marriage of Baldwin II's heir Melisande to the recently widowed Fulk V of Anjou, who ruled Jerusalem as co-sovereign (r. 1131–43), brought the kingdom within the ambit of the Angevin empire. Fulk was the father of Geoffrey V of Anjou and paternal grand-father of England's King Henry II, but his reign saw the start of serious internal

dissidence because many opposed the influence of the king's Angevin retinue. There was also now a major external threat; Zengi (c.1095–1146) had been imposed by the Seljuks as governor both of Mosul (1127) and of Aleppo (1128), and then recognized by them as an independent ruler. The two cities were thereby united under Zengi's rule, and he became the founder of a new dynasty of Turkic rulers. In 1144 the Zengid army invaded and conquered Edessa, the last of the crusader states to be established and the first to fall. This was recognized as a major crisis in the West, and the Second Crusade (1147–49) led by Louis VII of France and the German king Conrad III made Damascus its primary object of attack.

## CAPTURING DAMASCUS FOR THE TURKS

Zengi had targeted Damascus earlier when he launched a campaign against its Turkic ruling dynasty in the mid-1130s, but the alliance signed in 1139 between Damascus and Jerusalem had frustrated his goal of hegemonic power in Syria. By 1147, however, Damascus was in alliance with Zengi's son, Nur ad-Din, the emir of Aleppo. The siege of Damascus in July 1148 ended in utter failure and the disintegration of the entire crusade. Disputes about military strategy had divided the crusading leaders – and especially Conrad – from the nobility in Jerusalem whose reputation for fractious behaviour made it difficult to interest Western leaders in crusading during the decades that followed. These, however, were the years when Nur ad-Din, sustained by his interpretation of *jihad* as an anti-Western holy war, succeeded in entrenching a new pattern of power in the Middle East. His forces' defeat of the army of Antioch at the Battle of Inab (29 June 1149) exposed the principality to new levels of danger. Furthermore, the death in that conflict of the principality's ruler, Raymond of Poitiers, was a grievous blow to the collective interest of the crusader states.

By 1154 Nur ad-Din was in control of Damascus. Baldwin III (r. 1143–62) formed a protective alliance with the Byzantines in 1158, and this was renewed in 1168 by his brother King Amalric I (r. 1162–74). In the 1150s the Fatimid dynasty's authority over Egypt decayed, and in 1169 Nur ad-Din ordered his general, Shirkuh, to seize Egypt from the vizier Shawar. Shirkuh died just two months later, however, and supreme authority was transferred to his nephew Saladin who established himself as Sultan and asserted his independence of Nur ad-Din. Following Nur ad-Din's death in 1174 Saladin extended his authority in Syria.

## BALDWIN IV, THE LEPER KING

Manuel I Commenus had been a close ally of Amalric and had supported the Latin kingdom's own attempts at exerting authority within Egypt. The Greek emperor's death in 1180 removed an important source of support. When Amalric's son and

successor Baldwin IV (r. 1174–85) came to power he was able to exert his own authority, despite the fact that he suffered from leprosy. Baldwin could also call on the support of his uncle, Joscelin III of Edessa, whenever the authority of his cousin Raymond III of Tripoli seemed to be overbearing. Furthermore, the marriage of his sister Sibylla to William of Montferrat, a cousin of Frederick I Barbarossa and of Louis VII of France, carried with it the prospect of substantial Western support. However, William's death in 1177, soon after arriving in Jerusalem and leaving Sibylla pregnant with the future Baldwin V, was a major blow. Moreover, the influence of Raynald of Chatillon within the kingdom created enormous problems. Raynald's ruthless military strategy helped to defeat Saladin at the Battle of Montsigard (25 November 1177), but his reputation for extreme and wanton cruelty was by now fully deserved.

A leper king who could not be expected to live long, and an heir who was a mere infant, created a tense situation for the dynastic succession. Count Raymond III, along with his cousin Count Bohemond of Antioch, plotted to persuade the widowed Sibylla to marry into the Ibelins, a powerful and ambitious local family. But her brother, although an ailing king, stole a march on them by securing Sibylla's marriage to Guy of Lusignan, a nobleman who had recently arrived in the kingdom. Baldwin's disillusion with Guy's military performance prompted another strategic shift. The coronation of the sickly five-year-old Baldwin V in 1183 was designed to limit the influence of Guy and Sibylla in the immediate royal circle, and Raymond of Tripoli regained his authority. The infant survived his uncle by barely a year, and after he died in 1186 Sibylla reigned in Jerusalem as co-consort with Guy. However, Guy's influence, exerted in combination with his close associate Raynald, only contributed to the kingdom's problems.

## THE BUILDUP TO THE THIRD CRUSADE

An advantageous marriage had made Raynald lord of Oultrejourdain, whose fortresses controlled the trade routes between Damascus and Egypt. It was in this area that he launched an unprovoked attack on a Muslim caravan in 1186 – an action that led Saladin to declare war on Jerusalem. Raymond had returned to Tripoli in protest at Sibylla and Guy's joint rule, and had gone so far as to ally himself with Saladin, whom he

allowed to occupy his fiefdom in Tiberias. A reconciliation between Raymond and Guy in 1187 led to their joint command of the force sent to do battle with Saladin at Tiberias. But their failure to agree on a strategy led to the crusaders' defeat at the Battle of Hattin (4 July 1187), and following his capture Raynald was executed on account of his flagrant disregard for Muslim custom both in war and in peace. Guy was imprisoned in Damascus before being allowed to return to Jerusalem in return for a ransom payment.

Saladin's forces overran the whole of the Latin kingdom except for the port of Tyre, which was defended by Conrad of Montferrat, Baldwin V's paternal uncle. The surrender of the city of Jerusalem in October 1187 marks the end of the first kingdom of Jerusalem, although the principality of Antioch and the county of Tripoli managed to survive Saladin's onslaught on the Latin kingdom to their south. Jerusalem city was already swollen with refugees who had escaped from the countryside during Saladin's advance, and its population were allowed to escape to Tyre, Tripoli and Egypt from where they often fled back to Europe. Those who could not afford to pay for their freedom, however, often ended up in slavery. Confronted by this collapse, Western leaders launched the Third Crusade. Henry II of England and Philip II Augustus of France put aside their differences and issued a joint call to arms financed by a levy known as the

'Saladin tithe'. Following Henry's death in 1189 it was his son and successor, Richard I ('the Lionheart'), who led the English crusaders. The German emperor Frederick I Barbarossa also joined the expedition, and on 18 May 1190 his army captured Iconium, the capital of the sultanate of Rum. Three weeks later, Barbarossa's horse slipped while crossing the Saleph river, and he died after being thrown onto rocks. Most of his men then returned to Germany.

## THE LIONHEART IN THE HOLY LAND

Richard the Lionheart and Philip II Augustus of France started the crusade as allies, and it was their joint campaign in Anjou in the summer of 1189 that had forced Henry II of England to pay homage to Philip for his French territories. In July 1190 Richard (now king of England) and Philip set sail from Marseilles for Sicily en route to Palestine. The landing in Messina was initially an opportunity to resolve a dynastic conflict: Sicily's ruler Tancred had imprisoned Joan, who was the wife of his predecessor and also Richard's sister. Joan was released after her brother captured Messina on 4 October 1190, but the issue of the Lionheart's own betrothal now emerged as a thorny issue. Richard had been engaged to Philip's half-sister Alys, but he now declared that he intended to marry Berengaria of Navarre instead. An offended Philip left Sicily without Richard at the end of March 1191 and arrived in Palestine in the middle of May. His forces now joined those of Leopold V, duke of Austria, who was Barbarossa's successor as commander of the imperial troops.

Richard's armada left Sicily on 10 April 1191 but soon encountered a severe storm. His own ship was able to dock at Limassol in Cyprus, but several other ships bearing a substantial amount of treasure ran aground, whereupon Duke Commenus, the ruler of Cyprus, seized the booty. This act prompted Richard's retaliation, and he launched a swift military takeover of the island. In June 1191 he arrived in Acre where he and his men joined the crusader forces besieging the town.

Guy of Lusignan had been denied entry to Tyre by Conrad of Montferrat, and the king of Jerusalem had therefore shifted his military campaign to the south where he embarked in 1189 on a two-year siege of Acre. Queen Sibylla's death in 1190 had deprived Guy of the right to rule as consort, and the right of succession reverted to Baldwin IV's half-sister Isabella. Conrad's arranged marriage to Isabella therefore allowed him to claim the Crown, although Guy refused to cede his rights. The leaders of the Third Crusade therefore had to decide whom to back in this succession dispute once they arrived in the summer of 1191. Richard decided to back Guy, who was one of his vassals in Poitou. Philip of France, however, supported Conrad, who was a cousin of his father Louis VII. This added to the ill will between them, and Philip returned home after Acre fell to the Christians on 12 July. Another quarrel was in progress, too. Richard had offended Leopold by casting down the duke's flag which had been raised, along with the banners of the English and French Crowns and of the kingdom of Jerusalem, in Acre following its recapture. By the end of 1191 the duke, who was another significant backer of Conrad for the Crown of Jerusalem, was back in Austria.

Richard's victories at Arsuf (7 September 1191) and at Jaffa in early July 1192 recovered most of the coast for the Latin kingdom and dented Saladin's reputation for invincibility. But it was clear by now how difficult it would be to reoccupy and defend the city of Jerusalem. Richard moreover needed to return to England in order to defend his domestic position against his brother John. On 2 September 1192 therefore Richard and Saladin signed the peace treaty that ended the Third Crusade.

## A MUCH-REDUCED KINGDOM

The kingdom of Jerusalem, with its capital at Acre, survived for another century after the end of the Third Crusade as a much-diminished entity extending along the coast from Tyre to Jaffa. Saladin died soon afterwards, and his sons quarrelled over his territorial legacy. The embittered nobility of the greatly-reduced feudal kingdom considered themselves abandoned by their Western patrons, and the descent of Saladin's former realm into civil war caused its citizens to lament the lost opportunities of the past.

Conrad of Montferrat was elected to the throne in April 1192 by the nobility of the kingdom, but was murdered by members of the Hashshashin sect a few days afterwards. Leopold of Austria suspected the Lionheart of complicity in Conrad's murder, and his resentment at the removal of his standard from the walls of Acre still rankled. Richard's route back to England crossed Leopold's territories, and while the king was making the journey the duke took the opportunity to arrest and then imprison him. Richard was then transferred to the custody of Henry VI, the German emperor. The Lionheart was only allowed to return to England two years later in 1194 on payment of a ransom of 150,000 marks.

*BELOW This contemporary illustration depicts Richard I ('the Lionheart') being pardoned by Henry VI for his suspected complicity in the murder of Conrad of Montferrat, from the Liber ad honorem Augusti (A Book to Honour the Emperor) by Peter of Eboli, c.1196.*

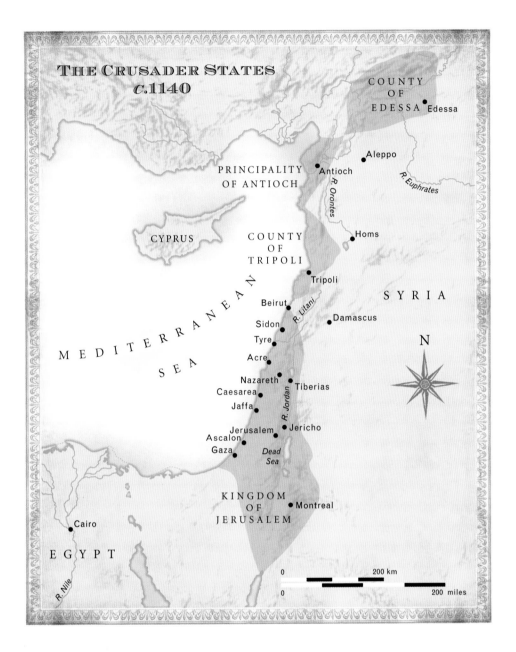

THE CRUSADER STATES
*c.*1140

COUNTY
OF
EDESSA · Edessa

PRINCIPALITY
OF ANTIOCH

· Aleppo

· Antioch

*R. Orontes*

*R. Euphrates*

CYPRUS

COUNTY
OF
TRIPOLI

· Homs

· Tripoli

SYRIA

MEDITERRANEAN SEA

Beirut ·

*R. Litani*

Sidon ·

· Damascus

Tyre ·

N

Acre ·

Nazareth ·

· Tiberias

Caesarea ·

*R. Jordan*

Jaffa ·

Jerusalem · · Jericho

Ascalon ·

Gaza · *Dead Sea*

KINGDOM
OF
JERUSALEM

· Montreal

· Cairo

EGYPT

*R. Nile*

0          200 km

0          200 miles

Conrad's resilient, and pregnant, widow Isabella had married Count Henry II of
Champagne, a political supporter of his uncle Richard of England, within days of the
assassination. Guy of Lusignan, meanwhile, was given a consolation prize and allowed
to buy the kingdom of Cyprus, which had been conquered by Richard on his journey
to Acre. When Count Henry died in an accident in 1197 Isabella married Amalric
of Lusignan, Guy's brother. Conrad of Montferrat, who had wanted the Crown of
Jerusalem so very badly, would nonetheless receive a posthumous reward. His daughter
Maria of Montferrat succeeded to the throne in 1205 on the death of her mother
Isabella and her stepfather Amalric.

# THE KNIGHTS TEMPLAR

*Increasing numbers of pilgrims were drawn to the Holy Land in the wake of the success of the First Crusade, but as they travelled through the Latin kingdom of Jerusalem's countryside they were often besieged by bandits. In c.1120 King Baldwin II of Jerusalem therefore approved the foundation of 'The Poor Knights of Christ and of the Temple of Solomon', whose original and sole aim was to provide protection for the pilgrims.*

These first 'Knights Templar' numbered some dozen soldiers who had embraced poverty, chastity and obedience on joining the new Order, and they observed a communal monastic discipline. Their headquarters was on Jerusalem's Temple Mount, raised – according to tradition – above the remains of the Temple of Solomon, and that location was evoked in the organization's title.

The pioneering knights gained the support of Bernard of Clairvaux, whose advocacy was instrumental in obtaining the Order's official recognition by the Church in 1129. A rapid growth in numbers followed, and the knights' status as the crusading movement's shock troops ensured that land and money were given or bequeathed to them by supporters from all over Western Christendom. In 1139 the papacy decreed the Order's exemption from obedience to local or national laws. This extraterritorial status, which included freedom from taxation, gave the Templars an international and self-regulating status. The individual vow of poverty remained, along with the requirement to hand over to the Order all of one's personal wealth and goods. But the knights' corporate wealth rivalled that of some European governments, and their financial and business interests were extensive. There was a Templar banking structure, originally developed to provide pilgrims with a safe deposit for their valuables while travelling, and Templar houses supplied the Order with local headquarters in the major European towns and cities.

A blend of the monastic and the military shaped the organization's administration, and each region of Europe and the Middle East with a significant Templar presence was ruled by a Master. At the apex stood the Grand Master, who was in overall control of military campaigning in the Middle East and of financial interests in the West. Dressed at all times in their white mantle with its red cross,

the Knights Templar were easily recognized, and their code of behaviour, forbidding physical contact with women and enforcing silence at meals, was designed to instill an austere communal identity. That solidarity was also the source of their reputation as formidable warriors: the red cross

emblazoned on the knightly robes symbolized martyrdom, with an honourable death in combat meriting a heavenly reward. The Templars did not just consist of aristocratic knights, however. At the height of the Order's influence, when its total strength was not much less than 20,000 men, the knights were a minority within that number.

Within the Order, the sergeants were of a lower social standing, and they dealt with the more mundane details involved in running the Templars' businesses and estates. The chaplains constituted a third clearly defined group.

As the crusading ideal waned, so, too, did the fortunes of the Knights Templar. The loss of Jerusalem city enforced their withdrawal to Acre in the 1190s, and the Knights' headquarters were relocated to Cyprus after the armies of the Mamluk Sultanate (then ruling both Egypt and Syria) seized the last remaining Templar fortresses in the north during the 1290s. By 1303 Mamluk forces had ejected the Knights from Cyprus. The Templars' relations with the other knightly orders that emerged out of the Latin kingdom, the Hospitallers and the Teutonic Knights, were sometimes difficult, and a reputation for secrecy had always surrounded them. The Order's initiation ceremonies were solemn occasions whose details were a closely guarded affair. But this secrecy was seized upon by the Templars' enemies as a sign of something more sinister, and conspiracy theorists who mistrusted them on account of their wealth were provided with ammunition.

The campaign of persecution that King Philip IV of France (1268–1314) launched against the Order in 1307 was a convenient way of expunging the massive debts owed by the French monarchy to the Templars, and confessions of idolatry, heresy and financial corruption were extracted under torture. In 1312 Pope Clement V formally dissolved the Order, having already instructed all Christian monarchs in Europe to seize Templar assets. Most of the Templars who were tried in the papal courts were acquitted, and many members of the disbanded Order joined the Knights Hospitaller, an organization that had also taken over many of the properties once owned by their rival.

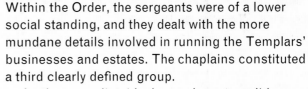

*The 14th-century* Roman de Godefroy de Bouillon *shows Templar knights approaching Jerusalem.*

# 1179
# 1244

# THE ALBIGENSIAN CRUSADE

*The papal-inspired crusades had a European as well as a Middle Eastern dimension, and expeditions launched in the 13th century secured the conversion of pagan peoples in the continent's north, such as the Norwegians and the Swedes. From the 1230s onwards members of the military Order known as the Teutonic Knights were also subjugating the Prussians – a Baltic people – and imposing Christianity on them. In Western Europe, however, the campaign (1209–29) to extinguish the Cathar heresy – a Christian religious sect that flourished in the Languedoc region of southwestern France – acquired a particular notoriety. These rebels of the Midi posed a direct and explicit challenge to the papacy's interpretation of Christianity, and the methods used to crush them were correspondingly violent.*

The papal conviction that it could both identify heresy and had the right to extinguish it in the name of orthodoxy testified to the institution's new self-confidence during this period. But the defeat of the Cathars also had important political and cultural ramifications since it gave the French Crown a new authority in the southwest of the country. This was the region, including Languedoc, which was widely known as Occitania. The province had its distinctive customs that it shared with neighbouring Aragon to the south, as well as its own Latin language (the *langue d'oc*). Many of these cultural features would survive for centuries, but the brutality of the Cathars' extirpation meant that there would be no political expression to that regional identity. The military campaign launched against the heretics came to be known as the Albigensian Crusade and took its name from the French town of Albi, which was seen as a focal point for the Cathar movement. Although the town had a predominantly Catholic population, it was nevertheless surrounded by numerous Cathar strongholds.

RIGHT *A depiction of Tannhäuser, the poet, clad in the habit of the Teutonic Order of Knights, in the Codex Manesse of 1340.*

## THE CATHAR DOCTRINE

The Cathars probably derived their name from the Greek for purification, *katharsis*, and their beliefs, along with their secretive initiation rites, placed them in a long tradition of religious dissidence that starts with the Gnostics of the early Christian centuries.

Catharism considered the world of matter to be intrinsically evil and opposed to the world of the spirit in which love predominated. The intensity with which the distinction was drawn explains why the movement's adherents are often described as dualists – a position that attracted the hostility of orthodox Christianity, which emphasized the redemption of the material world through the incarnation, crucifixion and resurrection. As believers in pure spirit, the Cathars denied that Christ could have become incarnate in mankind and still remain God. And they probably considered the Christian God to be a malevolent agent since, in the Church's own view, he had created matter. The early 13th-century Catholic Church, with its riches, great buildings and taste for political power, seemed to the Cathars to be the very embodiment of matter's pride, pomp and wickedness. These were just about the most dangerous set of beliefs it was possible to hold in medieval Europe.

Distinctively Cathar beliefs could be detected in the towns of the Rhineland and of northern France during the mid-12th century. By the late 12th century Cathars were well established in northern Italy and Languedoc, and in both of these regions they formed communities of believers who maintained that they were Christ's true followers and the true preservers of early Christian belief. The Church correctly identified the Cathars as a rival body, since they were organized in an ecclesiastical fashion with their own sacraments and services, bishops and clergy. Those called the *perfecti* (the perfect ones) were separated from mainstream society and constituted the heart of the movement. Those known as the *credentes* (the believers) attended religious services but otherwise lived normal lives in the everyday world. This, then, was a secret society whose adherents could not be identified easily, and that uncertainty contributed to the persecution's paranoid attitude towards them. Withdrawal from the flesh was extreme for both types of Cathars, and procreation was frowned upon since it meant creating more matter – and hence more evil. The *perfecti* therefore abstained from sexual intercourse. This was, however, permitted to the *credentes* as long as they restricted themselves to anal sex. Cathars refused to take part in wars, opposed capital punishment and were hostile to the tithe system that supplied revenue for the Church. They also refused to take oaths of any kind, claiming that such agreements subjected the spirit to the world of matter. These beliefs were unsurprisingly viewed by the authorities in both Church and state as an anarchic threat to the very foundation of civilized order.

The territory of what is now southwestern France was divided in the mid-12th century between the kingdom of Aragon and the county of Toulouse. By the standards of contemporary Europe it was densely populated and contained a large number of towns. Those Western European areas in which Catharism flourished tended to be urbanized, and by the mid- to late-12th century a high proportion of the Languedoc population seem to have embraced the heresy. They proved to be very tough nuts to crack. A

papal legate arrived in the area in 1147 charged with converting the dissidents, and Toulouse saw the arrival of two more such Church missions in 1178 and 1180. Official condemnations were promulgated at the Council of the Church held in Tours (1163) and then at the Third Council of the Lateran (1179). None of these initiatives had any impact. Moreover, the Cathars seemed to be not only well entrenched and protected by the local nobility but also very popular as individuals among the population at large.

## PREPARING FOR AN ANTI-CATHAR OFFENSIVE

The long papacy of Innocent III (1198–1216) saw a vigorous assertion of the universal nature of papal authority in relation to secular princes and a renewed emphasis on crusading activity. In 1198 Innocent decreed the Fourth Crusade, which was designed to recapture Jerusalem. He was also particularly exercised by Catharism. The pope considered the Languedoc's bishops to be obstreperous, and they certainly resented the powers given to papal legates sent to combat heresy in the region's dioceses. In 1204, therefore, the pope suspended a number of these bishops, and in the following year he appointed the dynamic Folquet de Marseille, a former troubadour poet, to be bishop of Toulouse.

Folquet worked closely with the Spanish priest Dominic de Guzman (St Dominic), one of the great religious figures of the age, on an extensive conversion programme, and a series of public debates were held between Cathars and Catholics. Few Cathars, however, were converted, and Dominic's experiences led him to establish in 1216 the Order named after him, the Dominicans. They exercised a preaching ministry specifically designed to combat heresy using well-honed arguments and exposition. But Dominic had also identified an important feature of the Cathars: many of those he had met in Languedoc were well-informed and cultured people rather than ignorant fanatics. As he told the papal legates who returned to Rome in 1208, having failed yet again to convert the Cathars:

> *'It is not by the display of power and pomp, cavalcades of retainers … or by gorgeous apparel, that the heretics win proselytes; it is by zealous preaching, by apostolic humility, by austerity … '*

The Church hierarchy needed to show the same qualities, but in defence of a stronger case: *'Zeal must be met by zeal … false sanctity by real sanctity, preaching falsehood by preaching truth.'* Confronted, though, by the reality of what had turned into a mass movement of opposition, the Church hierarchy and its political allies chose another way.

Raymond VI, count of Toulouse, was the region's most powerful noble and a significant Cathar defender. Towards the end of 1207 he was challenged by Pierre de Castelnau, the papal legate and former Cistercian monk who had been active for some years in the anti-Cathar mission. De Castelnau was the central figure in Pope Innocent's newly energized campaign, and several local nobles had already been excommunicated because of their support of the Cathars. Raymond is supposed to have threatened de Castelnau with violence after the legate accused him of being a heretic, and the count was subsequently excommunicated. On 15 January 1208 de Castelnau was attacked and murdered while travelling back to Rome, and the pope, along with many others, concluded that the knight responsible for the assassination was acting on Raymond's orders.

Pope Innocent now had an excuse for war, and he wrote to King Philip II Augustus of France requesting his support for a crusade that would crush Catharism. Rather than take part himself, the king sent Simon de Montfort, an adventurous, militarily skilful and conventionally pious aristocrat, to the south instead. De

Montfort's reputation for extreme brutality in warfare was well justified, and in 1209 his fellow nobles on the Albigensian Crusade elected him to be their leader. The French Crown was experiencing great success in asserting its authority in the north, and strategic calculation on its part dictated de Montfort's nomination to lead the crusade, while also allowing him to commit multiple murders during the campaign. King Philip Augustus also saw the crusade as an opportunity to deflect the energies of some of his more ambitious nobles, and he allowed them to claim southern territories. Quite apart from its religious dimension, therefore, the Albigensian Crusade was an attempt by the monarchy and northern French nobility to subjugate the hitherto independent-minded Midi. The region's hilly terrain, along with its mass of fortified towns, nonetheless frustrated the military strategies pursued by both sides and made for a prolonged campaign in which as many as half a million people, and possibly even more, may have died.

## CRUSHING THE CATHARS

Raymond-Roger Trencavel was the first Languedoc aristocrat to fall victim to the crusader force as de Montfort and his northern barons moved into the south. Although not himself a Cathar he had tolerated the faith's diffusion across his territories, and his own position showed how the crusade involved a pattern of feudal loyalties while also seeking to combat religious heresy. As viscount of Beziers and Albi, Raymond-Roger was a vassal of the county of Toulouse, and as viscount of Carcassonne he owed allegiance to his feudal overlord, Peter II, who was king of Aragon and a notably orthodox Catholic monarch. De Montfort was granted the Trencavel lands by the pope and paid homage for them to the king of France, thereby angering King Peter, who had previously been neutral. There was also conflict between the French Crown and the papacy following Innocent's official decree that Cathar lands could be confiscated. This angered not just the southern nobility but also King Philip II Augustus, since he remained the ultimate suzerain of lands that the papacy had declared to be open to seizure and spoliation.

BELOW *The fortified city of Carcassonne was a Cathar stronghold during the Albigensian Crusade.*

Up until 1215 it was the crusaders who won the more significant victories, and the siege of Beziers, with its subsequent loss to the Cathars, in July 1209 was particularly bloody. The mass of its population, both Cathar and Catholic, was killed and the city itself destroyed before the crusaders moved on to Carcassonne, which surrendered in mid-August. Raymond-Roger, having led the defence of his city, was taken prisoner at Carcassonne, with de Montfort possibly involved in his murder while he was under supposedly safe conduct. By 1213 Catholic forces were in control of most of the county of Toulouse, at which point Peter II, king of Aragon, intervened in defence of Raymond VI, who was his vassal as well as his brother-in-law. King Peter's defeat and death at the Battle of Muret (12 September 1213) led to temporary exile for Raymond, and the lands of the county of Toulouse, having been seized by the French Crown, were granted to de Montfort along with the territories of the dukedom of Narbonne. Peter II's defeat at Muret had a major long-term strategic impact, since it spelled the end of any southern French ambitions for the Aragonese kingdom.

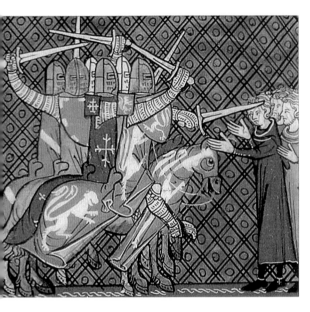

ABOVE *A 14th-century illustration from the* Chronicle of Saint Denis *depicting the crusaders massacring Cathars.*

During the next two years the Cathars and their aristocratic protectors were subjected to systematic campaigns of subjugation. Raymond VI, accompanied by his son who shared his name, returned at the head of an army in 1216. The future Raymond VII seized Beaucaire in the lower Rhone valley and defended it successfully against de Montfort's forces. In the following year his father retook Toulouse and entered the city in triumph, following which de Montfort mounted a prolonged siege in the course of which he was killed (25 June 1218) after a stone launched from a projectile within the city smashed his skull to pieces. In subsequent years the Albigensian Crusade faltered and the Cathars retook formerly besieged centres. From 1226 onwards, however, the French monarchy regained the initiative, and the treaty that Raymond VII was forced to sign at Meaux in April 1229 both ended the war and extinguished regional autonomy. The House of Toulouse was now dispossessed of most of its fiefs, and the Trencavels, lords of Beziers and Carcassonne, lost all their fiefdoms.

But the official end of military operations did not mean that the Cathars had gone away. One key result of the Albigensian campaign was the establishment of Inquisitions – formal bodies answerable to the papacy and staffed with clerical professionals charged with discovering error through cross-examination. These mobile institutions were very active in southern France from the 1230s onwards. The Cathars were now taking refuge in their few remaining strongholds, and for a whole year from the spring of 1243, the remote Cathar fortress of Montségur was besieged by the archbishop of Narbonne's army. Over 200 Cathar *perfecti* were burned by their captors after the castle fell on 16 March 1244. From then on the Cathars lacked aristocratic support, and their few

# OCCITANIA

*Occitan is a Romance language and, like its close linguistic cousins French, Italian and Catalan, it evolved out of vernacular forms of Latin during the early Middle Ages. Spoken today by over a million people in southern France, the Aran valley in the Spanish Pyrenees and along the Franco-Piedmontese border, Occitan is a remarkable linguistic survivor and offers a direct link with the culture of medieval Western Europe.*

Although Occitan also flourished in Navarre and Aragon during the central Middle Ages, it was displaced in these regions by Navarro-Aragonese, another Romance language, during the 14th century. The first texts written in standard Occitan date from the tenth century, by which time the language was already being used as a medium of literary and scientific communication as well as in works of jurisprudence. Written forms of Occitanian dialects, which include Provençal, Gascon, Languedocien, Limousin and Auvernhat, can be dated to at least the eighth century.

It was Dante, in his *De vulgari eloquentia* (1302–05), who created the category *lingua d'oc*. Observing the different words for 'yes' in Occitan, in various Italian and Iberian languages, and in French, he wrote: 'Some say *oc*, others say *si*, others say *oil*.' *Hoc illud* ('this is it') is the derivation of *oil*, and the *langue d'oil* refers to the language of medieval northern France that is the basis of modern-day standard French. *Oc* is derived from the Latin *hoc* ('this'), and Occitan's linguistic features demonstrate both the depth of Rome's cultural influence in the regions of Provence and Aquitaine as well as its persistence after the end of empire. The words 'Occitan' and 'Occitania' – a probable conflation of *Oc* and *Aquitanus*

(Aquitanian) – were first used in the 13th century and they are based on an archaic allusion to the Roman province of Gallia Aquitania which included large areas of southern France. Occitan was used by the mass of the population in the regions where it predominated during the Middle Ages, but it was also the language of courtiers and of aristocratic society. Through the poetry of the troubadours who adopted both Occitan's standard form and its different dialects, the language became the vehicle of a high culture. During the 15th century Occitania's cultural and political assimilation into the French kingdom was fast evolving, and by that stage the region's nobility were increasingly speaking French while the lower orders tended to use Occitan. French bureaucracy's enduring obsession with uniformity and regulation explains the persistence of its hostility towards Occitan from the time of the Cathars to the present day. The language was hard hit by Francois I's Ordinance of Villers-Cotterets (1539), which proscribed the use of any language other than standard French in official legislation. And the Jacobin leaders of the French Revolution waged a continuous campaign against the southern culture and language, seeing in both the expression of a dissent that undermined Republican unity and solidarity.

survivors lived as rural fugitives. There were sporadic attempted insurrections in southwest France but these were pathetic affairs. The Inquisitions had now become very powerful and the *perfecti*, when captured, were invariably burned. But the *credentes* could survive provided they recanted, and during the period following their official statement of repentance they were forced to wear yellow crosses sown onto their clothing as a sign of past error. A new chapter had opened in the history of persecution in Europe.

# THE GLORY OF ISLAMIC SPAIN

**711 / 1002**

*Spain's Islamic civilization reached its apogee during the tenth century and was centred on the city of Córdoba. This was home to the caliphate, the institution that exercised predominance over most of the Iberian Peninsula. With a population of about half a million, Córdoba was Western Europe's largest conurbation, and the caliphate's levels of economic prosperity, intellectual vitality and artistic originality made it an advanced civilization whose only possible European rival was Byzantium. Spain had by then experienced over two centuries of intense Islamic influence, and the caliph's government must have imagined it was set to endure on Spanish soil. But the invading army that had arrived from North Africa in 711 and set in motion a huge cultural transformation was only the latest in a wave of influences to affect the peninsula.*

By the end of the 11th century Spain's pre-existing Christian civilization was once again on the march, and determined to regain the lands it had lost. Spain had been Roman long before it became Christian, and Córdoba, conquered by the Roman army in 152 BC and seized from the Carthaginians, became capital of the imperial province of Baetica. The transformation of the Roman world during the fifth-century imperial retreat inevitably affected Spain, and during 415–18 the Germanic people known as the Visigoths (or Goths of the West) made an initial foray into the country following their leader Alaric's celebrated sacking of Rome in 410. Another Germanic grouping called the Vandals had, however, already established themselves in southern Spain by 409. It was from there that in 429 their leader Gaiseric transported his people en masse to North Africa, where the Vandals were initially Rome's federated allies – although they were to become the waning empire's implacable foes.

*RIGHT The Great Mosque of Córdoba, now a Christian cathedral, was built over a period of 200 years and completed by 987.*

## A CLASH OF CHRISTIAN FAITHS

The Visigoths became imperial allies in 418 and were settled for this purpose in Roman Aquitania, the region between the Garonne and the Loire valleys. In the fifth century

an increasingly independent Visigothic kingdom expanded from this base in Gaul, spread across the Pyrenees to most of Spain and moved its capital from Toulouse to Toledo. The Visigoths, like the Vandals, had converted to Christianity by the mid- to late fourth century, and both peoples had adopted the faith's Arian form, which denied that Christ was part of the Godhead. For Catholic Christians this exclusive emphasis on the saviour's human status was a heresy, and one which also had a major political and military consequence. The Franks were another Germanic people, and Clovis, who became their king in c.481, had subsequently converted to Catholic Christianity. He found the Visigoths' Arianism a useful pretext to declare war and succeeded in dislodging the Visigoths from Gaul following the Frankish army's victory of 507 at the Battle of Vouillé, near Poitiers.

Attachment to Arianism gave a group identity to Spain's Visigothic rulers and set them apart from their Catholic subjects. But the conversion of King Reccared to Catholicism in 587, followed swiftly by that of Spain's Visigothic nobility, gave rise to an intense brand of religious nationalism in the peninsula. Reccared's father, Leovigild, had already united most of the peninsula under his rule between 567 and 586, and his approval of mixed marriages was leading to the Romanization of the Visigoths. By c.600, therefore, Spain's national identity had acquired some distinctive roots and was strongly allied to the cause of the Church. One of the casualties of this Hispano-Gothic fusion was the country's large Jewish population, and the intolerance to which they were subjected led many Jews to welcome the arrival of an army of Muslim invaders in 711. Some 7000 soldiers had left Tangier under the command of the city's Arab governor, Taiq ibn Ziyad, consisting mostly of non-Arab Berber tribesmen along with a number of Syrians and Yemenis. The Visigothic nobility had only recently elected Roderick – in all probability Baetica's military governor – to the throne, and dissidents who supported the claims of the previous king's two sons joined the ranks of defectors. Toledo and Córdoba fell to Islam, and the arrival in the following year of another invasion force, again mostly Berber, meant that by 714 Islam was in effective control over most of Spain, a country that became collectively known as al-Andalus.

ABOVE *Chintila was the Visigothic king of Galicia, Hispania and Septimania from 636 until his death in c.640. His statue, sculpted by François de Vôge in 1753, stands in Retiro Park in Madrid.*

Immense religious and ethnic variety emerged as the new Arab ruling élite established its rule over a population consisting of Hispano-Romans and Visigoths. Cultural and political control was promoted by a policy allowing the peninsula's large numbers of serfs to become freemen provided they converted to Islam. Spanish Christians who kept their religion but adopted the Arabs' language and social customs were termed Mozarabs. Descendants of the pre-invasion population who converted to Islam were called Muwallads, and the Berbers who arrived in successive waves of migration had a major impact on population patterns. In 741 there was a major uprising of Berber troops garrisoned in Spain after their fellow tribesmen in North Africa rebelled against Arab rule. The subsequent arrival in the peninsula of a large army of Syrians sent to reassert Arab control ensured an even greater ethnic mix. Berber settlement had been especially strong in the northwest, and the 741 rebellion gave the Christian kingdom of Asturias, a northern outpost established in 718 by fleeing Visigothic nobles and officials, a chance to incorporate Galicia.

## THE STRUGGLE TO RESIST ISLAMIC EXPANSION

During this earlier period of Islamic rule al-Andalus remained part of the empire presided over by the Umayyad dynasty of rulers based in Damascus. Arab tribal rivalry within Spain was intense, but this did not diminish the desire for northern expansion, and that thrust was maintained until 732 when the Franks, under their leader Charles Martel, defeated an invading force near Tours. Defeat by Byzantium in Anatolia during 740 suggested that Islam might be reaching its territorial limits in the East as well as the West, and the caliphate of Syrian rulers was about to pay the price. Muslims who desired a continuous and consistently Islamic expansion had always considered the Umayyads too secular in style and were apt to dismiss the Damascus regime as merely 'the Arab state'. Nonetheless, it was the Umayyads who had broken with the ancestral Arab custom of allowing tribal leaders to elect their leader or caliph, and they established the new principle of hereditary rule within a dynasty. Following major revolts in Iran, Iraq and Khorasan, the Umayyad army was defeated in 750 at the Battle of the Great Zab river in Mesopotamia. The victors were the new 'Abbasid dynasty, whose forces set about the bloody business of exterminating the preceding regime's leading members and supporters.

'Abd al-Rahman, the former caliph's grandson, was 16 in the year of his family's deposition and managed to escape the slaughter. Accompanied by a few loyalists, the young prince at first led the life of a fugitive in North Africa, but in 755 he succeeded in making the journey across the straits of Gibraltar from Ceuta to al-Andalus. 'Abd al-Rahman was now leading an army composed mostly of mercenaries, but he also benefited from pro-Umayyad sentiment among the local population. The governor of al-Andalus owed a nominal obedience to the now 'Abbasid-controlled caliphate, but he was still the region's effectively independent ruler. Following a military defeat, his capital city of Córdoba was seized. The Umayyad prince proclaimed himself to be emir of Córdoba and as such the rightful ruler of al-Andalus, the peninsula conquered by his ancestors. The further arrival from Syria of Umayyad partisans and officials ensured the dynasty's survival in its new base.

## THE GLORY OF ISLAMIC SPAIN

**711** An Islamic army consisting mostly of Berber tribesmen leaves North Africa and arrives in Spain. Toledo and Córdoba, centres of the Christian Visigothic kingdom, fall to the invaders.

**714** Most of Spain is Muslim-controlled and becomes known collectively as al-Andalus.

**750** The Umayyad dynasty, rulers of the Islamic caliphate in the Middle East, are expelled from power by the 'Abbasids. Islamic Spain becomes politically independent of the 'Abbasids.

**929** 'Abd al-Rahman III adopts the title of caliph and thereby establishes his religious independence of the 'Abbasid caliphate. He restores his dynasty's authority over Islamic rebels in Spain.

**933** Fall of Toledo, last centre of Muslim resistance, to the Córdoban caliphate.

**976** Completion of Córdoba's Great Mosque.

**978–1002** Period in office of Abu 'Amir al-Mansur as chief minister of the Cordoban caliphate and effective ruler of Islamic Spain. The caliphate establishes its authority in northwest Africa, which is administered as the viceroyalty of Cordoba.

ABOVE *The Battle of Roncesvalles in 778, as depicted in the* Song of Roland, *is the subject of this illustration (c.1335/40) from a manuscript which forms part of the* Grandes Chroniques de France *(1274–1461). Roland lies dead on the ground, while a Christian knight prays over his body.*

Al-Andalus had therefore ceased to be a territorial province of the caliphate centred on Baghdad, and the institution termed the emirate of Córdoba ruled the peninsula as an independent territory. As emirs instead of caliphs, al-Rahman and his immediate successors were nonetheless claiming political rather than religious independence from the 'Abbasids, and they still had to confront major internal challenges. 'Abbasid partisans, followers of the former governor – especially in Toledo – as well as Berbers in the grip of messianic movements and who controlled most of central Spain, were all able to resist the expansion of the Córdoban emirate for some 20 years. By the late 770s 'Abd al-Rahman had defeated these particular opponents and was extending his authority to northeastern Spain, where a variety of local Arab leaders were contesting the right to local predominance. Regional overlords in Barcelona and Zaragoza invited the Franks to intervene with military assistance, but the arrival of an army led by Charlemagne prompted a change of heart. Realizing, in all probability, that so mighty an ally could turn into a threat, garrisons in the two cities refused admittance to their putative supporter, and Charlemagne's army had to retreat through the Pyrenees.

In the late summer of 778 the rearguard of the Franks' army was attacked at the mountain pass of Roncesvalles and then massacred by warriors drawn from the local Basque population. Roncesvalles was a major humiliation for Western Europe's greatest military power, and the capture of Zaragoza by emirate forces in 783 was a further containment of the Frankish Christian threat along the border zone. Major bouts of dissidence among the Arab nobility, lasting for a generation from the end of the eighth century, would nonetheless pose a significant threat to the emirate's control of the peninsula. There were other dangers, too. Muwallads might have converted to Islam, but they and their descendants had a keen sense of their own native Iberian identity, and many of them rebelled as a group in the second half of the ninth century. Mozarabs protesting against the increasing Arabization of their fellow Christians were a major public order problem in the mid-ninth century. Embracing martyrdom, they embarked on a systematic campaign of reviling the prophet's name in public – an offence punishable by death from 850 onwards. Asturias, with its capital at Oviedo, emerged during this time to become an important Christian frontier state, and especially so after the discovery of St James's supposed tomb at Compostella. With its expansion to the south, the territory became known as the kingdom of León from 910 onwards, and Mozarabs flocked there in increasing numbers.

## New Islamic power bases

The emergence by 909 of the new and independent caliphate associated with the Fatimid dynasty based in Tunisia changed Islam's international power alignments. As caliph of the West, 'Abd al-Rahman III established his religious independence of the 'Abbasids, and in 929 he adopted the caliphal title of *Al-Nasir li-Din Allah* or Victor for the Religion of God. With his authority thereby enhanced, he countered the Fatimids' naval aggression in the western Mediterranean and subsidized local revolts against their rule in North Africa. Spain itself had seen numerous rebellions during the preceding reign (that of the new caliph's grandfather 'Abd Allah), and it took some 20 years of campaigning before central authority was restored. Toledo, focus of the last major Muslim resistance to the caliph, fell in 933. León paid homage but retained its ancestral independence despite the prolonged campaign waged against it.

'Abd al-Rahman III's preoccupation with the danger of local dynasties emerging to undermine his rule was therefore understandable enough. That is the reason why he made frequent changes to the personnel of provincial governorships. Moreover, an entire new city, Madinat al-Zahra, was built near Córdoba to house the bureaucracy and royal household, whose expansion showed the caliph's determination to assert dynastic control. The greatest architectural expression of Andalusian Spain's Islamic civilization is the Great Mosque at Córdoba, which was finished by 976 after two centuries of almost continuous construction and embellishment. Erected on land bought from Christians, the mosque was intended to show the vitality of an enduring culture, and the cathedral that had stood on the site was demolished. No other building in tenth-century Western Europe came close to offering a comparison with the magnificence of Córdoba's mosque, whose architectural motifs of the horseshoe arch and ribbed dome announced the arrival of a new stage in the history of Islamic architecture. The roofs of the prayer hall's 19 aisles were supported by more than 850 columns made of porphyry, jasper and coloured marble; a two-tiered system of arches consisting of white stone and red brick linked the aisles and columns; domes were covered with mosaics, floral decorations rose from their base of stucco and alabaster panels were covered with Quranic texts. Only the East could provide a parallel to this assertion of combined cultural glory and political might, and Córdoba's claim to rival the magnificence of 'Abbasid Baghdad was now well founded.

## Prosperity and coexistence

This consolidated Spain prospered economically, with coins of pure gold and silver being struck at the newly established national mint. The governing regime also enjoyed remarkable successes in external policy. The Fatimids had to abandon their Western campaigns and concentrated their ambitions subsequently on Egypt, where they gained dynastic control in 969. Umayyad Spain could therefore expand into the power vacuum that had emerged in the Maghrib of northwest Africa. It was this area that would be transformed into the viceroyalty of Córdoba under the dynamic command of Abu 'Amir al-Mansur who, as the caliphate's chief minister (978–1002), was Islamic Spain's effective ruler. He exerted an easy predominance over the Arab aristocracy and controlled a government whose high officialdom contained many slaves personally appointed by al-Mansur. He also had complete command of his own well-trained army, made up largely of Berbers who were fanatically attached to his personality and leadership. His patronage of poets and scholars was in the highest traditions of Islamic and Arabic culture, and al-Mansur's regime, like that of his immediate predecessors, was a tolerant one by the standards of the age.

The Arabic term *dhimmi* covered all non-Muslims who were not slaves, and as subjects of Córdoba's emirate and subsequent caliphate they were tolerated within certain limits. Jews and Christians had to pay a special tax called the *jizya* and sometimes incurred higher rates on other taxes. They could not carry weapons, marry a Muslim woman, receive an inheritance from a Muslim, or give evidence in an Islamic court of law. Christians outnumbered Muslims in Spain, and that fact alone meant that a programme of mass conversion was impractical. Neither Christians nor Jews, were forced to live in ghettoes and they were not actively prevented from following their faith – though they did have to wear a special badge. And successive rulers employed highly educated *dhimmi* at a high level in government. Jews and Christians had certain

# ANDALUSIAN LIFE

*A Muslim-Christian-Jewish coexistence, however unequal, was the matrix for Europe's most literate society. Córdoba was in conscious intellectual rivalry with Baghdad, and as a result its profusion of libraries, collections of manuscripts and translation centres emulated the 'Abbasid capital's achievements. Al-Andalus's astronomers, with their reliance on measurement and observation, played a major role in displacing the Ptolemaic system and its theory-based insistence that the orbit of the planets was circular rather than elliptic.*

Observational science recorded major advances in medicine, and al-Andalus's doctors invented surgical techniques such as autopsies and anaesthetics – as well as instruments including the bone saw and surgical needle. The amenities of life, in terms of a varied diet and improved hygiene, made daily life a good deal more enjoyable in Islamic Spain than in other regions of medieval Europe. As part of an international Muslim culture, Spain imported from the Middle East crops that were new to Europe, such as rice, apricots, citrus fruits, aubergines and cotton, and improved irrigation systems meant that such produce could now be grown extensively in al-Andalus. Trading networks with the rest of Europe, India and China required accurate maritime navigation, and the maps that guided the merchants and sailors of Córdoba's caliphate were based on careful geographical observation. The contracts underpinning Islamic Spain's import and export businesses pioneered the system of buying and selling on commission. Modern banking practices, including cheques, can be traced back to the methods used by investors who backed Islamic Spain's merchants; monies deposited in Baghdad, for example, could then be cashed in Spain. Islamic technology pioneered the windmill, the first examples of which were operating in the Middle East by the eighth century before their introduction through al-Andalus to the rest of Europe. By the 11th century watermills could be seen at work in Spain, and Islamic culture in general placed a high value on a regular and abundant supply of clean water. The cities of al-Andalus boasted drinking fountains, sanitary sewers and public baths, as well as Europe's first system of municipal rubbish collection.

*The Arabic inscriptions on this planispheric astrolabe – a device used to compute the movements of the planets and stars – states that it was made in Toledo by Ibrahim ibn Said al-Sahli in AD 1067.*

advantages as administrators, since they were wholly dependent on their patrons and unattached to any potentially fractious Muslim groupings. The period of comparative toleration was at its height in the late tenth century and lasted until the dissolution of the caliphate from *c.*1009 onwards. Al-Mansur presided over the last great age of Islamic Spain, until its territorial unity fragmented in the 11th century with the advance from the north of the Reconquista, Christian Spain's campaign of territorial recovery.

# 1204 — 1302

# THE KINGDOM OF NAPLES

*Imperial ambition was a recurring phenomenon in 13th-century Europe. Philip II of France's successes led contemporaries to dub him 'Augustus', Germany's ambitious Staufen princes cast themselves in the mould of classical Rome's emperors, and by the end of the century Edward I's campaigns of conquest in Wales and Scotland were furthering the Anglicization of Britain. It is therefore unsurprising that the Fourth Crusade's leaders established a 'Latin empire' after they captured Greek imperial territory, including the city of Constantinople; Baldwin IX, count of Flanders, was crowned its ruler on 16 May 1204. Venice's republic grabbed Crete and Corfu for itself, and three vassal states, imitating imperial precedent, owed Baldwin a feudal allegiance: the duchy of Athens, the kingdom of Thessalonike and the principality of Achaea on the Peloponnese.*

The aristocrats who fled from occupied Constantinople to the Greek territories in Asia Minor (modern Turkey) established two empires that were ruled from Trebizond on the Black Sea and from Nicaea adjacent to the new Latin empire's eastern borders. These empires' hatred of the Latin intrusion was shared by another successor state to Byzantium – the despotate of Epirus on the western coast of the Greek mainland. All three powers spent decades quarrelling with each other in a shifting pattern of alliances which also involved the Seljuk Turks to the east and the Bulgarian empire to the north. But the empire of Nicaea, under its ruler Michael VIII Palaeologus, eventually took the lead in an offensive that defeated the Latin empire of Constantinople in 1261. Byzantium was restored, with Epirus and Trebizond continuing as independent Greek states.

*RIGHT This statue of Charles of Anjou, by Tommaso Solari (1820–89), stands within the facade of the royal palace, Naples.*

However, the notion of a Latin Catholic sitting on the throne in Constantinople, and thereby linking the ancient Roman empire's Eastern successor with the traditions of the West, was an enduring ambition. During the late 13th century it was Louis IX's youngest brother, Charles of Anjou, who took up that cause. Once installed in 1266 as king of Sicily – a jurisdiction that included both the island itself and the southern Italian

ABOVE *The Battle of Benevento on 26 February 1266 was fought between Charles of Anjou and Manfred of Sicily. Manfred's death resulted in 17 years of French rule over the kingdom of Sicily (from a series of 13th-century frescoes in the Ferrande Tower, Pernes-les-Fontaines, France, that tell the story of the reconquest of Sicily by Charles of Anjou and the Battle of Benevento (1266), where Manfred is killed).*

mainland – he, too, looked to the East covetously. The Sicilian Vespers rebellion of 1282 forced Charles to withdraw from the island of Sicily, which was subsequently ruled by Aragon. Although Charles went on to found a dynasty, he and his successors had to content themselves with the Italian Peninsula's southern half, a territory that became known as the kingdom of Naples.

## CHARLES OF ANJOU – FROM COUNT TO KING

Charles of Anjou's role as a prince started unpromisingly. He was Louis VIII's youngest son, and his mother, Blanche of Castile, lavished attention on his eldest brother Louis during the decade or so when she ruled France as regent following her husband's death in 1226. Charles was initially ignored in the allocation of titles and lands under the apanage system. He only became count of Anjou and of Maine in 1247 because his elder brother, John Tristan, had died, and Louis IX preferred the company of his other younger brothers Robert of Artois and Alphonse of Toulouse. This family indifference may explain Charles's assertive character. Nevertheless, marriage to Beatrice, the heiress to Raymond Berengar IV of Provence, gave him his own power base as count of Provence from 1246 onwards.

Provence was part of the kingdom of Burgundy and, owing an ultimate allegiance to the Holy Roman Empire, it was accustomed to a fairly relaxed administration. Marseille, Arles and Avignon enjoyed a good deal of autonomy as imperial free cities, and the Provençal nobility enjoyed historic liberties. Charles appointed committees of inquiry into his rights as ruler and these investigations, conducted by obliging lawyers in 1252 and then again in 1278, gave him the answers he wanted. But insistence on his full rights – and the need to pay accompanying fees – had typified Charles's administrative style as soon as he arrived in Provence. When he went north again in 1247 to be invested as count of Anjou the imperial cities combined to form a defensive league against him. The count's more prolonged absence on the Seventh Crusade in 1258–60 gave his local enemies a chance to mount a prolonged revolt which he defeated with his accustomed vigour on returning to Provence. Arles and Avignon submitted in the summer of 1251 as did Marseille a year later.

Provence's agricultural wealth and the commercial prosperity of its towns produced the revenues that enriched Charles, but ruling the county could not satisfy all his ambitions. Then came a proposal that he should be king of Sicily, a territory regarded as its fiefdom by the papacy. The notion was first mooted in 1252 by Innocent IV and resulted from the usual papal neurosis about the Staufer. However, Louis IX vetoed the proposal that Charles should usurp Conrad IV, Frederick II's son, as ruler of the Sicilian kingdom.

During the next decade Charles settled down to being a highly successful, if somewhat frustrated, ruler of Provence, and the county's political élite grew accustomed to his brisk but efficient government. However, the seizure of power in Sicily by Manfred, Frederick II's illegitimate son, in 1258 changed the dynamics of power in the central Mediterranean. The papacy was once again confronted by a vigorous and resourceful Staufer on its southern frontier and Manfred's manoeuvring in central and northern Italy aroused its traditional fear of encirclement. An alarmed papacy therefore renewed its offer of the kingdom of Sicily to Charles. In July 1263, with Louis IX's support, Charles signed a treaty with Urban IV granting him the Sicilian throne.

In the years following his victory at the Battle of Benevento (26 February 1266) Charles ruled the Italian south with an exactitude already familiar to his Provençal subjects. He was also now planning a major offensive against the Byzantines, and he persuaded Louis IX that a campaign to restore the Latin empire of Constantinople could form part of a wider crusade. In 1267 he signed a treaty with the exiled emperor Baldwin II, who transferred to Charles the overlordship of Achaea, the Latin empire's vassal state that had survived the re-establishment of the Greek empire. The Villehardouin family, who were princes of Achaea, therefore became Charles's vassals, and he supplied them with the men and materials necessary to continue an anti-Byzantine struggle within the Peloponnese. Charles had already seized Corfu, as well as most of the Aegean islands, and he was therefore well placed for a full frontal attack on Michael VIII Palaeologus.

## THE KINGDOM OF NAPLES

**1204** A 'Latin empire of Constantinople' is established by the Fourth Crusade's leaders following the capture of Greek imperial territory.

**1246** Louis IX's youngest brother, Charles, becomes count of Provence on marrying Beatrice, heiress to the county, and is invested (1247) as count of Anjou and of Maine.

**1261** Michael VIII Palaeologus defeats the Latin empire and restores Byzantium.

**1263** Urban IV grants Charles of Anjou the throne of Sicily, a papal fiefdom that includes the island of Sicily and the southern Italian mainland.

**1266** After defeating Manfred of Sicily at the Battle of Benevento, Charles starts to rule as king of Sicily.

**1281–82** Charles prepares for a military offensive against the Byzantium empire.

**1282** Rebellion spreads from Palermo to the rest of Sicily. King Peter III of Aragon becomes King Peter I of Sicily.

**1302** Frederick III is recognized as ruler of the island kingdom of Sicily, and the rule of the House of Anjou-Naples is restricted to the southern Italian kingdom.

# Preparing to attack Byzantium

Byzantium's emperor nevertheless had one card to play in his defence. Michael wrote to Louis IX, and suggested a *rapprochement* between the Latin and Greek Churches. Besides which, he argued, would not an attack on Constantinople by the king's brother interfere with Louis's eagerness to launch a crusade defending the crusader states against Baybars, the Mamluk sultan of Syria and Egypt? Charles went through the motions of postponing his conquest plans, but his alternative strategy was typically adroit in its self-interest. The caliph of Tunis had been Manfred's vassal, and Charles wished to re-establish the Sicilian kingdom's suzerainty over Muhammad I al-Mustansir. The fact that the caliph was rumoured to be contemplating conversion to Christianity lent weight to Charles's suggestion that the Eighth Crusade be directed initially against Tunis as an easy target. Louis IX accordingly sailed for Tunis and, following the king's death almost immediately after landing there, Charles conducted the siege of the town which ended in al-Mustansir's renewal of his vassalage to the kingdom of Sicily.

There may have been a plan to use the crusading fleet in order to launch an attack on Byzantium, but its destruction by storms while returning to Sicily put paid to any such proposal. However, there were other pickings within easy reach, and in 1272 Charles proclaimed himself king of Albania after he had conquered lands along the Albanian coast that had previously been part of the despotate of Epirus. He still thought that Byzantium was within his grasp, but a reunion of the Greek and Latin Churches now

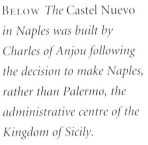

BELOW *The* Castel Nuevo *in Naples was built by Charles of Anjou following the decision to make Naples, rather than Palermo, the administrative centre of the Kingdom of Sicily.*

seemed imminent, and since Michael Palaeologus was in serious discussions with the papacy on the subject, Charles's ambition remained frustrated.

Pope Gregory was, however, in a position to grant Charles a consolation prize: the kingdom of Jerusalem. Deprived of the city of Jerusalem and with its capital in Acre, the tiny kingdom that clung to the Syrian coast was not much of a gift. Hugh III of Cyprus had been crowned its king in 1269, but the faction-ridden local nobility disgusted him and in 1276 he returned to his island throne . This left Mary of Antioch as a claimant, and she was ready to sell her rights to Charles of Anjou. With papal approval the deal was done in 1277, and following the application of some strong-arm tactics by Charles's agents the local nobility swore fealty to their new king.

Simon de Brion's election to the papacy as Martin IV on 22 February 1281 was an encouraging moment for Charles. The count had gone so far as to imprison two obstreperous Italian cardinals to ensure that the conclave voted unanimously for the French cardinal who had been Louis IX's chancellor in 1259–61. Michael VIII had found it difficult to sell the idea of a Church reunion in Constantinople, and the new pope helped Charles by excommunicating the Greek emperor. In 1281–82, therefore, and with papal approval, Charles could at last prepare to go to war against Byzantium.

Initial land campaigning designed to break out from Charles's Albanian base provoked a Byzantine counter-attack which put his army to flight. Campaigning in Achaea had also gone badly, with the principality proving a problem in other respects. The deal of 1267 meant that Charles was now lord of Achaea as well as its suzerain, following the death without issue in 1271 of his son Philip, who had been his vassal in the Peloponnese principality. But the Villehardouin family contested his succession, and although possession of Achaea gave Charles's Angevin dynasty a major role in Frankish-occupied Greece, squabbling over the succession ensured over a century of civil wars. Still, in the summer of 1282, Charles's hopes must have been bolstered by the sight of the 400 ships he had assembled at the great port of Messina in readiness for the attack on Constantinople.

## A REVOLT IN SICILY

On the evening of 29 March, however, just as the church bells of Palermo started to ring in readiness for the service of Vespers, a quarrel broke out between French officials and some locals. A contemporary account of the evening describes a Frenchman pestering a young married woman, whose husband then attacked the lout and stabbed him to death. Whatever the cause, a spark had been lit and in the ensuing massacre the local Palermitans killed as many of the French as they could find. The rebellion spread after local leaders were elected in Palermo, and six weeks later Charles of Anjou's French government had lost control of most of the island of Sicily. By the end of April even well-fortified Messina was lost to the French, and the rebels set fire to Charles's armada.

Why did this happen, and how spontaneous was it? Charles's French administrators could certainly be harsh, and his decision to base himself in Naples had isolated him from the island of Sicily. And there was a long history of Italian communalism behind the demands sent to a predictably unsympathetic papacy: the rebel leaders wanted their cities to be self-governing and directly answerable only to Martin IV as their suzerain. To some extent therefore this was a popular revolt. But the rebellion following the Sicilian Vespers incident was also part of the diplomatic politics of European princes.

After the pope had rejected their demands rebel leaders sent a message to King Peter III of Aragon, whose wife Constance was Manfred's daughter and a claimant to the Sicilian throne. Peter was well placed to champion the claim made in the summer of 1282 since his navy – a newly built fleet intended to protect his subjects' trading interest in north Africa – was located at Tunis just a couple of hundred miles to the south of Sicily. There was also another element to the Sicilian Vespers incident: Peter's Aragonese kingdom contained numerous Sicilian refugees who hated Charles. These exiles tended to be Ghibellines who opposed papal territorial power in Italy, and in the past Charles had shown no qualms about killing people who held such views. In 1272 he had declared war on Genoa, a city run by Ghibellines whose revolts, partly financed by the Greek emperor Michael VIII, spread across north Italy. By 1275 the Ghibellines had forced Charles to withdraw from Piedmont, but their hostility remained intense.

John of Procida, Manfred's former chancellor and once a counsellor to Frederick II, was an all-important point of contact between all these groups, and the strength of his devotion to the Staufen memory was equalled only by his detestation of Charles. In 1282 John was 72, but this gifted conspirator's age did not stop him from being an effective liaison between the emperor Michael in Constantinople, the Aragonese court and Charles's opponents in Sicily.

The Sicilians' appeal to Peter and Constance of Aragon was accepted, and on 30 August 1282 the Aragonese fleet docked at Trapani. The king promised a restoration of ancient Sicilian liberties rather than free communes, but the undertaking was good enough for the islanders and he was acclaimed Peter I of Sicily on 4 September at Palermo.

Charles could still rely on the papacy for support. Martin IV first excommunicated Peter of Aragon and then declared that Charles of Valois, son of France's King Philip III ('the Bold') should rule Aragon. These actions were part of a pattern of consistently craven support for Charles of Anjou, and Martin's subservience to French interests

had a serious long-term effect in undermining the papacy's spiritual authority as an independent power. The pope's further announcement of 1284 that the war against the Sicilians would be an Aragonese Crusade devalued the vocabulary of an ideal that was once supposed to unite all Christian princes and their subjects.

Christendom itself therefore was a major casualty of the Sicilian Vespers incident. The war to which it gave rise lasted until 1302, and as an essentially Franco-Spanish conflict it showed the energy of national governments guided by rulers' ambitions. The intervention of Philip III of France in 1284 saw his major force advancing on Aragon through Roussillon to advance the claim of Charles of Valois. This force, however, was decimated by disease, and in 1285 the French king died at Perpignan. Despite the deaths in the same year of Charles of Anjou and of Peter of Aragon, the war continued. By 1302 Charles of Anjou's son and successor, Charles II of Naples, had to concede the futility of any further attempt at invading Sicily, and Frederick III, the son of Peter III of Aragon, was confirmed as the island's king.

ABOVE *The Sicilian Vespers – a rebellion that took place on 30 March 1282 in Palermo against French rule in Sicily under Charles of Anjou – led to a war that lasted until 1302. This depiction of the event that may have triggered the uprising was painted by Francesco Hayez (1791–1882) in 1846.*

# THE HOUSE OF ANJOU-NAPLES

*The alliance that Charles of Anjou formed with Hungary's Arpad dynasty had momentous consequences. His son Charles (1254–1309), the future Charles II of Naples, married Maria, the daughter of Stephen V of Hungary (1239–72). His daughter Elisabeth, married Stephen's heir, Ladislaus (1262–90). Maria claimed the throne of Hungary after Ladislaus IV died without issue, but the Hungarian aristocracy turned to Andrew III (c.1265–1301), a Venetian nobleman descended from an earlier Arpad monarch, Andrew II (1177–1235).*

Queen Maria transferred her Hungarian dynastic rights to her eldest son, Charles Martel of Anjou (1271–95), who died young, and with Andrew III finding it difficult to assert his authority the Angevin claim was supported by Hungary's Church leaders. Charles Martel's son, Charles Robert (1288–1342), pursued his claim to the throne in Hungary from 1300 onwards, and his coronation as Charles I of Hungary in 1312 marks the start of the Hungarian Angevins' dynastic history. Primogeniture should have also made him his grandfather's heir in Naples, but Charles II chose his youngest son Robert of Anjou (1277–1343) as successor.

Crowned king in 1309, Robert was an enlightened patron of the arts, and as leader of the Guelph party in Italian politics he resisted the territorial ambitions of the emperor Louis IV (1282–1347) in north Italy. Ancestral guilt about Charles I of Hungary's exclusion from the line of Neapolitan succession nonetheless clung to Robert, and following the death of his own son and heir he wished to make reparation. He therefore arranged for his grand-daughter Joanna (1328–82) – who had become his heir – to marry prince Andrew, Charles I of Hungary's younger son and the brother of Louis I (1326–82), who succeeded to the Hungarian throne in 1342. The Angevin dynasty's Italianizing influence had by now raised Hungary to new levels of cultural achievement and economic growth, and in 1370 Louis also became king of Poland in succession to his maternal uncle, Casimir III. In his will, King Robert of Naples specified that Prince Andrew and Joanna were both to be crowned monarchs of Naples in their own right. Joanna, however, refused to share sovereignty, and in August 1344 she was crowned sole monarch. In 1345 her husband Andrew was murdered by Neapolitan

aristocrats determined to prevent his coronation, and although a trial held under papal auspices in Avignon acquitted Joanna of complicity the event undermined her authority.

Determined to avenge his brother's murder, Louis invaded Naples on several expeditions conducted in 1346–48 and again in 1350 but failed to establish himself as the kingdom's permanent ruler. The beleaguered queen's decision to adopt Louis I of Anjou (1339–84), a younger son of John II of France, as her heir established a junior Angevin line in opposition to the senior line whose rights of succession were represented by Charles of Durazzo (1345–86), a direct descendant of Charles II.

Joanna's support for the Avignon papacy during the western schism led in 1381 to her official condemnation by Pope Urban VI as a heretic. He bestowed her kingdom, which was a papal fief, on Charles of Durazzo, who arranged for Joanna to be murdered in 1382. The prince of Durazzo then ruled as Charles III of Naples, and he also tried to seize the Hungarian throne after Louis I died and during the minority of Louis's heir, Mary (c.1371–95). Here though he was less successful. The Hungarian Queen Mother Elisabeth arranged for Charles's assassination on 7 February 1386, and Mary was reinstated. Mary's husband Sigismund (1368–1437), originally a German prince whose father was the emperor Charles IV, became entirely devoted to the Hungarian cause, and his long reign as king of Hungary from 1387 onwards ended any prospect of an Angevin restoration.

Charles III was succeeded as king of Naples by his son Ladislaus (1376–1414), who nonetheless had to fight Louis II of Anjou (1377–1417) for his inheritance. Louis II reigned in Naples for ten years (1389–99) before being ejected by forces loyal to

The marriage of Sigismund, son of the emperor Charles IV, and Mary of Hungary can be seen in the background of this illustration from the 1468 edition of the Chronicles written by the French historian Jean Froissart (c.1337–c.1405).

Ladislaus, whose sister and successor Joan II of Naples (1373–1435) was the last Anjou-Durazzo to reign in Naples. Local anti-French sentiment was revived by the behaviour of Joan's husband, James of Bourbon (1370–1438), the count of la Marche who acquired the title of king on marriage. After a riot broke out in Naples in 1416 James had to remove the French administrators he had introduced to the kingdom. Renouncing his regal title, James had left Naples by 1419 and the senior Angevin line of Neapolitan monarchs became extinct when Joan died. She had settled the succession on René of

Anjou (1409–80) of the junior Angevin line, but his reign was brief (1438–42). Following a successful siege of Naples in 1441–42, Alfonso V (1396–1458), king of Aragon and of Sicily, accomplished the tremendous feat of reuniting the island of Sicily with the southern Italian mainland in one kingdom, which he ruled as a dependency of Aragon.

# 1337 | THE
# 1453 | HUNDRED
# | YEARS' WAR

*The conflict that consumed English and French energies for well over a century from 1337 to 1453 was, in fact, a series of wars punctuated by periods of peace. Dynastic rights were at the core of the hostilities, with England's Plantagenet kings asserting against the French dynasty of the Valois their claim to be kings of France. The war ended in the expulsion of the English forces from France – with the exception of Calais and the area surrounding the city. But the impact of the war transcends the story of dynastic rivalry, for the conflict also witnessed momentous developments in military technology and gave birth to a new and energetic sense of national identity in both England and France.*

Although England's dynasty of Anglo-Norman rulers had retained Normandy as a fief for themselves and their heirs, as dukes of Normandy they were nonetheless obliged to swear fealty to the French Crown. William the Conqueror and his heirs resented this vassalage, and by the same token France's Capetian dynasty disliked the fact that a constituent part of their realm was being governed by a foreign power. These tensions were compounded by the rise to power of the Plantagenets (sometimes known as the Angevins), since they were a thoroughly Anglo-French dynasty. At the height of their power, England's Plantagenet kings controlled not just Normandy but also Maine, Anjou, Touraine, Poitou, Gascony, Saintonge and Aquitaine. England's kings therefore not only ruled more French lands than did the French Crown, but also owed vassalage to a dynasty far less powerful than themselves.

## THE BACKGROUND TO WAR

RIGHT *The Battle of Crécy on 26 August 1346 is depicted here in the 14th-century section of the* Grandes Chroniques de France *(1274–1461).*

The weakness of England's position during the reign of John (1199–1216) allowed Philip II Augustus of France to seize most of the ancient English territorial holdings. At the Battle of Bouvines (1214) in modern Flanders King Philip II Augustus defeated Otto IV, the German emperor, and Otto's ally King John of England. John's humiliation was a major factor in his decision to capitulate to the demands of the English baronage and to sign the *Magna Carta*. Philip's victory meant that he could now assert control

over Anjou, Brittany, Normandy, Maine and Touraine. As a result, the Angevins' French territories were reduced to parts of Gascony. It was this humiliation, compounded by further defeats in the Saintonge War (1242) and the War of Saint-Sardos (1324), that the English aristocracy were now determined to avenge.

The extinction of the main line of the Capetian dynasty provided the English with a pretext for war. Philip IV left three male heirs on his death in 1314: Louis X, Philip V and Charles IV. He also left a daughter, Isabella, who was the wife of Edward II of England and the mother of Edward III. Louis X died in 1316 and his son, John I, died months afterwards. Philip V now claimed the Crown for himself and used the ancient Salic law and its prohibition of female succession to the French throne in order to set aside the claims of Louis's other child, Joan. Charles IV used the same authority to set aside the claims of Philip V's daughters when the king died in 1322.

In 1324 the short War of Saint-Sardos, fought in Gascony, provided a foretaste of the mighty struggle to come. Charles IV of France besieged the English fortress of La Réole, which was forced to surrender after a month of steady bombardment. England's humiliation was complete. The entire duchy of Aquitaine had once been the possession of the English Crown and now only Bordeaux and a narrow coastal strip remained. This cause of national shame had a major domestic consequence: the deposition of Edward II in 1327 by the discontented English nobility and the succession of his son Edward III – a very different kind of ruler. When Charles IV died in the following year it seemed to many – and not just those with English sympathies – that Edward was the legitimate heir to the French throne. Charles was the last representative of the senior line of the Capetian dynasty and his child, born posthumously, was a girl. Edward was not just Charles's nephew and closest surviving male relative, he was also the only living male descendant of Philip IV. The French aristocracy were, however, appalled by the prospect of being ruled by an English king, and in order to justify their hostility they fell back on the Salic law. This prohibited not only succession by women but also succession by those whose claims descended through a female relative. They turned instead to Philip of Valois, a Capetian who was the nephew of Philip IV. He was already regent and was subsequently crowned Philip VI in 1328, the first king of the Valois dynasty.

French ambitions on the eve of the conflict centred on Gascony, still held by the English as a fief of the French Crown rather than as their own territorial possession. Edward had been allowed to keep it, but an agreement made in 1331 meant that in return he had to give up his claim to the French Crown. This was an uneasy compromise, and in 1336 Philip made plans to take over Gascony while

Edward was preoccupied with making war against the Scots – by now a well-established French ally. In 1337 Philip claimed the whole of Gascony as his own fiefdom, and Edward in return asserted his claim to be the rightful king of France.

## ENGLISH NAVAL MIGHT

The initial stages of the war went badly for the English, who had allied themselves with Flanders and also with various individual nobles elsewhere in the Low Countries. Paying subsidies to these allies and meeting the costs of maintaining armies on foreign soil placed huge strains on English finances, and by 1340 these alliances were abandoned. The French naval offensive deployed ships and crew supplied by the republic of Genoa, and the disruption to England's trading patterns was considerable – especially the export of raw wool to Flanders and the import of wine and salt from Gascony. At the Battle of Sluys in 1340, however, the English were able to assert their naval supremacy and for the rest of the war the English Channel was effectively defended from any threat of French invasion. The focus of conflict thereafter shifted to Gascony and to Brittany where the two powers supported rival claimants to the duchy, but in both areas the fighting of the early 1340s was inconclusive.

ABOVE *An anonymous portait of Edward III, who reigned as King of England between 1327 and 1377.*

However, in July 1346 in a major military offensive, Edward led an expedition to France which landed on the Cotentin Peninsula on the Normandy coast. Caen was captured swiftly and Edward then advanced northwards towards the Low Countries, pillaging as he went. At Crécy the two armies confronted each other in battle and the result, greatly influenced by the English and Welsh archers with their longbows, was a decisive defeat for the French. Edward was now able to proceed northwards unopposed, and following a siege he captured the city of Calais in 1347. This was a major coup for the English army, which could once again maintain its troops in a fortified settlement on French soil. Developments in Scotland were also favouring England by this time, and David II was captured following his defeat in the Battle of Neville's Cross in 1346.

## THE EXPLOITS OF THE BLACK PRINCE

The next stage of the war saw the rise to prominence of Edward III's son and namesake, the prince of Wales, also known as the Black Prince. In 1356 the prince landed his troops in Gascony and advanced towards Poitiers, where a major victory was gained in battle over the French. This success was once again attributable to the English and Welsh archers. France's new king John II (*Jean le Bon*), a patron of the arts and an indifferent soldier, was captured and taken to England where he was held in captivity for four years while the ransom to release him was being raised in an economically weakened France.

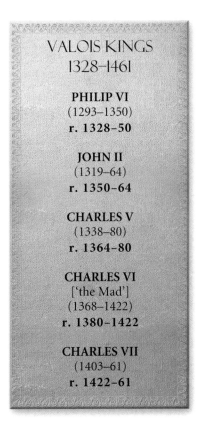

### VALOIS KINGS 1328–1461

**PHILIP VI** (1293–1350) **r. 1328–50**

**JOHN II** (1319–64) **r. 1350–64**

**CHARLES V** (1338–80) **r. 1364–80**

**CHARLES VI** ['the Mad'] (1368–1422) **r. 1380–1422**

**CHARLES VII** (1403–61) **r. 1422–61**

RIGHT *An illustration depicting the murder of Etienne Marcel, 1358. Marcel was about to open the gates of Paris to the king of Navarre's armed bands, but Jean Maillart prevented him, and killed him before the Porte Saint-Antoine (from* The Chronicles of Jean Froissart*).*

By now much of the French countryside was collapsing into a state of anarchy, with professional soldiers turning to brigandage and pillaging the land. In 1358 there was a major peasant rebellion (the *Jacquerie*) and deep divisions were also emerging among the French élite. Charles the dauphin was trying to rule as regent in his father's absence, and in October 1356 he summoned the Estates-General, a representative body consisting of the three orders of clergy, nobility and townspeople. Étienne Marcel, leader of the Paris merchants, enjoyed the support of many nobles in his refusal to grant money to Charles and in his attempt to impose substantial restrictions on royal power. Charles's resistance led Marcel to support the king of Navarre, whom he hoped to place on the French throne and whose armed bands were on the outskirts of Paris by the beginning of 1358.

English forces were keen to capitalize on this domestic French crisis, and in 1358 Edward III once again launched an invasion force but was unable to capture either Paris or Rheims. Charles was able to call on support from the provinces in reasserting control over Paris and its urban mob, whose violence had alienated previously sympathetic members of the nobility. By the terms of the Treaty of Brétigny (1360) a third of western France – Aquitaine, Gascony, western Brittany and the countship of Calais – was ceded to England, whose Crown held these territories without having to pay homage. A ransom of three million crowns was fixed as the price to be paid in instalments for the king's release. Although England gave up Normandy and, at least in theory, the claim to the French Crown, the treaty marked the high point of English fortunes in the Hundred Years' War, and it now ruled a much-expanded Aquitaine. The enormous sums paid in ransom by the French boosted their enemy's treasury for the rest of the century and consequently increased the English capacity to wage war. As a guarantee of the future payment, and after paying one million crowns, John II had to give up two of his sons as hostages to the English. When his son Louis escaped from England in 1362 King John II decided to give himself up. An amiable captivity in England seemed preferable to the burdens of exercising kingship in France, and on his death in 1364 John was succeeded by his son who reigned as Charles V.

## THE FIRST PERIOD OF PEACE

During the first period of peace (1360–69) Charles contemplated two issues: how best to regain the French lands lost to the English and how to rid the countryside of those mercenary soldiers who had been disbanded and were now causing social chaos. He found a solution in Bertrand du Guesclin, a minor noble from Brittany who had learnt advanced guerrilla techniques while engaged in the duchy's internal conflicts. Du Guesclin had crushed the forces of Charles II of Navarre in Normandy in 1364, and Charles V now placed him in command of the mercenary bands whose energies could be used to further the cause of the French Crown.

Castile in the 1360s was consumed by a civil war, with the English supporting the cause of Pedro the Cruel while his opponent and brother Don Enrique enjoyed French support. Du Guesclin's men forced Don Pedro out of Castile in 1365, at which point he attracted the support of the Black Prince, who was then ruling in Aquitaine as his father's viceroy. At the Battle of Najera in April 1367 the Anglo-Gascon force inflicted a heavy defeat on du Guesclin's men. It was the Black Prince's last major victory, and he subsequently developed the dropsy which would later claim his life. His rule in Gascony-Aquitaine became increasingly autocratic, and when Pedro defaulted on his debts the prince resorted

*Continued*

### THE HUNDRED YEARS' WAR

(Henry IV) seizes the English throne from Richard II.

**1415** Henry V declares war. English gain victory at Agincourt. After further victories at Caen (1417) and Rouen (1419), Normandy is English controlled.

**1420** Treaty of Troyes: Charles VI recognizes Henry V as his heir.

**1421** A Scottish army that has arrived in France defeats the English at the Battle of Bauge.

**1422** Death of Henry V and of Charles VI. The infant Henry VI is crowned king of England and of France. War continues.

**1429** Jeanne d'Arc helps to relieve the English siege of Orléans. Rheims opens its gates to the dauphin's army and he is crowned as Charles VII.

**1435** Treaty of Arras: the Burgundians agree peace with Charles VII.

**1449** French recapture Rouen, as well as Caen (1450), and Bordeaux and Bayonne (1451).

**1453** An Anglo-Gascon force is defeated at the Battle of Castillon. Calais is the English Crown's sole foreign territorial possession.

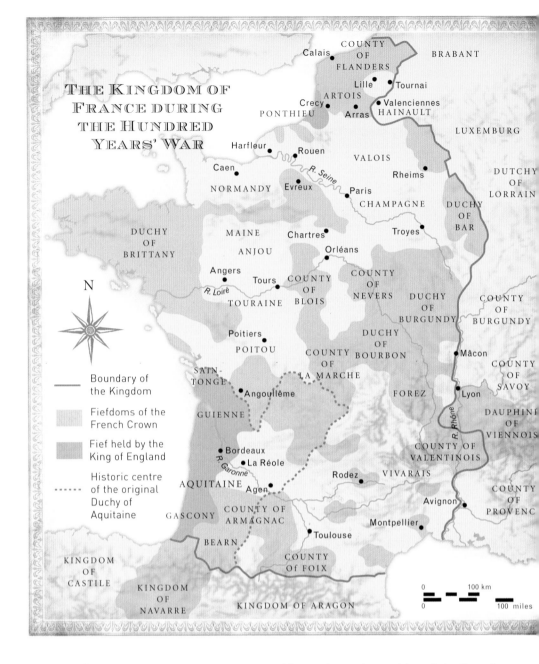

The Kingdom of France during the Hundred Years' War

to extraordinary taxation measures. Gascon nobles at that point petitioned the French Crown to come to their aid, and Charles V summoned the prince to Paris to answer charges. When he refused to do so the king charged him with disloyalty and deemed that the English had broken the terms of the peace treaty. In May 1369 Charles declared war and hostilities resumed.

## HOSTILITIES RESUMED

The second major phase of the Hundred Years' War saw a steady improvement in French fortunes. Charles opted for a policy of attrition that was calculated to engage English forces across a broad front while seeking to avoid a major battle. In pursuing this policy the French relied on the effective strategies of du Guesclin, who was appointed constable of France in 1370. He drove back the major English offensive in northern France using both hit and run raids and the persuasion of bribery. The French could also rely on the navy of Castile, since du Guesclin had captured Pedro the Cruel and the region's throne was occupied from 1370 onwards by France's ally, Enrique. England now suffered from a dearth of effective commanders. The Black Prince's illness meant that he was deprived of his command in 1371, and his father, the king, was too old to take to the field of battle. The loss of John Chandos who, as *seneschal*, was the administrator of Poitou, and the capture of their Gascon vassal Jean III de Grailly, deprived the English of two of their greatest military leaders. In 1372 du Guesclin avenged an historic French defeat by retaking Poitiers, and five years later his forces captured Bergerac. Charles's policy of negotiating with cities and regions the French had lost was also highly effective, and by 1374 he had regained all the lands ceded under the peace treaty with the exception of Calais and Aquitaine. The death of the Black Prince in 1376 and of Edward III in 1377 meant that the prince's son Richard of Bordeaux succeeded to the throne during his minority. Du Guesclin's death in 1380 and the resumption of a major Scottish military offensive in the 1380s, including the Battle of Otterburn (1388), meant that it suited both sides to engage in peace negotiations. These were eventually concluded in 1389.

## THE SECOND PERIOD OF PEACE

The period of the second peace (1389–1415) was one in which both countries saw a resumption of domestic challenges to the authority of the Crown. Charles V's brothers, who dominated the regency council that ruled in the name of his infant son, quarrelled among themselves and the authority of the Crown diminished accordingly. When Charles VI started to govern in his own name he proved to be a trivial figure, and his descent into madness in 1392 put his uncles back in power. An open contest for power developed between two factions. The Orléanist group – subsequently known as the Armagnac – supported the king's brother, Louis of Valois, duke of Orléans. Those who championed the cause of the king's cousin, John II, duke of Burgundy, were known as the Burgundians. The Burgundian group were responsible for the assassination of Louis, duke of Orléans, in 1407, and thereafter leadership of those opposed to John of Burgundy passed to Bernard VII, count of Armagnac. By 1410 both these factions were seeking English assistance in a period that was effectively one of French civil war.

The English Crown was also embroiled in domestic conflict. Richard II failed to quell the Irish uprising that preoccupied him for most of his reign, and his cousin Henry Bolingbroke seized the throne in 1399. From 1400 onwards Henry IV was challenged by a major Welsh rebellion under the leadership of Owain Glyndwr, and until 1410 much of Wales was lost to the English. In the north the English regime change led to a series of renewed Scottish attacks along the border. These were countered by an English invasion in 1402 and the defeat of the Scots at the Battle of Homildon Hill. However, that battle sowed the seeds of another conflict, since Henry and the earl of Northumberland quarrelled over the fruits of their victory. A long and bloody struggle ensued between the two for control of the northern English region, and this was only finally resolved in 1408 when the Percy family had to concede defeat. These troubles, along with the resumption of major French and Scandinavian raids on English shipping, meant that England was in no state to renew the French campaign until 1415.

## AGINCOURT AND AFTER

England's declaration of war in 1415 sought to capitalize on the French domestic mayhem that followed cessation of hostilities between the two nations in the late 1390s. In 1414 Henry V had turned down an offer from the Armagnac faction to support his claim to the throne in return for their restoration of the frontiers established under the Treaty of Brétigny signed in 1360. Henry's declared war aim was the restoration of the French territories possessed by the English during the reign of Henry II (1154–89).

In pursuit of this highly ambitious goal, Henry arrived with an army at Harfleur in August 1415 and, after taking the town, he marched on towards the safety of English-occupied Calais. However, he now found himself outmanoeuvred and his supplies were running low. He therefore decided to make a stand at Agincourt, a site north of the River Somme. In the ensuing battle (25th Ocober 1415) a comparatively larger and better-equipped French army was defeated by the English. Subsequent English propaganda may have inflated the disparity in numbers in order to emphasize the scale of the victory, but there can be no doubt that, for the French, Agincourt was a defeat on the scale of Crécy and Poitiers. Henry went on to take most of Normandy, including Caen in 1417 and Rouen in January 1419. Normandy was once again under English control for the first time in two centuries.

These were great victories for English arms, but they also owed much to the intensity of French factionalism. Charles, duke of Orléans, was captured by the English at Agincourt, and Bernard VII, count of Armagnac, was murdered in 1417 by a mob of Burgundian supporters in Paris. After 1417 the Burgundians controlled both Paris and the king himself, and their conflict with the Armagnacs meant that French forces could not concentrate on the campaign against the English in Normandy. Although the two factions agreed to a truce in 1419, the Burgundians retained their ambitions and the grouping decided to ally themselves with England.

It was this Burgundian influence that brought pressure to bear on Charles VI, who had now descended into insanity. Under the terms of the Treaty of Troyes signed in 1420 the French king recognized Henry V of England as his heir. Henry would marry Charles's daughter Catherine, and Henry's heirs were recognized as rightful rulers of France. The dauphin, later Charles VII, was declared to be illegitimate and thereby disinherited. Late in 1420 Henry entered Paris in triumph, and the Anglo-French agreement was ratified by the Estates-General.

ABOVE *Henry V is portrayed in this elaborately gilded anonymous painting of the 15th century.*

## A change in French fortunes

It was at this point, however, that the Scottish dimension to the conflict re-emerged. A substantial Scottish force led by the earl of Buchan landed in France and engaged the English in battle. Thomas, first duke of Clarence, was killed at the Battle of Bauge in 1421 and most of the other English commanders were either killed or captured. The death of Henry V at Meaux in 1422 was followed by that of Charles soon after. Henry's infant son was crowned as Henry VI, king of England and France. The Burgundians continued to support him as English allies, but the Armagnacs' fidelity to the cause of Charles's son ensured the continuation of the war. By 1429 the English were besieging Orléans, a city that seemed on the point of surrender. It was at this stage that a remarkable peasant girl named Jeanne appeared, and her message transformed French prospects.

Jeanne d'Arc maintained that she had received a vision from God telling her that it was her destiny to drive the English out of France. In 1429 she appeared before the dauphin and persuaded him that she should be sent to Orléans, where she had a galvanizing effect on morale. The French troops subsequently went on the offensive and forced the English to lift the siege. The French proceeded to take several English positions along the Loire valley, and at the Battle of Patay (1429) a French army defeated a superior force led by John Talbot, first earl of Shrewsbury. Not even the famed archers of England and Wales, hitherto an invincible military resource, could withstand the French advance. With his position thus strengthened, the dauphin was able to march to Rheims where he was crowned Charles VII that same year.

Jeanne was subsequently captured by the pro-English Burgundian faction, sold to the enemy and burned at the stake. For a while the French advance ground to a halt as both sides engaged in peace negotiations. The breakdown in relations between the English and the Burgundians heralded the end of the war. The infancy of King Henry VI of England had been marked by quarrels between his uncles who ruled as regents. One of these uncles, Humphrey, duke of Gloucester, was married to Jacqueline, countess of Hainault. Humphrey decided to invade the province of Holland in order to regain her former territories, and this action brought him into direct conflict with Philip III,

ABOVE *A late-15th-century miniature portrait of Jeanne d'Arc, who inspired French soldiers with her leadership and divinely inspired sense of mission.*

duke of Burgundy. In 1435 Duke Philip changed sides, and the Burgundians therefore decided to sign the Treaty of Arras, a development that enabled French royal forces to regain control of Paris. From now on the Burgundian faction had to concentrate on defending their interests in the Low Countries, and that strategic need dictated their withdrawal from the French civil war.

In the years that followed it became obvious that Charles VII had made good use of the long truces that punctuated the war in France, since he went on to pursue long-term changes in French military and civilian administration. A more professional army and a more centralized state, supplemented by the du Guesclin strategy of avoiding battle, meant that the French could inflict regular defeat on the English. Rouen was retaken in 1449, as was Caen in 1450, and Bordeaux and Bayonne fell the following year. The final engagement of the Hundred Years' War was fought at Castillon in 1453, when the superior cannon of the French commander Jean Bureau defeated John Talbot's Anglo-Gascon force.

## The consequences of war

A period of over a century was inevitably one that saw major military, social and political changes. The Hundred Years' War reflected those developments, while also contributing to them. Parliament's power to approve taxation gave 14th-century England a new source of centralized authority, and the country's feudal levy was replaced by a paid army whose professional captains recruited troops. In terms of technology, the war gave a significant boost to the artillery; the longbow – and at a latter stage of the conflict firearms as well – grew to rival the cavalry in importance. English innovations in military strategy also transformed the art of war, and the victories at Crécy and Agincourt owed much to the deployment of men-at-arms occupying fixed defensive positions. The typically English deployment of lightly-armed mounted troops – later called dragoons – who dismounted in order to fight would be adopted on a pan-European scale. These changes brought about a gradual decline in the use of heavy cavalry, which came to be seen as expensive and inflexible. The social and cultural position of the institution of knighthood declined as a result.

But despite enjoying these institutional and strategic advantages, England was faced with an insuperable difficulty: the enemy's territory was simply too extensive for it to be occupied for any substantial period of time. France's land mass was three times the extent of England's, and the French population was four times greater. English forces did occupy large parts of France during the war, but since such areas needed to be garrisoned, the ability of the occupying army to campaign and strike at the enemy was compromised. Shrewsbury's army at Orléans had 5000 men, but that was not enough to take control of the city since it was greatly outnumbered by the French troops within the city and its environs. Once the inspiration of Jeanne d'Arc had raised the morale of French troops their victory was well-nigh inevitable. John Talbot was one of the most aggressive and effective of all English commanders, but even he could not prevail against the inherent strategic disadvantages of the English position in France.

These prolonged wars also had profound effects on the civilian population. The French countryside experienced widespread devastation, but the suffering also contributed to a new sense of national identity. When victory came at last it was seen as being due to the French government's ability to organize men and materials more effectively than in the past; the country's feudal structures were giving way to the evolution of more systematic and centralized methods of government. England's culture was affected in similar ways, with a national spirit of resistance being reflected in the rumours that a French invasion would mean the extirpation of the English language. From the time of the Norman Conquest the culture of England's ruling élites had been French. But by the end of the 14th century that dominance had passed. England's economic base also shifted. Before the war England had been a massive exporter of raw wool to the southern Netherlands where weavers then turned the wool to fine cloth. The unpredictable alliances of the dukes of Burgundy disrupted that trade, as did the high levels of taxation imposed on exports by the English Crown in order to help pay for the war. As a result weavers in England started to develop their own textile industry, and cloth from their looms aquired an international renown.

## CHANGES IN MILITARY STRATEGY

The war confirmed the longbow's technological superiority over the crossbow. While the longbow required immense strength and great expertise to use, it was extremely accurate. The crossbow, on the other hand, was relatively easy to use and had great fire power against both plate and chain mail, but it was a cumbersome and heavy weapon that took time to reload. Bowmen serving with the Welsh and Scottish armies had taught their English enemy a painful lesson: deployed in fixed positions, they could inflict immense damage from a distance and so destroy a cavalry charge. The same strategy was deployed by the English on French soil: after choosing a site of battle they would fortify their position and subsequently destroy the enemy. But although the triumph of the longbow was a significant feature of 14th-century Anglo-French warfare, it became less important in the early 15th century; by then, advances in plating techniques meant that

ABOVE *After each of his four elder brothers died without producing an heir, Charles VII became king of France in 1422. This contemporary portrait was painted in c.1444–51 by Jean Fouquet (1420–81).*

armour could resist penetration by arrows. The introduction of gunpowder and cannon to the field of battle in the late 14th century transformed the art of war, and artillery was a deciding factor in the French victory at the Battle of Castillon (1453), the last major engagement of the Hundred Years' War.

New kinds of weapons made for new kinds of armies. Victory now came to kings and other rulers who could raise large armies consisting of a rank-and-file armed with longbows and firearms, and who had the resources to employ and pay mercenary soldiers. This new professionalism displaced the earlier military model of armies consisting of knights summoned by their superior lords to do battle when required. A new sense of national solidarity also meant that kings could obtain through taxation the monies needed to pay for these large armies. This new access to great martial power meant kings could now use military means to quell internal dissent as well as to counter the threat of foreign invasion. It therefore became possible for a monarch to raise a standing army – a military force that existed in times of peace as well as of war. The French monarchy was the pioneer of that development, and although the innovation spread throughout continental Europe it encountered resistance in England. The military basis of knighthood was undoubtedly whittled away during these conflicts, but its cultural aspect in terms of the chivalric code remained powerful.

ABOVE *This anonymous contemporary illustration shows a castle being stormed as its walls are breached during a 15th-century siege. The soldiers are using crossbows, cannon and harquebuses (an early form of the rifle).*

## THE IMPACT OF WAR ON FRENCH AND ENGLISH MONARCHIES

By the mid-15th century it had become very obvious that the monarchies in France and in England were very different kinds of institutions. In France the Estates-General had tried to assert its own independent power at the very nadir of the nation's military fortunes. The Estates had the power to confirm or disagree with the *levée* – the main tax imposed by the Crown on its subjects. Étienne Marcel's leadership saw the Estates exploiting that source of power and attempting to impose major restrictions on the powers of French monarchs. Under the proposed Great Ordinance the Estates were to have the power to collect and spend the *levee*, to meet regularly as an independent body and to play a role in government as well as exercising some judicial powers. But the collapse of that campaign in the violence of the 1350s, when the *Jacquerie* threatened a form of mob rule, meant that the nobility rallied to the cause of the Crown. The Great Ordinance would be abandoned and the Estates-General would not develop along the lines of England's consultative parliament. It was this strengthened monarchy that helped to win the war for France, and the association between the country's national identity and the institutional power of its kings became one of profound historical importance.

In England, too, the institution of monarchy acquired a new dimension as the focus of national identity in the face of a threat from abroad. But the English Crown's domestic authority in the mid-15th century was far weaker than that of its French counterpart. The Peasants' Revolt of 1381 had some parallels with the French *Jacquerie*. Some 100,000 of the aggrieved marched on London to protest at the high taxation imposed to pay for the war and at the subjection of many of the peasantry to serfdom by the English nobility. Authority was soon restored. The rebellion's leader Wat Tyler was killed by the king's men, and the peasantry returned to the countryside with their grievances unresolved. Taxation levels therefore remained high, and both the Crown and the nobility were enriched as a result of the acquisition of large parts of France – especially during the war's earlier stages. But by the latter stages of the conflict the English treasury was essentially bankrupted by the high costs of waging the war in France and by the need to administer and maintain its conquered territories. Lack of money contributed to a loss of regal authority, and England descended into a prolonged civil conflict as the rival noble houses of Lancaster and York vied with each other for control of the English Crown during the 'Wars of the Roses' conducted intermittently between 1455 and 1485.

English disillusion with the great continental adventure was profound, and at the end of the war Calais was the Crown's sole foreign possession. But although so much had been lost to England in territorial terms, perhaps the deepest impact of the war was a psychological one. England had withdrawn from France and was now defining itself in conscious opposition to the rest of the European continent. Viewed from the continental mainland, England appeared to be a marginalized and insular country. But England's geographical position, and the country's maritime traditions, also enabled it to take advantage of the opportunities which beckoned across the Atlantic in the great age of discovery that was now dawning.

THE PLANTAGENET DYNASTY DURING THE HUNDRED YEARS' WAR

**EDWARD III**
(1312–1377)
**r. 1327–77**

**EDWARD, PRINCE OF WALES**
['the Black Prince']
(1330–76)

**JOHN OF GAUNT**
(1340–99)

**RICHARD II**
(1367–1400)
**r. 1377–99**

**HENRY IV**
(1366–1413)
**r. 1399–1413**

**HENRY V**
(1387–1422)
**r. 1413–22**

**HENRY VI**
(1421–71)
**r. 1422–61, 1470–71**

# THE PARLIAMENT OF ENGLAND

*The term 'parliament' came into use in the early 13th century to describe a national forum for discussion, and the institution's origins lay in the consultative Great Council, consisting of the nobility and senior clergy, which had been regularly summoned by English monarchs since the Norman Conquest.*

Parliamentary constitutionalism was built on *Magna Carta*'s enunciation of fundamental rights and its declaration that the king's will was bound by law. Renounced by King John after he signed it in 1215, the document was reissued by Henry III's regent William Marshal and then by the king himself in 1225 when he attained his majority. By 1297, when Edward I's parliament issued it yet again, the charter was fundamental to the English legal tradition. Following *Magna Carta*'s adoption the convention was established that parliaments ought to be summoned when monarchs wished to raise money through taxation, and by the mid-13th century knights of the English shires were occasionally attending parliament to advise the Crown – especially on financial matters.

The nobility and senior clergy played an especially important administrative role during Henry III's minority, and aristocratic resentment at his failure to consult once he started to rule led to the adoption of the Provisions of Oxford (1258). Henry had to agree to the establishment of a supreme administrative council of 15 barons whose performance was monitored by thrice-yearly meetings of parliament. Simon de Montfort, 6th Earl of Leicester (and son of the anti-Cathar crusader) emerged as the leader of this constitutionalist movement. But in 1264 Henry obtained a papal bull which exempted him from having to abide by his oath to uphold the Provisions. In the military hostilities that followed, Henry was defeated and taken prisoner by de Montfort's army at the Battle of Lewes (14 May 1264). Many of the nobility became alarmed at this turn of events.

In December 1264 de Montfort summoned the first English parliament to be convened without a preceding royal authorization. The senior clergy and the baronage were summoned as well as two knights from each shire, and the presence of two burgesses from each borough, chosen by a form

of democratic election, was a real innovation. De Montfort's system was adopted by Edward I during the 'Model Parliament' of 1295, by which time the knights and burgesses were collectively known as 'the Commons'. The Provisions of Oxford had been allowed to lapse following de Montfort's defeat, and death, at the Battle of Evesham (4 August 1265). Nonetheless, the knights and burgesses who attended parliament had continued to gain in authority, and it became widely accepted that discussion of taxation usually required the summoning of the Commons. The idea however that knights and burgesses should attend every parliament only gained ground in the mid-14th century.

In 1341 the Commons started to meet separately from the nobility and clergy, and Edward III's reign saw the establishment of the principle that the support of both Houses of Parliament and of the monarch was needed before any law could be approved or any tax levied. The Hundred Years' War is therefore part of the story of English constitutionalism, since the king was forced to seek parliamentary approval for the very high levels of taxation needed to meet the costs of campaigning. Parliamentary consent had also been important in approving the deposition of Edward II and in establishing his son's legitimate right to rule. Edward III nonetheless tried to avoid parliamentary scrutiny as much as possible. During the Good Parliament (1376), the Commons were critical of the way the war was being conducted and its members demanded a novel right to scrutinize public expenditure.

*Edward I presides over parliament in c.1278 in this anonymous 16th-century illustration. He is flanked symbolically by Alexander III of Scotland and Llywelyn II of Wales.*

longtain voyage. quil souffra de porter seulemet vng
las de soye a vng ymage de sainct george pendat a icelluy.
Aussi se ledit colier dor auoit besoing de reputacion il pora
estre mise en la main de souurier iusques a ce quil soit
repare. Lequel colier aussi ne pourra estre enrichy de ~
pierres ou daultres choses / reserue led ymage qui pourra
estre garny au plaisir du cheualier. Et aussi ne pourra
estre ledit colier vendu engaigie dōne ne aliene pour
necessite ou cause quelconque que ce soit

Alexander Rex
Scotorū

lewellin
princeps
wallie

# AVIGNON AND THE SCHISM

## 1301 — 1417

The traditionally close association between the papacy and French monarchy broke down during the pontificate of Boniface VIII (r. 1294–1303) as a result of Philip IV's attempt to tax the clergy. However, the relationship was restored following the election of Bertrand de Goth, archbishop of Bordeaux, to the papacy in 1305. For security reasons the conclave of 1304–05 was held in Perugia rather than in Rome, where armed conflict had broken out between powerful aristocratic groupings, the most important of whom were the Colonna and the Orsini families. Moreover, the electors were divided between the French and Italian members of the College of Cardinals, and the new pope, Clement V (r. 1305–14), chose to be crowned in Lyon. Clement's court therefore stayed in Poitiers for the first four years of his papacy. The destruction by fire of much of the Lateran palace, the official papal residence, in 1307 provided another reason for staying away from Rome.

In March 1309 Clement removed his court to Avignon, part of the county of Provence, whose feudal overlord was the king of Naples. This event heralded a longer-term shift of policy. Clement and his successors, as leaders of the Latin Church, would base themselves in Avignon for almost 80 years – a period when competition between Europe's national monarchies was putting the idea of a united Christendom under increasing strain.

Pope Gregory XI (r. 1370–78) who, like his seven predecessors in Avignon was a Frenchman, returned the papal court to Rome in January 1377. However, the conclave to elect his successor in the following year saw a renewed Franco-Italian split. The local mob agitated for the election of a Roman, but it was Bartolomeo Prignano, the archbishop of Bari and a Neapolitan by birth, who was chosen by the cardinals. As Urban VI (r. 1378–89), the pope embarked on a vigorous reform of some of the financial abuses that had crept into the curia during the years of exile in Avignon, and

RIGHT *This gilded bronze statue of Pope Boniface VIII was sculpted in 1301 by Manno di Bandino, two years before the pope died.*

**1305** A conclave meeting in Perugia elects Bertrand de Goth, archbishop of Bordeaux, as Pope Clement V. He decides to be crowned in Lyon. Since Rome is riven by aristocratic infighting, Clement keeps his court in Poitiers.

**1307** Fire destroys the Lateran Palace, Rome.

**1309** Clement removes his court to Avignon.

**1377** Gregory XI returns the papal court to Rome.

**1378** Bartolomeo Prignano, archbishop of Bari, is elected as Pope Urban VI by a conclave split on a Franco-Italian divide. Dissenting French cardinals withdraw to Anagni and elect Robert of Geneva, archbishop of Cambrai, as the anti-pope Clement VII who establishes a rival papal court in Avignon.

**1378–1417** The Western schism: five anti-popes resident in Avignon maintain their legitimacy in opposition to the popes established in Rome.

**1417** The general Church council meeting at Constance (1414–18) sets aside the rights of all papal claimants and elects Oddone Colona, archpriest of the Lateran basilica, as Pope Martin V.

he castigated the cardinals for accepting gifts and favours from secular rulers. But an intemperate manner limited Urban's effectiveness, and a group of French cardinals withdrew to Anagni where they issued a manifesto of grievances and declared that they had been pressured by the mob to elect an Italian pope. The dissenting cardinals then elected Robert of Geneva, archbishop of Cambrai, to the papacy in September 1378. As the antipope Clement VII (r. 1378–94), he set up his own court in Avignon in opposition to the official papacy. Robert's four successors continued the line of dissident anti-popes during the period of the Western schism, which was only finally resolved in 1417 when a general Council of the Church meeting at Constance (1414–18) set aside the rights of all the current papal claimants and elected a new pope, Martin V (r. 1417–31).

## THE IMPERIAL PAPACY

The papacy of Innocent III (r. 1198–1216) marks the high point in the effective assertion of papal authority, with Lotario dei Conti bringing his legal scholarship to bear on the definition of the papal claim to universal rule. All power came from God, and all rulers were therefore answerable to the pope who was God's representative on Earth, the chosen instrument of the divine will and autocratic ruler of an universal Christian empire which was superior to all secular expressions of might. The holder of the papal office was therefore not just the high priest of God's Church but also humanity's supreme judge in legal cases and a universal king whose majesty dwarfed all secular princes. It was this *plenitudo potestatis* or fullness of power that distinguished God's vice-regent and gave him the authority as priest-emperor to mediate between God and man: '*God is honoured in us when we are honoured, and in us is God despised when we are despised.*'

This exalted conception of papal authority shaped the views of Benedetto Caetani, a scion of the minor nobility and whose family owned estates in the region of Anagni to the southeast of Rome. Caetani, like Pope Innocent, was trained as a jurist and his career as a member of the curia was a distinguished one. After becoming a cardinal in 1281 he often worked on diplomatic missions as a papal legate sent to the royal courts of Western Europe. Caetani was elected to the papacy in 1294 as Boniface VIII, and his statement '*Ego sum Caesar, ego imperator*' showed the extent of Innocent III's influence on Caetani's frame of mind. Catastrophe – both personal and institutional – marked Boniface's papacy, and although his own lack of judgement contributed to that collapse the major reason lies within the evolution of European power politics that had moved decisively against the idea of a monarchically supreme papacy. *Clericis laicos*, a bull issued by Boniface in 1296, showed his readiness to confront the kings of France and England over the issue of taxing the clergy.

## CLERICIS LAICOS

Popes had long since allowed kings to tax the clergy in order to raise money for papal-sponsored crusades, but *Clericis laicos* made the strident assertion that papal approval was always necessary before kings could even think of diverting Church revenue to secular purposes. In retaliation Philip IV forbade the export of bullion from his territories, and supplies of French money to the curia in Rome dried up in the late 1290s. The extravagant assertion in the 1296 bull that the laity *en masse* had always been hostile to the clergy was an example of the papacy striking attitudes, and in the following year Boniface was forced to concede that kings could tax the clergy in circumstances of

national emergency. It had already been necessary for Boniface to explain to France's Philip IV that none of his statements applied to customary feudal taxes due to the king from Church lands.

Papal self-confidence was, however, boosted by the success of the jubilee year in 1300, a tradition instituted by Boniface and in the course of which pilgrims who came to Rome were assured pardon and remission of their sins. The pope was therefore in no mood to compromise when the news arrived of a major attack by Philip on Bernard Saisset, one of Boniface's key supporters in the French Church. Saisset was a Languedoc aristocrat steeped in his region's culture and language. In his years as abbot of St Antonin in Pamiers from 1268, and then as bishop of the local see since 1295, he had led the local resistance to the French monarchy – an institution that he and his followers regarded as an alien and northern Frankish force bent on destroying the liberties and customs of the south. Philip had Saisset arrested as a treasonous supporter of Occitan independence, and the bishop was charged in October 1301. But before any further judicial proceedings could take place Saisset would need to be deprived of his see by Boniface and thereby stripped of clerical protection. Only then could he be tried for treason. Boniface unsurprisingly refused Philip's demands in this regard and insisted that Saisset be released and sent to Rome where he would face any judicial investigation.

## DISPUTES BETWEEN KING AND PAPACY

By the end of 1301 relations between pope and king had broken down entirely. The public letter issued in December was entitled *Ausculta fili* ('Listen, my son') and told the king: '*Let no one persuade you that you have no superior ... for he is a fool who so thinks.*' At the same time Boniface announced that a council of the French bishops would be held the following November in Rome. Philip retaliated by holding his own assembly on Church affairs in Paris in April 1302, and the clergy and laity who obeyed his summons to attend rejected the notion – not itself advanced by Boniface – that the pope was France's feudal overlord. On 18 November 1302, in response to the Paris assembly, Boniface issued the papal bull *Unam Sanctam*. Its statement that '*it is absolutely necessary for salvation that every human creature should be subject to the Roman pontiff*' was an extreme declaration of the papacy's supremacy as both a spiritual and a temporal institution. Following the bull's release the pope contemplated further measures, including Philip's excommunication. The king then summoned another anti-papal assembly and that body, attended by senior French ecclesiastics, gave vent to a collective rage accusing Boniface of idolatry and heresy.

Philip had by now decided that only Boniface's removal from office could resolve matters. Guillaume de Nogaret, a former professor of jurisprudence at Montpellier and

OELVMCLONIT MEDIVMOVE IMVMOVE TRIBVNAL·· LVSTRAVITOVE ANIMO CVNCTA POETA SVO·· DOCTVS ADEST DANTES SVA OVEM FLORENTIA SAEPE·· I CONSILIIS AC PIETATE PATRE·M·· NIL POTVIT TANTO MORS SAEVA NOCERE POETAE·· QVEM VIVVM VIRTVS CARMEN IMAGO FACIT··

senior adviser to the king, persuaded Philip that Boniface should be seized and brought to France where a special council of the Church would then depose him. It was a risky venture, and Nogaret had to proceed in secrecy. He first gathered a band of mercenaries in the Apennines and made contact with the Colonna family who were bitter enemies of Boniface's clan, the Caetani. Sciarrillo Colonna, whose uncle and brother had been deprived of their positions in the College of Cardinals by Boniface, joined the group of some 2000 soldiers led by Nogaret. On 7 September 1303 they arrived at Pope Boniface's family palace in Anagni where he was seized and subjected to three days imprisonment, beating and humiliation. The mob stopped just short of killing him. Sciarrillo is said to have hit the pope in the face, and that 'slap of Anagni' became a Europe-wide *cause célèbre.*

Anagni had also been the home town of Innocent III, and it was in the local cathedral that the pope had excommunicated Frederick II in September 1227. It was an all too appropriate setting, therefore, for the humiliation of the papacy by a secular power that

ABOVE *This fresco from the Duomo of Florence shows Dante Alighieri holding a copy of his* Divine Comedy. *He stands symbolically under Heaven, between the gates of Hell, the mountain of Purgatory and the walls of Florence.*

was consigning Innocent's elaborate doctrines to history. Even Dante Alighieri, no friend of the pope and a fierce opponent of the notion that the papacy was a universal monarchy, was appalled by Boniface's humiliation. *De Monarchia*, written in 1312–13, is a considered rejection of theocracy and a defence of the imperial power's autonomy. Both emperor and pope, Dante maintained, had been given power by God to rule over their respective domains. But he still viewed the pope as exercising a spiritual power derived from God, and the repugnance the poet felt at the shameful treatment of Boniface is given a literary form in the *Divine Comedy*'s description of a new Pilate imprisoning the vicar of Christ (*Purgatorio*, XX, vv. 85–93). The local population at Anagni rose up and released Boniface, who returned to Rome a few days after his release. But the ordeal had badly shaken up the 78-year-old pontiff, and he died a month later.

The election of the very pliant Clement V in 1305 signified a papal capitulation to French force, and the pope obliged Philip by supporting the campaign of persecution he launched in 1307 against the French members of the order of the Knights Templar. Philip nonetheless pursued his vendetta against Boniface beyond the grave. In 1309 he persuaded the pope to instigate post-mortem judicial proceedings to investigate charges of heresy and sodomy against Boniface. It was not unusual for opponents of Philip's royal will to be accused of sodomy – as in the case of the Knights Templar – but the Church council that met at Vienne in 1311 dropped all charges against Boniface for lack of evidence.

# The papacy at Avignon

In 1309 Clement moved the papal court to Avignon. Avignon was a self-governing city located within another enclave – the lands of the *comtat* or county of Venaissin. The *comtat* had been inherited as its possession by the papacy in 1274, and both territories came under the over-lordship of the counts of Provence. Since the days of Charles of Anjou, the junior, or Angevin, branch of the French royal house had ruled the county of Provence. In the early 14th century these Capetian-Angevins were also rulers of the southern Italian mainland as kings of Naples.

Joan I, queen of Naples, sold Avignon to the papacy in 1348, with the result that both *comtats* then formed a unified papal domain. The region of Avignon therefore did not form part of the French Crown's territorial holdings, but the French influence on the papacy in the years of its exile from Rome was profound, both politically and culturally. French cardinals were the dominant force in the running of the curia, and the rituals of the papal court imitated those adopted by French kings. The austere magnificence of the new papal palace at Avignon, built during a quarter of a century from the late 1330s onwards, was the setting for one of Europe's most lavish courtly societies, with the papacy's zealous emphasis on a centralized approach to the raising of revenue helping to pay for the splendour.

The system of *benefices* – the income enjoyed by the holder of an ecclesiastical position – could be abused with candidates buying posts (a practice known as simony). Spiritual duties might then be farmed out to incompetents or not performed at all, and there were plenty of opportunities for enjoying the fruits of more than one office (pluralism). The tithe system was a venerable one by *c*.1300, but it was the Avignon papacy that systematized the *annates* by which the income gained in the first year of holding a high office, such as that of bishop, was remitted to the papacy. The Avignon Exchange was one of Europe's first foreign exchange markets, with agents of the great Italian banking houses acting as intermediaries between the Apostolic Camera (the papacy's central board of finance), the papacy's creditors and also its debtors – those who remitted to it the taxes and tributes. Regions that lacked an organized money market – Scandinavia, for example, and most of central and Eastern Europe – still sent coined money to Avignon by land or by sea, though these were precarious methods.

## A backlash begins

A reaction against the papal lushness was not slow in coming, with the followers of John Wycliff (*c*.1324–84) in England, the Hussites in Bohemia and the groups of the Fraticelli in Italy registering their revulsion at the parade of riches, and preaching a return to apostolic values of poverty and simplicity of life. There were intellectual critiques, too. *Defensor Pacis* (1324), by Marsilio of Padua (*c*.1275–*c*.1342)), goes beyond Dante's hostility to a monarchical papacy and seeks to justify the emperor's supremacy over the pope. In 1328 the English philosopher and Franciscan William Ockham (*c.*1288–*c.*1348) had to flee Avignon, where he had been teaching, after concluding that the papacy was in error by not following the mendicant poverty of Christ and his disciples. Ockham's *Dialogus* (1332–48) is a major work of political theory with its emphasis on property rights, rejection of absolutist monarchy and the advocacy of limited constitutional government.

Both Ockham and Marsilio were excommunicated on account of their writings, whose political context is supplied by the conflict between Pope John XXII (r. 1316–34) and the emperor Louis IV (r. 1328–47) who revived an ancient debate by rejecting the pope's accustomed right to crown an emperor. Backed by the German nobility, Louis invaded Italy with an army in 1327, and on entering Rome he installed the anti-pope Nicholas whose brief period of influence (1328–29) anticipated the later schism. This episode inevitably made the papacy even more dependent on French support, and Clement VI (r. 1342–52), a former archbishop of Rouen, excommunicated Louis in 1346.

Clement's bull *Unigenitus* (1343) justified papal 'indulgences', which relieved the penitent of some of the temporal punishments for sins committed – and that system lent itself to later abuse by professional 'pardoners' who sold indulgences. But although sanctity might not have been one of his attributes, Clement was a keen patron of musicians and composers, and it was he who commissioned the paintings on the walls of two of the papal palace's chapels.

Pope Gregory XI (r. 1370–78) had the wit to see that the papacy needed to be in Rome if it was to retain its authority in Italy. In reaching this conclusion he was much influenced by Catherine of Siena, a Dominican nun and prodigious correspondent whose letters advocating the pope's return were sent to the clerical and lay leaders of Italian opinion. However, the subsequent Western schism of 1378 to 1417 did great damage to the idea of a universal Church, with England, the empire, Poland and northern Italy supporting the pope in Rome, while France, the Spanish kingdoms and the kingdom of Naples backed the Avignon anti-popes.

In the early 15th century the conciliar movement sought to renew the Church by locating its authority within representative councils whose meetings would supplement the traditional role of the papacy. But despite the return to Rome, and the presence once again of just one 'supreme pontiff', the papacy looked increasingly like one other European power jostling for position among more formidable competitors.

ABOVE *An early 15th-century woodcut of The Pardoner from the* Ellesmere Chaucer, *an illuminated manuscript of Geoffrey Chaucer's* Canterbury Tales.

# PETRARCH – CHAMPION OF ROME'S RENAISSANCE

*Critical accounts of the papacy's period in Avignon started early and many take their cue from the Italian poet Petrarch who, while staying in the city in the 1340s, wrote: 'I am astounded to see these men loaded with gold and clad in purple, boasting of the spoils of princes and nations.'*

Petrarch's polemicism ignores the fact that many Avignon popes were able administrators. John XXII (r. 1316-34) for example sanitized Church finances, and Benedict XI (r. 1334-42) campaigned against clerical corruption. Successive Avignon popes, seeking to defuse the persistent disputes between French and Italian cardinals, built up the curia as the Church's central administration. Nepolistic appointments were sometimes made as a result. Increasing bureaucracy and centralization were the unintended consequences of the papacy's attempt at reforming itself.

Although Francesco Petrarca (1304–74) was born in Arezzo he was partly brought up in Avignon where his father, a lawyer, had moved the family in order to be near the papal court that he found to be a lucrative source of business. After a period spent studying law (a profession he loathed) at Montpellier and Bologna, Petrarch moved back to Avignon in the mid-1320s, and by *c.*1330 he was working in the household of Cardinal Giovanni Colonna. But it was Rome that drew him, and a visit to the city in 1337 inspired Petrarch to write *L'Africa*, an epic poem composed in Latin and which described the defeat by Scipio Africanus of the Carthaginian general Hannibal during the Second Punic War (218–201 BC). The Colonna family in Rome liked the poem, and Petrarch benefited from their patronage while working on the project. The theme first came to him while walking in the mountains of the Vaucluse near Avignon, and Petrarch's treatment of Scipio as a heroic figure is central to the poet's artistic vision of the glories of the Roman past together with the urgent contemporary need to revive the classical tradition in the arts and letters. A comparison between the decadence of Avignon, a city of 'licentious banquets' and 'foul sloth' in Petrarch's words, and the sublimity of Rome is therefore implicit to his programmatic account of a 'renaissance'. *L'Africa* was dedicated to King Robert of Naples, who liked it enough to award Petrarch with a laurel crown in 1341. The ceremony, held in Rome on Easter Sunday, consciously evoked the emperor Augustus's patronage of Horace, Ovid and Virgil. Ceremonial trumpets sounded, the king clad his laureate poet in a special robe, and Petrarch's speech of acceptance would in time be seen as a manifesto for the Italian renaissance. This was a *trionfo* inconceivable in Avignon, Petrarch's 'Babylon of the West'.

*Petrarch's statue stands outside the Uffizi Palace in Florence.*

FRANCESCO PETRARCA

161

# THE GOLDEN AGE OF FLORENCE

*Like many European towns, Florence adapted and survived in the centuries following the collapse of the Western Roman empire. Florentia ('the flourishing one') was founded by Julius Caesar in 59 BC, and its position at the confluence of the Arno and Mugnone rivers, as well as road links to the Po valley region, gave the town important trading advantages. But early medieval Florence first needed to re-establish its primacy as a regional centre, since the Lombard monarchy – which controlled most of seventh-century central and northern Italy – decided that Lucca should be the capital of its duchy of Tuscany. Florence's position further inland also exposed it to attack from the Byzantines, who were still established in Italy's northeast. Lucca moreover offered a more direct land route to the Lombard capital of Pavia. Florence overcame these disadvantages and attained a cultural and financial pre-eminence during the central middle ages.*

RIGHT *Florence's massive cathedral of Santa Maria del Fiore, with its red tiled dome, is closely flanked by the octagonal Baptistery and by the campanile designed by Giotto di Bondone in the 1330s.*

The march (or margraviate) of Tuscany was established following Charlemagne's conquest of the Lombard kingdom in 774, and this frontier area to the Carolingian empire's south consisted of a collection of counties that included Florence. Lucca remained the seat of the margrave – who owed allegiance to the Holy Roman emperors – until the mid-11th century, and by then Florence was fast evolving as the Tuscan region's main administrative centre. Bureaucracy, however, went hand in hand with Florence's emerging intellectual and cultural role, with the city's ruling élite being strongly committed to the Gregorian reform and therefore supporting the papacy against the empire. Pope Gregory VII (r. 1073–85) was backed by Matilda, margrave of Tuscany from 1076 onwards and owner of the castle at Canossa where the emperor made his temporary submission to the papacy in 1077. Although many of Tuscany's cities – including Lucca – rebelled sporadically in favour of the empire, Florence's loyalty to Matilda was never in doubt. Her marriage in c.1189 to the future Welf II, duke of Bavaria (r. 1101–20), brought a trans-alpine cohesion to the anti-imperial cause. Although her husband left the margrave after a few years on discovering that

## THE GOLDEN AGE OF FLORENCE

**1182** Florentine merchants establish the city's first guild, the *Arte dei Mercanti*.

**1210s** The commune is divided between pro-imperial Ghibelline and pro-papal Guelph aristocratic factions.

**1250–1260** The *Primo Popolo*: a merchant-dominated form of democracy.

**1260** Battle of Montaperti: Ghibelline Siena defeats Florentine forces. Florence's Ghibelline nobles return to power.

**1266** Battle of Benevento: Charles of Anjou's victory confirms Guelph dominance in Italian politics.

**1267** Ghibelline expulsion from Florence.

**1282** The *popolani* regain political predominance.

**1293** The Ordinances of Justice adopted by the commune prescribe a republican government for the period of the *Secondo Popolo*.

**1378** Marginalized non-guild workers, aided by some members of the lesser guilds, seize power. The *popolo grasso* crush the rebellion.

**1397** Giovanni de' Medici establishes the family bank.

her lands were bequeathed to the Church, the marriage contributed to Florence's fateful association with the Guelph faction – the Italian political expression of the German Welfs' pro-papal policy.

Florentine solidarity, evident when the city defended itself successfully against Henry's army in 1082, bound Matilda to her subjects, and she was correspondingly generous in the granting of local liberties and privileges. By the time of Matilda's death in 1115 Florence, entrenched behind fortified walls that had been greatly extended during the imperial siege, had all the appearance of a typically independent Italian commune. In 1125, a defensive collective identity turned into opportunistic aggression; following the death of the emperor Henry V, who had no legitimate direct heirs, Florentine forces attacked and conquered the neighbouring city of Fiesole. During its early history as a commune Florence was run by the local nobility with merchant support, and although the emperor Frederick Barbarossa tried to limit Florentine political autonomy by re-establishing the margraviate of Tuscany in 1185, that proved to be a short-lived experiment. Barbarossa had deprived Florence of its *contado*, the territories surrounding the city, but in 1197 it regained control of its lands by once again taking advantage of a hiatus in imperial affairs following the death of Barbarossa's successor, Henry VI.

## THE COUNTRY COMES TO TOWN

Economic development accompanied Florence's population growth. The spread of new suburbs meant that the River Arno, once at the city's perimeter, now became its arterial centre of communications and a source of energy for local industries reliant on waterpower. Florence now looked atomized compared with the classical regularity of *Florentia*'s intersecting streets, and the landed gentry who had moved in from the countryside reproduced within their urban enclaves the designs of those fortified castle-like compounds, complete with towers, that had been raised to defend their rural estates. The dozens of towers that dominated Florence's skyline symbolized the fragmentation of central authority, since the nobility used them to protect their households in times of civic disorder. With the establishment in 1182 of the *Arte dei Mercanti*, merchants had their own means of representative self-assertion, and in the decades that followed Florence's ever-growing number of artisans and tradesmen established numerous specialist guilds.

By the 1190s, following the example of most other Italian cities, the commune of Florence was using the office of the *podestà* (a magistrate-like official) to allay civic strife. Usually a nobleman, the *podestà* invariably came from another Italian region and was therefore likely to be neutral when adjudicating on local conflicts during his allotted year in office. The innovation worked in Florence for a generation or so, but by the 1210s the commune's allegiances were divided to noxious effect between the pro-imperial Ghibelline nobility and the equally aristocratic Guelph leadership who often supported the interests of the guilds.

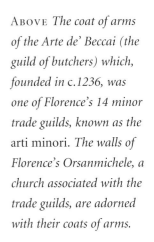

In 1244 the Ghibellines were dominant, and they tried to strengthen their position by bringing elements of the mercantile grouping into government. But in 1250 the merchants turned on their new-found patrons and established a form of democracy during the period of the *Primo Popolo*. The new government ordered that the towers be reduced in height since they symbolized aristocratic factionalism. From 1252 onwards the gold florin, which supplemented the silver florin first introduced in 1235, showed the prosperity and ambition of this mercantile society. A new government needed a new building to house its various councils, and in 1255 construction work started on the *Palazzo del Popolo* (now called the *Bargello*) whose crenellated form, complete with a tower, was another instance of the rural fortification being replicated within the city. The Battle of Montaperti (1260) saw the Florentine army's defeat by the forces of Siena, a strongly Ghibelline rival within Tuscany. It also meant the end of the *Primo Popolo* experiment. A resurgent Ghibelline nobility dismantled the democratic structures and ordered the destruction of palaces, towers and houses owned by Guelph aristocrats. This vindictive policy continued until 1266, when the Ghibellines suddenly found themselves in a precarious position following Charles of Anjou's defeat of Manfred, the Staufen king of Sicily, at the Battle of Benevento (26 February).

ABOVE *The coat of arms of the Arte de' Beccai (the guild of butchers) which, founded in c.1236, was one of Florence's 14 minor trade guilds, known as the* arti minori. *The walls of Florence's Orsanmichele, a church associated with the trade guilds, are adorned with their coats of arms.*

Charles's victory was one fraught with Italian implications. The cause of the empire, embraced by the Ghibellines, had received a decisive setback, and since the papacy had used its Florentine bankers to help finance a papal-French-Angevin axis of power in Italy the city's commercial interests as well as its political advantage now lay within that orbit of influence. A Guelph restoration and a Ghibelline expulsion became imperative. By the spring of 1267, and with Pope Clement IV's support, the commune had achieved both measures and that meant the end of the Ghibellines in Florence. Charles of Anjou was made *podestà* for ten years by the commune and, ruling the city through his lieutenants, he imposed a Guelph-dominated regime. Florentine troops were to the fore among Tuscany's combined Guelph forces when they defeated the Ghibellines at the Battle of Campaldino (1289), and that victory lent an additional authority to the Guelph leadership in Florence.

## ARCHITECTURE: THE ILLUSTRATION OF GLORY

By the end of the 13th century Florence was one of Western Europe's largest cities. Its population of some 100,000 had been boosted by immigration from the surrounding countryside, and reserves of capital accumulated through trade and financial services

were being used to give architectural expression to Florentine glory. Medieval Europe's major cities required the presence of a castle and a cathedral in order to control the urban environment and to regulate citizens' lives. In the case of Florence its first major public building, the *Bargello*, fulfilled the role of a castle, and construction work started on the city's new cathedral of Santa Maria del Fiore in the mid-1290s. But the monastery was quite as important for the medieval city, and Florence was a major centre for the new religious Orders who built in the Gothic style – the city's vernacular school of architecture.

In the second quarter of the 13th century the Franciscans started construction work on their monastery dedicated to the Holy Cross, and it was re-designed in the 1290s to assume its present form. The great church of the Dominicans, Santa Maria Novella, having been first raised on the site of an earlier church in 1246, was completed by the 1350s. Along with the monasteries of the Augustinian, Servite and Carmelite Orders, these substantial complexes exerted huge social influences on their immediate localities; they contributed culturally and economically as well as having a religious purpose.

## DEFINING FLORENCE'S GOVERNMENT

Nonetheless, Florence's intra-mural politics continued to be fractious. The period after the *Primo Popolo* witnessed

*ABOVE Construction begin on the* Palazzo della Signoria, *now known as the* Palazzo Vecchio, *in 1299. The palace was built upon the site of an older tower belonging to the Foraboschi family, which is now marked by the location of the present tower.*

the renewed self-assertion of the *popolani* – those merchants and trades-people who were organized into the more significant guilds and who defined themselves in conscious opposition to the *magnati* or nobility. In 1282 the *Popolo* movement became the dominant element within the commune, and the constitutional transformation it effected 11 years later included the *magnati*'s formal exclusion from Florence's political life.

The Ordinances of Justice (1293), as adopted by the commune, provided a republican constitution for the city's *signoria* or government. Its nine members, the *priori*, were chosen from the guilds at two-monthly intervals. The head of those elected was the *gonfaloniere*, who served the republic as its chief public representative during his brief period in office. In governing Florence the *signoria* had to consult two other elected councils: that of the *dodici* (12) and of the *sedici* (16). They could also call on the expertise of councils specializing in matters such as warfare, security and commerce, and which would be formed by election as and when the need arose. In 1299 work started on constructing the *Palazzo della Signoria* (now the *Palazzo Vecchio*) that housed the government of the *Secondo Popolo,* and its fortified appearance showed the defensiveness of the attitudes accompanying the republican assertion. From the time of its formation onwards this structure of government was subjected to internal strains, with the lesser commercial classes or *popolo minuto* differentiating themselves from greater ones or *popolo grasso* who were dominant in the *arti maggiori* (major guilds).

Florence's chronic tendency to fragment could also be seen in the tensions that became endemic in the 1290s between the 'Blacks' and the 'Whites' (the *Neri* and *Bianchi*) who adhered to the aristocratic families of the Donati and the Cerchi respectively in the struggle for influence. Following the Ghibellines' expulsion the victorious Guelphs had split: the Black Guelphs stuck to a pro-papal line while the White Guelphs were critical of the papacy and more likely than their adversaries to embrace the new constitution. After the *priori* forced both the Donati and the Cerchi leaders into exile in 1300 the Blacks appealed to the pope. The mediator he chose, the French prince Charles of Valois, occupied the city with an army. Charles then delivered Florence to Corso Donati, who established the Black government that sent many of the White Guelphs, including Dante Alighieri (*c.*1265–1321), into exile.

Fourteenth-century Florence was exposed to external threats from Ghibelline-controlled Milan as well as from Lucca and Pisa. When Castruccio Castracani, duke of Lucca, inflicted a military defeat on the Florentines in 1325, the administration turned for support to the Anjevin rulers of the kingdom of Naples, who shared their antipathy to the empire. In 1326 the city placed itself under the direct rule of Duke Charles of Calabria, heir to the Neapolitan kingdom, by electing him to be its *signore* (lord) for ten years, though that experiment ended when the duke died unexpectedly two years later and the commune found that its liberty had been restored. Florence again had to call on Naples for support when it was threatened by Mastino II della Scala, *signore* of Verona and north Italy's most successful warrior-prince in the 1330s. This resulted in a brief period of imposed tyranny in 1342, which ended in a popular uprising and the restoration of the traditional liberties.

Florentines had long been accustomed to both domestic turbulence and external threats, but the mid-14th century saw new environmental dangers as well as a terrifying public health crisis. New bridges (which include the Ponte Vecchio) had to be built across the Arno after major flooding destroyed the earlier structures in 1333. And the epidemic known as the 'Black Death' hit Florence particularly hard from the late 1340s onwards. A far greater catastrophe, however, was the collapse in the 1340s of Florence's banks. This followed their involvement in shadily speculative financial instruments and entrapment in a bubble of currency speculation created and controlled by Venetian high finance. That financial cataclysm led to a continent-wide banking crisis, collapse of credit, and trade contraction that lasted for decades.

## An instructive insurrection

Florence's democratic structures were based on the great guilds, and this fact alone meant that *popolani* could be a synonym for an oligarchy dominated by the *popolo grasso*. In 1378 the commercial élite were quarrelling among themselves, and specialist wool workers known as the *ciompi* – who were not affiliated to any guild – seized their moment. Large numbers of the disenfranchised working groups, such as the tanners and dyers, joined the *ciompi* in petitioning the *signoria* for the right to establish guilds that would protect their interests. In late July these dissidents, backed by radical elements within the marginalized minor guilds (*arti minori*), such as those of the bakers and mill-workers, seized the government by force. But although new guilds were formed, including one for the *ciompi*, the insurrection leaders failed to maintain their solidarity. By the end of the summer an alliance of the greater and lesser guilds had crushed the *ciompi* leadership, whose guild was subsequently disbanded. In the following years the *popolo grasso* re-established its dominance.

The events of 1378 lived on in the memory of the Florentines and contributed to a mounting and general disillusion with both the theory and the practice of the city's republican constitution. Victories were still possible, however, and Florence's conquest of Pisa in 1406 made the republic a maritime power for the first time in its history. But workers in the *arti minori* continued to be alienated from the *popolo grasso*, and important elements within an élite haunted by the recollection of civil disorder concluded that they needed better protection. Different sectors of Florentine society therefore had their own, albeit mutually contradictory, reasons for allowing the local de' Medici family (who were also Europe's premier bankers) to effect an early 15th-century revolution in government by keeping the republican constitution while denuding it of significance. That Medicean transformation needed to be subtle, since Florentines were proud of their city's history and conscious of its grounding in republican values that had produced greatness as well as violence. Cosimo de' Medici (1389–1463) ran the bank established by his father Giovanni (1360-1429) and rarely held public office, but connections acquired through patronage and money meant that he could control Florence by exerting his personal influence. Just like his grandson, Lorenzo (1449–92), Cosimo was Florence's sole ruler, and the Medicis' sedulous avoidance of the title of 'prince' allowed Florentines to maintain their communal self-esteem and to pretend that the link with the republican past was still in place.

Above *A marble portrait of Cosimo de' Medici from c.1464, believed to have been sculpted by Andrea del Verrocchio. This is the oldest surviving portrait of the Medici patriarch.*

# GIOTTO AND REALISM IN ART

*Although Florence is the city that defines the* rinascimento, *its history also challenges the idea that 'renaissance' and 'medieval' are mutually exclusive categories.*

The career of Giotto di Bondone (c.1267–1337) is a case in point. He was born either in Florence or its surrounding rural hinterland, and tales of his preternatural skill form part of the Giotto tradition – as in the case of the fly he drew on a canvas being worked on by Cimabue (c.1240–c.1302) and which looked so lifelike that the painter tried to wave it away. The story was first related by Giorgio Vasari (1511–74) in his *Lives of the Most Eminent Painters* (1550), a work written over two centuries after Giotto's death and which sought to demonstrate that Florentine artists were the best and earliest exemplars of renaissance originality. In Vasari's account of the matter Giotto's naturalistic style is contrasted with the stiffness of earlier Tuscan artists, who were still working in a tradition influenced by the icons of Byzantium – as in the case of Cimabue and Duccio (c.1255/60–c.1318). Their stylized and mosaic-like approach to painting can thus be labelled 'medieval' and even 'Gothic'.

But the psychological impact that is a hallmark of Giotto's figures is also present in the work of the preceding generation. The Virgin present in Cimabue's 'Maestà' (1280s) is an approachable intercessor, and the animation of Duccio's own 'Maestà' (1308–11) comes from the spiritual intensity of the 20 angels and 19 saints who crowd round the Madonna. Giotto certainly brought a new dramatic focus to his representations of the Passion, as in the celebrated 'Lamentation' (c.1305) painted in the Scrovegni Chapel in Padua. The artificially elongated figures and swirling drapery of the Byzantine tradition have now disappeared, and our involvement as engaged spectators is partly a result of Giotto's supremacy as a draughtsman who can set the scene and control the perspective. But this is still an artist who is indebted to his masters; the gestures of those who surround the saint's dead body in the 'Mourning of St Francis', painted for the Bardi Chapel in Florence's Santa Croce, evoke the stylized grief of Byzantine mosaics and icons. Giotto's art, like that of his Florentine contemporary Dante, escapes facile categories, and to see him as just the pioneer who prepared the way for a later renaissance is to miss the point of genius.

*'Lamentation' (c.1305) by Giotto di Bondone is a fresco painted in the Scrovegni Chapel in Padua. The Holy Family and the disciples mourn the dead Christ whose body has been taken down from the Cross.*

# 722
## —
# 1492

# THE
# RECONQUISTA

*The re-conquest of the Iberian peninsular territories occupied by Muslim invaders was a process that lasted, on one interpretation, for some seven and a half centuries. Christian forces secured their first major victory as early as 722, just over a decade after the first invaders arrived in Spain from North Africa. The Battle of Covadonga was fought by members of the Visigothic aristocracy who had fled to the mountainous Asturias region in the far north, and their victory led to the establishment of a Christian kingdom that became a base for the re-conquest of Spain. The end of Islam's territorial power in Spain came in 1492, when the emirate of Granada fell to the united kingdoms of Aragon and Castile after a ten-year military campaign. Granada had, however, been an anomalous outpost since 1238 when it became Castile's vassal state, and by that stage the rest of Spain had already been re-conquered for Catholic Christianity.*

The *reconquista*, which gathered pace in the 11th century, was a product of the conviction that Iberian Christianity had only a precarious toehold on the southern European border with Islam. Hunger for land and the urge to populate empty territories played their part as the Christian leaders moved southwards, taking some of their subjects with them. Towns that were being repopulated were granted *fueros* or charters by Christian rulers, and the popularity of these written guarantees of liberties and immunities helped to ensure higher population levels from the mid-tenth century onwards. *Fueros* created a direct relationship between rulers and townspeople, and they therefore offered an attractive escape route from lordship (or feudalism) and its local obligations. But Western Europe's first major crusading enterprise also stirred hearts and minds with an intensity whose effects would be lasting both in Spain and in Europe. The continent's Christian culture, still so experimental in the 11th and 12th centuries, learnt from the *reconquista* the hard lesson of negativity: in order to exist and flourish it had to be an oppositional force, one defined by its enmity. The papacy's decision to launch a series of crusades in the Middle East owed much to the Iberian experience, and

subsequent Spanish rulers whose rationale of power included a Christian missionary element were similarly indebted. It was not for nothing that Francisco Franco chose Burgos, the Castilian city that was a major base for the re-conquest, as the symbolic location for his self-proclamation in October 1936 as generalissimo of the Spanish army and head of state.

## CHARLEMAGNE'S CHRISTIAN BORDER STATES

Charlemagne's army returned to Spain in the late 790s following the earlier, and disastrous, expedition of 778, and his formation in 795 of a Frankish-controlled Spanish march had created a buffer zone along the border between Umayyad Spain and his empire's southern limits. The march extended from the Basque region in the west and along the Pyrenean frontier. Following a victory for the Franks in 801 it also

ABOVE *Loarre Castle was a major Christian fortification, built by Sancho III in Aragon in the early 11th century, on the frontier between the Christian and Muslim lands. The castle was much restored during the 20th century.*

**795** Charlemagne establishes the Spanish march, a buffer zone whose separate counties will evolve into the independent principalities of Navarre, Barcelona and Aragon.

**791–842** Alfonso II rules the Christian kingdom of the Asturias in northwest Spain. His forces conquer Basques to the east and Galicia to the west.

**924** The Asturias kingdom, following its southward expansion and incorporation of the county of Castile, becomes known as the kingdom of León.

**939** León's southern boundaries extend towards the River Douro.

**970** Death of Fernan Gonzalez, count of Castile, who has established his county's independence of León.

**1002–31** The Córdoban caliphate disintegrates into petty principalities (taifas).

**1004–35** Sancho III ('the Great') rules Navarre: he annexes Castile, and León becomes his protectorate. He bestows (1029) Castile on his son Ferdinand (1017–65).

**1037** Ferdinand, count of Castile, turns his county

*Continued*

incorporated the county of Barcelona. This was one of Europe's most ethnically diverse regions consisting of Basques, Jews, Germanic Visigoths and native Iberians, as well as Hispano-Romans whose ancestors had populated Spain when it was a Roman imperial province. Frankish-appointed governors, called *walis*, administered each of the march's 17 counties.

As Carolingian power declined in the ninth century the *walis* became increasingly independent and hereditary rulers of their own fiefdoms, and they started to call themselves counts. It was this region of the march that would later become part of the principalities of Navarre, Catalonia and Aragon, and right from its Carolingian origins onwards it was something of a socio-economic experiment. Settlers were attracted into this sparsely populated and strategically vital area by Charlemagne's land grants. These allowed extensive rights and immunities in return for a promise of military service when required. A military aristocracy, based in the myriad small castles that dotted the landscape, was thereby created. Its martial obligations, owed first to Charlemagne and subsequently transferred to the regional counts, anticipated later European developments in lordship and feudal duties.

Although these Christian border states regarded Islam as their foe, they were also keen to establish their independence from their northern neighbour, the kingdom of the Western Franks. To this end, each of them was quite content to play off their Muslim and Christian neighbours against each other. Navarre, centred on its capital Pamplona, was a hereditary kingdom by the 820s, and Barcelona's counts – the region's predominant magnates – were passing on their holdings to their sons from the 880s onwards. Borrel II asserted the county of Barcelona's formal independence of France's Capetian rulers in 948, and all of these frontier states of the ninth and tenth centuries had remarkably stable boundaries. Nevertheless, they were mostly small entities, and the same mountains that protected them from invasion also limited their ability to break out and take on al-Andalus (the Arabic name for the part of the Iberian Peninsula held by the Muslims). The kingdom of the Asturias in Spain's northwest was, however, better placed for expansion, and during the long reign of Alfonso II (r. 791–842) his forces conquered Basque dissidents to the east as well as the province of Galicia to the west.

The discovery of St James's supposed bones in the Galician town of Santiago de Compostela turned the Asturias into a major pilgrimage centre from the early ninth century onwards, and the shrine was an important element in the kingdom's leadership of the *reconquista*. Alfonso II's reliance on plunder in order to maintain his kingdom, based on the city of Oviedo, makes him a characteristic medieval ruler. The tribute that he exacted gave him the means to raid Muslim-held towns

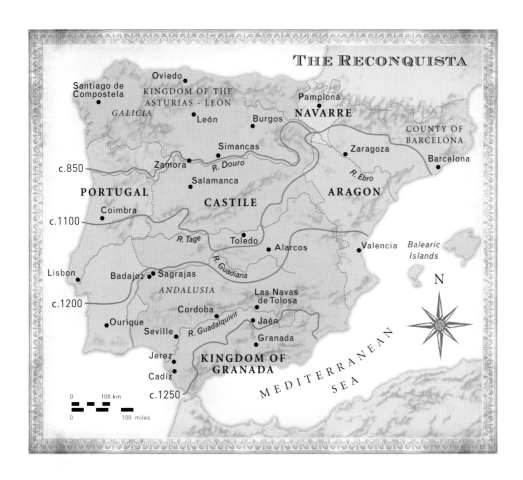

such as Lisbon and Zamora. A more consistent pattern of continuous expansion to the south developed after his time, with the Asturian possessions in the regions of Castile and León being fortified and systematically repopulated.

## LEÓN – SPRINGBOARD TO POWER

Alfonso III (r. 866–910) made the city of León his new capital, and from this base he campaigned to establish control over the lands to the north of the Douro river. A major reorganization of his kingdom saw Galicia and Portugal becoming duchies, and Castile was founded as a county. The southward movement of peoples from Galicia and Asturias changed the region's centre of gravity. From 924 onwards it was known as the kingdom of León, and although the Cordoban caliphate was at the height of its power in the tenth century Leónese forces were still able to mount damaging attacks on both Toledo and Seville.

The Battle of Simancas (19 July 939) was a great moment in the history of León, and the victory gained by the forces of Ramiro II (r. 931–51) over the caliph's army extended his kingdom's boundaries towards the Douro. Ramiro's army was, however, in a coalition with forces loyal to Fernan Gonzalez, the ruler of Castile who was now

Continued

## THE RECONQUISTA

into a kingdom and, having defeated his brother-in-law militarily, becomes king of León. Ferdinand I's son, Alfonso VI, succeeds (1065) to the throne of León and (1072) becomes king of Castile when his elder brother, Sancho II, is assassinated.

**1085** Toledo is taken by León-Castile.

**1090–94** Almoravid forces invade from North Africa and conquer most *taifas*.

**1118** Aragon's army retakes Zaragoza.

**1137** Dynastic union between the county of Barcelona and the kingdom of Aragon.

**1139** Portugal attains independence from León-Castile.

**1170** The Almohad dynasty has replaced the Amoravids as rulers of Islamic Spain.

**1212** Aragon, León-Castile, Navarre and Portugal unite in battle to defeat the Almohads. Cordoba is retaken (1236).

**1238** The emirate of Granada becomes Castile's vassal.

**1248** Ferdinand III of Castile retakes Seville.

**1492** Aragon-Castile conquer Granada.

using his position of power in order to assert his county's independence of León. Such manoeuvrings show that for most of the tenth century the Christian states of Spain had little conception of the *reconquista* as a strategic campaign which might co-ordinate their individual interests and efforts. By the end of the century, however, Navarre had made itself the Iberian region's greatest Christian power, and its ruler Sancho the Great (r. 1004–35) had shown little fastidiousness in pursuing that goal. A marriage alliance meant he could annex Castile, a powerful army helped him to conquer the two adjacent Christian marcher states of Sobrarbe and Ribagorza, victory in war against King Bermudo III turned León into Sancho's protectorate and Barcelona's count came to pay homage to Navarre.

The reign of Sancho III the Great covers the period of the Cordoban caliphate's disintegration into a number of small principalities termed *taifas* in the generation following the death of al-Mansur (*c*.938–1002), chief adviser to the caliph and effective ruler of al-Andalus. Al-Mansur was the greatest military strategist ever to confront the *reconquista*, and at the Battle of Cervera fought near Burgos on 29 July 1000 he inflicted a great defeat on Castile's army. But the succession disputes that arose after al-Mansur's death plunged the caliphate into civil war, and by the 1030s it had disappeared to be replaced by myriads of emirs running their own *taifas*.

Sancho divided his legacy among his sons, but he had shown how a tough hegemon could build up a Christian coalition, and his son Ferdinand, who had been allocated the county of Castile, shared a similar resolve. After waging a successful war on León, whose monarch was his own brother-in-law, Ferdinand succeeded him on the throne in 1037 and in the same year he turned Castile into a monarchy. The dynasty of Navarre had become the greatest power in Christian Spain, but it was the united realm of León and Castile – along with its contiguous areas in Galicia and the Asturias – which was the real political centre of Spanish Christianity. As king of León and of Castile, Ferdinand kept up the pressure on the Muslim-run *taifas* until his death in 1065, and the system of tributes known as *parias* was designed to weaken his Islamic subjects both financially and politically.

Ferdinand's son succeeded his father as Castile's King Sancho II, and then defeated his brother Alfonso in battle to become king of León in the months preceding his assassination in 1072. Alfonso had fled for safety to the *taifa* of Toledo (one of his Muslim client states), and Sancho's murder meant that he could now reunite León and Castile. The great event of Alfonso VI's reign (r. 1072–1109) was the conquest of Toledo in 1085, and the city's designation as an archbishopric made it the spiritual centre of Spanish Christianity. Alfonso had already proclaimed himself 'emperor of all Hispania' in 1077, and the close links he established with the papacy and European monarchs opened his kingdom to external influences. The Roman liturgical rite was now adopted by the Spanish Church, and the *reconquista* started to attract non-Spanish crusaders including, especially, the French.

## MESSIANIC BERBERS TAKE CHARGE

Although Arab-led, the Muslim conquest of Iberia had always relied on large numbers of Berbers from North Africa, both as fighters and as settlers. Confronted by the Christian advance, the rulers of al-Andalus decided to summon an additional force of Berber auxiliaries in 1086, and the warriors who crossed the Straits of Algeciras under the command of Yusuf ibn Tashfin ensured that Alfonso VI suffered a rare defeat in the Battle of Sagrajas (23 October 1086). As well as being a Berber, Yusuf also belonged to the Almoravid dynasty, whose rule already extended over Morocco, Algeria and through the southern Sahara into Senegal. Fortified by a vividly fundamentalist Islamic faith, the Almoravids regarded al-Andalus as a Muslim society that had weakened and whose defeats were a form of divine retribution. When Yusuf returned in 1090, therefore, he came at the head of an army of conquest whose enemies were now the emirs of al-Andalus.

The qualified toleration extended to its Christian and Jewish subjects by the Córdoba caliphate started to be threatened in the early 11th century. However, the Almoravid regime was set on a course of outright persecution, and that policy gave a new solidarity to the government of Islamic Spain. By 1094 Yusuf had removed most of Spain's local Muslim princes from power and the *taifas*, with the exception of Zaragoza, were absorbed within a single Almoravid caliphate. The dynasty's rule contained the *reconquista* for some two decades, but it was coming under increasing pressure in its North African base from the Almohads, another dynasty of Islamic Berbers and whose fanaticism rivalled that of the Almoravids.

Zaragoza maintained its resistance to the Almoravids until 1110. Its emir played a major role in the Almoravids' loss of authority, because following the defeat he and his army became allied to Aragon. In 1118 the Aragonese force seized Zaragoza, and the city became the capital of a Christian kingdom that was in the vanguard of the *reconquista*. Towards the west the Almoravids' defeat at the Battle of Ourique (25 July 1139) was another immensely significant event, since it enabled Prince Afonso Henriques to proclaim himself as Afonso I, Portugal's first king, and to declare his realm's independence of the kingdom of León and Castile.

ABOVE *A 12th-century painting of Alfonso VI, king of León, Castile and Galicia, from the Cathedral of Santiago de Compostela.*

The Almohads had replaced the Almoravids as emirs of Marrakesh in 1149, and in the years that followed they would also displace them in al-Andalus. In 1170 the Almohad capital was transferred to Seville, and although the regime lasted in al-Andalus for half a century its indifference to the arts and sciences made for a melancholy contrast with the sophistication of the Islamic Iberian past. The Almohad dynasty was nonetheless an effective warrior class and the victory gained by its Berber forces at the Battle of Alarcos (18 July 1195) undermined the Castilian kingdom's self-confidence. That defeat, however, instilled in the Christian states a new conviction that unity was the key to success. At the Battle of Las Navas de Tolosa (16 July 1212), fought near Jaen in modern Andalusia, the forces of Castile were joined by those of Navarre, Aragon, León and Portugal as well as by a French contingent. Together they inflicted the defeat on the Almohads that signified the end of the *reconquista* of the central Middle Ages.

It fell to Ferdinand III of Castile to consolidate the conquest by taking Córdoba in 1236 and Seville in 1248, with Jerez and Cadiz falling soon after. The Almohads were forced to retreat to North Africa, though here, too, they suffered a gradual attrition of authority, and when the last of the dynastic line was murdered in 1269 he held only Marrakesh. In the 1230s, therefore, Spain's Islamic far south was a power vacuum, and it was the Nasrid dynasty that seized the moment of regional opportunity. In 1237 Mohammed ibn Nasr established his authority in Granada, which then became the capital of his kingdom, and in the following year he accepted his status as Castile's vassal emir.

## Preserving the 'purity' of Spain

The Alhambra Palace was built by the Nasrid dynasty, but its architectural glories were a nostalgic tribute to the past rather than a guide to contemporary reality: Granada was obliged to raise troops for Castile and suffered major territorial losses as a result of Castilian invasions. The self-confident and united realms of Aragon and Castile conquered the kingdom of Granada in 1492, and it was taken over by the Castilian administration. By the terms of the Alhambra Decree (31 March 1492) issued by Ferdinand of Aragon and Isabel of Castile, all Spanish Jews had to either become Christians or leave the country. The Inquisition that the monarchs established in Spain in 1478 was already investigating the cases of various 'new Christians'. *Conversos* were former Jews and *Moriscos* were ex-Muslims. Both groups were suspected of a merely opportunistic conversion to Christianity and of a maintaining a secretive observance of their ancestral faith. *Conversos* and *Moriscos* could also be defined as individuals whose ancestors had converted during the *reconquista*, and their cases could therefore involve investigation of events that had occurred at least two or three centuries previously. An obsession with the 'purity' of Spain meant that the *reconquista* lived on as a set of attitudes long after the completion of Iberia's territorial re-conquest in the name of Christian faith.

# THE ALHAMBRA

*The architectural complex that Spain's Muslims called the* Calat Alhambra *('the red fortress') was completed in the second half of the 14th century on a plateau bordering the city of Granada. It is the colour of the local clay used in its construction that gives the Alhambra its name although the building's external walls were originally white-washed.*

Craftsmen were working on the earliest parts of the building in the mid-13th century but the history of the site as a fortification extends back to the late ninth century when a primitive red castle is known to have existed on the hill.

The idea of an enclosed palatine structure which is the ruler's domestic base, his administrative centre, and also a locale for public and religious ceremonies is middle eastern in its origins. Eighth century Baghdad's palace society under its Abbasid rulers was a particularly influential example of that architectural conception. The finest example of such a complex in early medieval Europe was the Great Palace in Constantinople, a series of pavilions which adjoined the basilica of Hagia Sophia. The palace, originally raised by the emperor Constantine but substantially redesigned in subsequent centuries, provided the rulers of Byzantium with an institutional base, a ceremonial setting, and domestic quarters. Charlemagne's early ninth century Aachen, with its palatine chapel, administrative offices and residential area, was a west European application of the same model.

The Alhambra's earliest architectural feature consists of an *alcazaba* or citadel: defensive capability was a primary consideration during the earliest phase of construction on the site, and the entire complex is enclosed by a fortified wall with 13 towers. Designed and decorated by Muslim, Jewish and Christian artists and craftsmen during a period of over a century, the palace-fortress shows the vitality of differing cultures in medieval Granada. A sophisticated irrigation system provided water for the numerous fountains, pools, bathhouses and gardens whose design furnishes the Alhambra with some of its most elaborate stylistic effects.

*The distinctive clay and Islamic architecture of the Alhambra with, to the right, the renaissance facade of the palace built during the reign of the emperor Charles V.*

# SAINTS, RELICS AND HERETICS

*The saints honoured by the Christian faithful during the medieval centuries were a specific group within the wider category of souls who had been admitted to heaven. When alive, the venerated saints had demonstrated exceptional holiness, and miraculous events that had occurred before and after their deaths were attributed to them. These interventions in the physical world took many forms: curing the sick and healing the lame as well as performing actions calculated to defeat their petitioners' enemies. Above all, the saints could help to undo some of the consequences of sin – that fallen state which was, according to the Church, the universal human condition. It was their possession of virtus or power – a force bestowed on them by God – that enabled these saints to act in support of individuals who had asked them to intercede with the Creator.*

The saints were souls who existed in the Almighty's presence, and they were therefore well placed to help an anxious humanity. This they achieved not just through miracles but also by advocating before God the cause of prayerful penitents who speculated anxiously about their chances of gaining admittance to the court of heaven after death. For many medieval minds a persuasive analogy existed with the courtly societies of this world's palaces, since here, too, there were powerful intermediaries in the form of courtiers who might be induced to represent outsiders who lacked influence.

RIGHT *Saint Thomas Aquinas is shown on the far left of this fresco (c.1437)* Coronation of the Virgin, *by Fra Angelico (c.1390–1455) from the church of San Marco, Florence.*

Saints were carefully categorized. Martyrs such as the apostle Paul had deliberately chosen to suffer and die for the faith. Saints who died of natural causes included 'confessors' who had lived exemplary lives. These included the fourth-century soldier Martin of Tours (316–97), who was especially venerated by successive French kings. 'Doctors of the Church' such as the Dominican Thomas Aquinas (1225–74) merited canonization as saints because of their lucid exposition of Catholic orthodoxy. The practice of honouring such exceptional people was an ancient one, and the commemoration of the early martyrs had helped to maintain Christian solidarity in the second and third

*c.*325 The emperor Constantine's mother Helena is credited with the discovery in Jerusalem of the remains of the True Cross.

*c.*700 Following the Islamic conquest of Syria and Palestine, Eastern Christian refugees have arrived in Western Europe – along with their collections of relics.

1155 A mass grave is uncovered in Cologne and is believed to contain the remains of Ursula and her 11,000 co-martyrs. The European relic market is flooded as a result.

1204 The crusaders' sack of Constantinople leads to the mass export of relics to Western Europe.

1322 Pope John XXII denounces as heretical the view that Christ and his disciples owned nothing.

1415 Jan Huss, a Czech reformer influenced by John Wycliffe, is put to death by the Church Council meeting at Constance.

1420–34 The Hussite Wars: the followers of Jan Huss engage in armed conflict in Bohemia and other central European regions.

centuries when the faith was often proscribed. Celebratory meals were held at martyrs' tombs such as the ones on the outskirts of Rome, and small shrines were sometimes built over them, as happened at Peter's tomb on the Vatican Hill. The emperor Constantine's mother Helena was credited with having discovered the remains of the True Cross in Jerusalem during the mid-320s, and the role of women in looking after relics and establishing shrines remained important throughout the Middle Ages. Large numbers of women attended the ceremonies held at the shrines and the church services commemorating saints' lives.

## RECOGNIZING SANCTITY

Saints who gained official recognition from the Church authorities were accorded a *cultus* or public honour. The *cultus* took many different forms. The Church nominated certain days – usually the anniversary of their death – for the saints' liturgical commemoration during the performance of the mass or the monastic office. Particularly important saints would be the focus of major celebrations sometimes involving a procession of relics. Individual dioceses and monasteries had their own liturgical calendars specifying celebrations for saints whose appeal was particular to the locality or specific to the religious Order, and the popularity of saints remained highly regionalized right across Europe during the Middle Ages.

Official recognition of some kind was always needed before a saint's cult could be established, but decisions about who should be venerated showed a degree of local initiative which clerical hierarchies often struggled to control. Establishing a relationship with certain chosen saints was one of the few ways in which the illiterate and the marginalized could exercise their freedom and assert their solidarity, and a saint's body of supporters was often described as his or her 'family'. For example, in the case of a saint who was the patron of a monastic community, that family would include not just the monks and the nobles who had endowed the foundation but also the serfs who worked the community's lands and the pilgrims who came to seek the saint's help. During the early medieval centuries bishops sought to establish a measure of control over who could be a saint within their dioceses. By the 12th century the papacy was exerting its own centralized authority by asserting a unique prerogative to issue the special bulls which canonized saints. This was also the time when the institution was preoccupied with a tight definition of orthodoxy and of its polar opposite – heresy.

## HOLY REMAINS

Among the relics or *reliquiae* ('the remains') left behind by the saints, it was the bones that attracted most attention. The Church taught that on Christ's return to Earth on the day of the Last Judgement the body of every human

LEFT *The golden shrine of Saint Elizabeth of Hungary, who died in 1231, once contained the saint's body. The shrine, located in Marburg, Germany, was plundered, and some of its relics are now to be found in Sweden and Austria.*

being would be reassembled from the pieces that had once constituted it. This was the bodily resurrection, and it applied to the venerated saints no less than to the rest of the dead. A tomb or a reliquary casket did not just contain inert bones, therefore. These objects continued to be part of the saints' identities and would be assembled to form their glorified bodies after the Last Judgement. To pray before the relics was to be in the physical presence of the saint – a real and identifiable personality offering a direct link with God who was the unique source of all power. Relics could also include physical objects used by the saints, such as items of clothing and books. Items brought into contact with relics – for example, pieces of cloth pressed onto a shrine or vials containing water used to wash a saint's body – could themselves become relics, albeit of a minor kind.

Relics were sometimes mere fragments of bones, and these could be placed inside altars or within reliquaries (a container for relics). Relics were also bought by the rich who used them in private devotions. The major shrines of the Middle Ages were more likely to contain a whole body or at least a significant collection of the relevant body parts. These frequently ornate structures were raised either over the original tombs or in places to which the bodies had been moved – as happened with James's shrine in Compostela and Thomas Becket's at Canterbury. The remains of Faith, a young girl tortured to death in c.300 by the Roman authorities, were originally to be found in her home town of Agen in Aquitaine. Faith's refusal to make pagan sacrifices, along with her spectacular torture on a red-hot brazier, made her a celebrity saint, and her bones were stolen in the ninth century by a monk from the Benedictine foundation at nearby Conques. It was here, on the pilgrimage route to Compostela, that Faith's relics became an object of mass devotion in the great 11th-century Romanesque abbey of Sainte Foy.

Eastern Christians had pioneered the veneration of relics, as evidenced by the scale of their devotions at the relic-rich holy places of Christendom in Syria and Palestine. The leadership of the Latin Church in Western Europe was often sceptical about the practice until at least the seventh century, and bishops tried to limit and control its local observance. However, the Islamic conquests in the Middle East led to a mass migration of Eastern Christians whose arrival in Western Europe – along with their relic collections – gave a new boost to the cult of relic veneration. Successive waves of popular devotion forced the clerical hierarchies to revise their views. The iconoclastic controversy that consumed the Greek Church for most of the eighth century and the first half of the ninth century also had an effect. Icons or pictures of the saints performed many of the roles (including miracles) attributed to relics, and the Byzantine emperors who supported the icon-breakers may well have wished to emphasize thereby their own unique authority as intermediaries between their subjects and God. Many Greeks were so devoted to their icons that they fled to Italy where they increased the numbers of those seeking to honour the saintly intermediaries. Nonetheless, the Church hierarchy remained wary, and the clergy tried to maintain control by subjecting relics to a process of authentication and by imposing order on the rituals marking their veneration.

From the 11th century onwards development of feudal practices and of the institution of lordship, which included the exchange of gifts, paralleled another upswing in the popularity of both saints and relics. Vassals who placed themselves under the protection of a local lord by offering him their service could be seen as secular counterparts to the pious, who might seek to gain the protection of saintly souls by bringing gifts to the shrines. Many churches and monasteries had to be rebuilt and extended because of the saints' popularity during the high Middle Ages. The great increase in the number of pilgrims drawn to Saint-Denis near Paris, for example, was one of the reasons why Abbé Suger embarked on a massive redesign of the abbey in the 1130s. The period also saw a steady growth in the numbers of female saints and their relics. From c.1050 onwards the monks at the Benedictine abbey of Vézelay in Burgundy began to claim possession of Mary Magdalene's relics. Later, the European relic market was flooded following the discovery in 1155 of a mass grave in Cologne alleged to contain the bones of Ursula and her equally legendary 11,000 co-martyrs. New trading contacts with the Middle East made as a result of the crusades, as well as the crusader's sacking and looting of Constantinople in 1204, swelled the number of imported relics. Sainte-Chapelle in Paris was built in the 1240s by Louis IX (1214–70) specifically to house the remains of saints.

# HOW RELIGIOUS ORDERS VIEWED SAINTS

Religious Orders could differ quite sharply in their attitudes to veneration of the saints. Cistercian monks followed an ideal of separation from mainstream society and Bernard of Clairvaux (1090–1153) led the movement to international recognition. But when the monks of Clairvaux prayed to their sainted founder they asked Bernard specifically not to perform miracles at his tomb in the monastery since they had no wish to deal with large numbers of pilgrims. The Franciscans, an austerely mendicant Order pledged to poverty, did not tend any significant shrines in France, although they did perform that task in Italy – and especially so at Assisi where their great founder Francis (1181/2–1226) was buried.

This was also a time when many saints acquired a rapid posthumous recognition, as in the cases of Louis IX and Bernard of Clairvaux, who were canonized in 1297 and 1174 respectively. The canonization of Dominic de Guzman (1170–1221), just 13 years after his death, rewarded his insight in establishing the Order of Preachers – a body of intellectual friars whose itinerancy and skills as communicators equipped them to move easily among the new urban centres of Europe. The rapid bestowal of a *cultus*

BELOW *This painting by Giovanni de Paolo (1403–83) dated 1455, shows Saint Clare of Assisi miraculously saving a child from being savaged by a wolf.*

recognized a saint's inspirational general example and ability to intercede. And in the case of these swift promotions the background was rarely one of mass devotion at particular graves and shrines. But the bodies of these near-contemporary saints were nonetheless carefully preserved, and often by members of a religious community. Such was the case with Clare of Assisi, a follower of Francis and founder of the Order that bears her name, who was canonized just two years after her death in 1253.

## Late medieval piety

A new intensity in lay spirituality was evident during the later Middle Ages, a time when shrines dedicated to the Virgin Mary and to Christ increased in numbers and popularity. The doctrines of the Assumption and Ascension taught that the bodies of the Saviour and his mother had been removed to heaven in their entirety, and since these shrines could therefore contain no fragments of bones the faithful had to content themselves with other objects. Chartres Cathedral became one of the great Marian centres of devotion since it claimed to possess the Virgin's tunic. Many statues of the Virgin, some of them painted black, were endowed with miraculous properties, and the many paintings recording her Annunciation showed Mary as a devout contemporary aristocrat reading in her bedchamber. Images of Christ's face became increasingly popular and the Eucharist (Christ's body and blood) came to be treated as a particular kind of relic. The Benediction of the Blessed Sacrament may have been an innovation of Francis of Assisi, and this ceremonial adoration of the host (the consecrated bread) was one of late medieval piety's most typical devotions.

ABOVE *These richly decorated pages come from a book of hours printed in Paris by Phillipe Pigouchet for the French publisher Simon Vostre in 1498. Such works were kept at home for purposes of personal devotion and study.*

The saints now lived on in many forms. Priests could commend them in sermons, and excerpts from hagiographies (collections of saints' biographies written in the vernacular) were read out to the laity. Books of hours – containing information about saints' lives – were consulted at home by the rich and literate. Images of saints were widespread on churches' painted walls, and they were ubiquitous in the Greek empire once the iconoclastic fury had passed. Confraternities (organizations of lay people that promoted special works of Christian piety) were an important part of medieval social life, and the saints adopted as patrons by these groups' members were honoured in elaborate ceremonies.

The zeal with which entire communities would approach saints who offered a specialist expertise was as great as ever. The 14th-century figure of Roch (or Rocco) of Montpellier was deemed useful when the plague struck, and Margaret, an Anglo-Saxon princess

who became Queen of Scots (*c.*1045–93), had been emblematic of the devout and philanthropic ruler ever since her canonization in 1250. Catherine of Alexandria, who was condemned in *c.*305 to die on the breaking wheel – a Roman instrument of torture – acquired a huge following in late medieval Europe. Her relics were to be found at the monastery, located on Egypt's Mount Sinai, that bore her name, and the pilgrimage route to her remains was one of the major international trails followed by the devout.

## DARING TO BE DIFFERENT

Heretics held views that contradicted the Church's orthodoxy. Although the Cathars were the most notorious examples there were many other sects who were treated with equal intolerance. The followers of Peter Valdez (*c.*1140–*c.*1218) in southern France and north Italy started as mainstream Christians who were especially attracted by New Testament injunctions to shun riches and to preach the gospel to the poor. Their zeal in doing so attracted the hostility of Church leaders who thought that preaching was a job for priests rather than for lay enthusiasts. It was their persistence as lay preachers, rather than any doctrinal reasons, that led to the Waldensians' initial condemnation as heretics by the Church in 1184. Having been given the label, they then started to embrace a whole set of genuinely heretical beliefs. By the early 13th century the Waldensians constituted a separate ecclesiastical structure that rejected both the idea of a priesthood and the notion of sacraments. Waldensians, rather like the Cathars, despised the official Church's association with riches and hierarchical power, and the sect stressed that spiritual insight and an ability to communicate with God was a result of individual merit rather than a reflection of the sacraments' efficacy.

Direct access to the Bible translated into vernacular languages was central to the Waldensians' appeal. The same is also true of the Lollards who followed John Wycliff in late 14th-century England and of the Hussites who followed their example in Bohemia a generation later. In all these cases it was the fear of being rejected by an individual conscience informed by its own interpretation of the New Testament that led the Church to anathematize the dissenters as heretics.

ABOVE *This illustration from* Foxe's Book of Martyrs *(1563) shows the Lollard John Badby being boiled to death in a barrel in 1410.*

Although Francis of Assisi embraced a ministry that preached the corrupting effects of riches, he and his immediate followers in the Order of Friars Minor ('the Franciscans') were impeccably orthodox in terms of Church doctrine. But when the official Franciscans changed their Order's rules after the death of the founder so that it might own material goods, an alternative grouping called the 'Spiritual Franciscans' emerged. These dissidents stated that all Franciscans should adhere to the founder's poverty and mendicancy. Their advocacy of the view that Christ and his disciples had owned nothing, was denounced as heretical by Pope John XXII in 1322. Most of the 'Spiritual Franciscans' eventually submitted but the Fraticelli, a disparate mass of splinter groups, continued to preach apostolic poverty in 14th-century Italy. Their denunciations of the established ecclesiastical order showed how the people rejected as 'heretics' by popes, bishops and councils of the Church could nonetheless display an enduring spiritual vitality.

# MYSTICS

*The Christian mystics of medieval Europe claimed to have been granted a special revelation: God had revealed himself to them in visions whose effects infused their entire being with the knowledge and love of the divine.*

Most were orthodox in their attachment to the Church's teachings, as in the case of England's Margery Kempe (c.1373–c.1438) and Dame Juliana of Norwich (c.1342–c.1416). Hildegard of Bingen (c.1098–1179) started to have visions when she was a young child, and this German abbess would have been remarkable in any age with her polymathic gifts as a composer, playwright, poet, expert botanist and highly acclaimed public preacher. She conducted four extensive preaching tours across Germany. Hildegard also enjoyed the support of Bernard of Clairvaux – always something of a litmus test in demonstrating orthodoxy – in calling for further reforms of the Church from within, including the abolition of simony. Others with mystical gifts were more of a problem for the Church authorities.

Joachim of Fiore (c.1135–1202) was inspired by the New Testament's Book of Revelation and by the Gospel's proclamation of an imminent and transformational kingdom of God. Born in Calabria, where he founded an abbey at Fiore which adhered to a tough interpretation of Cistercian monastic discipline, Joachim was a voluminous author whose writings revolve around the notion of three distinct phases in humanity's history. The Old Testament era had been the Age of the Patriarchal Father, who ruled through the exercise of power

*Hildegard of Bingen is depicted in the frontispiece of* Scivias, *dictating the details of a vision to her scribe,* Volmar. Scivias *sets out the 26 visions that Hildegard experienced during her lifetime.*

and by inspiring fear. The New Testament period was the Age of the Son, whose greater wisdom was evident in the foundation of a Catholic and sacramental Church. The Age of the Holy Spirit, or Third Age, would be the next stage in this progressive ascent, and its emphasis would be on egalitarian and communal values. A Church hierarchy would become unnecessary during the period that was dawning. Furthermore, the divisions between Jews, the Greek Church and the Western Latins would be transcended within a new dispensation guided by the spirit of the Gospel and by God's love, rather than by a slavish adherence to the letter of the law.

Joachim's humility and evident holiness of life saved him from persecution, and he even enjoyed the active support of Pope Lucius III (r. 1181–85). Thomas Aquinas disapproved of his teachings but, equally unsurprisingly, Joachim was a popular figure among many Franciscans, and Dante thought he was possessed of a genuine gift of prophecy. Joachim gave something of a hostage to fortune by nominating, albeit tentatively, the year 1260 as the time when the Third Age would actually start. Once that year had come and gone his posthumous reputation came under increasing attack, and in 1263 he was officially condemned as a heretic by the Church.

# 285
## c.1350

# MEDIEVAL SOCIETY

*At the beginning of the early medieval period Western European society was characterized by a fragmentation of authority and widespread de-urbanization whose causes can be attributed to the formal division of the Roman empire in 285. Economic, military and political resources tended to be concentrated in the East thereafter, and in the West the countryside was increasingly dominated by an aristocracy of landowners and senior soldiers, mostly based in large villas and newly fortified towns. The estates of Western Europe were worked by slaves, by freedmen who had once been slaves, and also by coloni – formerly independent farmers who had subordinated themselves to the great landowners in order to gain protection against imperial tax collectors and the demands of military conscription. Such landowners could dispense local justice and even assemble private armies. The Western economy became ruralized and regional. Trade with the Mediterranean economies diminished, and most of the goods bought and sold were locally produced.*

It was into this world that the Germanic tribes known to the Romans as *barbari* and *externae gentes* ('barbarians' and 'foreign peoples') moved in increasing numbers from the late fourth century onwards. With the frequent co-operation of local Roman officials, and enjoying the support of provincial citizens, the tribal leaders came to rule in the provinces of Gaul, Iberia, Italy and Britain, and it was in these regions that they established themselves as kings.

RIGHT *Peasants work the fields in front of the Château de Lusignan in this image from the* Très Riches Heures du Duc de Berry, *a 15th-century book of hours.*

Communities in areas of medieval Europe that had been part of the Roman empire were able to build on the institutional and architectural heritage of the Roman past. Rome's unit of local government was the *civitas*, which was composed of a local town and its surrounding countryside. These *civitates* were much more numerous in Italy and in the Western provinces compared with the areas in the empire's north and east, and each had its bishop. During the fifth and sixth centuries bishops in southern France and

**285** Rome's empire is divided: resources will be concentrated in the East, while authority fragments in Western Europe.

*c.*500 Bishops in southern France and Italy assume local governmental responsibilities in the *civitates* of the former Roman empire.

*c.*900 The manorial system is widespread across Western Europe.

*c.*950–*c.*1250 Europe has long, hot summers and mild winters. Agricultural productivity and population levels increase.

*c.*1000 Landowners have driven formerly free peasants into serfdom.

*c.*1050 Emergence of knighthood. 'Lordship' – a reciprocal exchange of loyalty and duty – is becoming the Western European social model.

*c.*1150 Aristocratic families now define themselves exclusively according to the patrilineal line and are associated with an inherited property, often a castle, which supplies the family name.

*c.*1200 Serfdom continues to expand in Eastern Europe but declines in the West.

*c.*1350 Europe's population levels plummet due to famine and plague.

Italy increasingly assumed the roles previously performed by Rome's provincial officials. Bishops now controlled the civil administration of their local *civitas* and were responsible for securing its supplies.

## LANDLORDS AND SERFS

The social patterns associated with the late Roman countryside – its landlords, peasants and slaves – survived for almost half a millennium after the dissolution of imperial authority. The same is largely true of its characteristic landscape of cultivated fields, orchards and dense forests. One major development, well established by the ninth century, was the manorial system which organized the relationship between landlords and peasants in working the land. Manors may well have evolved out of the social structures associated with the late Roman villa. The *demesne* was the part of the manor that the landlord, using peasant labour, farmed for his own purposes. The remainder was farmed by the peasants for their subsistence while paying the lord a rent, which could take the form of agricultural produce, provision of their own labour, or cash.

As central royal authority diminished in the post-Carolingian ninth and tenth centuries landowners had every incentive and opportunity to cultivate their lands more intensively and to exercise their territorial rights of lordship more vigorously. Many formerly free peasants and slaves now came to belong to a new social grouping, the serfs. *Servus* had previously been used to describe slaves and now referred to the serfs who, while not personally owned by their lords, were nonetheless tied to his lands. (The new word for a slave, *sclavus*, owed its origin to the Eastern European Slavic societies which produced, and exported, so many slaves.) The number of serfs continued to increase until the late 12th century, when the development of a more money-based economy made free and rent-paying peasants a more attractive proposition to landlords than bound serfs. The institution gradually disappeared in Western Europe from that time onwards. In Eastern Europe, however, serfdom actually increased in importance with an alliance between monarchs and lords leading to the formation of huge agrarian estates whose produce was designed to feed the growing Western market.

The aristocracy in the West also exploited its position by taking over the *bannum* – the public power to command and punish – that had been the prerogative of monarchs before the ninth-century decline in royal power. Local courts allowed the nobility to enforce its will, to expand cereal cultivation by clearing forests and to keep the rest of the woodland to itself for hunting purposes. Peasants and serfs did not just provide the nobility with labour. They were now being forced to use the mills and markets that were owned and run by nobles. They were also obliged to settle in villages whose growth in size paralleled the spread of a system of parishes, centred on the local church and paid for by the imposition of a tithe – one-tenth of the dependent classes' agricultural produce.

## Technological advances

Between the year 1000 and the mid-14th century, Europe's population may well have doubled to nearly 75 million. That increase was concentrated in the continent's north, where a trebling of population levels illustrated the effect of the protein-enriched and meat-based diets that became possible as a result of better farming techniques. The bean, imported from the Middle East to Muslim-conquered Spain, was brought north to the rest of the continent, and better pasturage led to a great increase in the number of cattle that could be bred for European consumption.

Technological breakthroughs associated with horses, water mills and windmills powered the rural economic advance. The ox had been the traditional beast of burden, but the draft horse, shod with iron horseshoes enabling the hooves to negotiate their way through damp northern European soils, was quicker and more efficient. By the late-tenth century the addition of the horse-collar, which enabled a burden to be hauled using the shoulders rather than the neck, increased the animal's pulling power.

The increasing numbers of water mills, which ground grain into flour, capitalized on Western Europe's extensive river network, while windmills – a technology imported from the Middle East – supplied power in areas where rivers were scarce. European forests and mountains produced the timber, fuel and metallic ores that provided raw materials for new technologies. Many areas were denuded of their forests as a result of the demand for timber used in constructing new ships, public buildings and private houses. Advances in metallurgy produced better quality swords, daggers and armoury for soldiers. Technological sophistication could also be seen in the glazed pottery and glassware frequently used in even quite modest households, and the houses of the mass of the population were increasingly being built of stone rather than wood and thatch.

ABOVE *A miller and windmill are depicted in the* Luttrell Psalter *of c.1340. Windmills became common in Europe from the late 13th century onwards.*

Climatic fluctuations gave the North Atlantic region a warm period (*c.*950–*c.*1250), and the productivity of medieval Europe's rural economy benefited from long hot summers and mild winters. These conditions also assisted the construction of the great Gothic

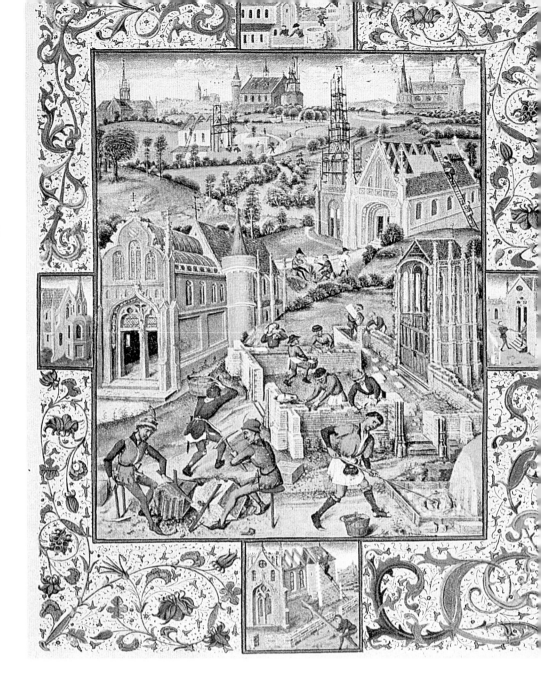

RIGHT *Peasants and masons build a new city in the 14th century, from a French manuscript version of the prose romance* Girart de Roussillon.

cathedrals of the central Middle Ages, since builders had longer periods of clement weather for their out-door work. The architectural skill, technical knowledge and managerial capacity that enabled cathedrals to be built were also evident in the growth of towns from the 11th century onwards. Large numbers of peasants, freed from the need to work the land as a result of increased agricultural productivity, migrated to urban centres.

## THE GROWTH OF TOWNS AND CITIES

Carolingian Europe's few cities were small-scale affairs. Some were redesigned Roman towns – especially in Europe's Mediterranean south – and most early medieval European urban centres existed to serve the needs of kings, bishops and monasteries. Subsequent urban development, however, reflected the economic needs of local lords, and in northern Europe in particular new cities came into being as centres for the local markets. From the tenth century onwards, large numbers of mercantile and craft-based guilds were becoming established within towns in order to protect their members' interests. Merchants' guilds played a particular role in the emergence of self-governing cities or communes – a development that underlined the distinctiveness of urban life and set it apart from the rural world of the village and estate. Nonetheless, cities had to protect their food supplies, chains of communication and trade routes. In both northern and southern Europe, therefore, the surrounding rural region was closely linked to the city.

Many of Europe's newly flourishing urban and civic centres were associated with new manufacturing processes. The cities of the southern Low Countries, for example, had a particular expertise in dyeing, weaving and finishing wool. Other towns specialized in the manufacture of metalwork and armaments, and some operated as market centres for products that could not be produced locally, such as wine. These specialist goods were then transported and distributed along extensive trade routes, and the rivers of Western Europe, where many cities were located, provided an important network of communications.

The formulation dividing society into those who fought, prayed and laboured enjoyed great vogue in the 11th and 12th centuries, and the structure of the second order, the clergy, was well established by *c*.1200. As the European economy developed and diversified from the 12th century onwards those who 'laboured' came to include merchants, financiers and lay professionals as well as peasants and artisans. The distinction between warriors and 'labourers' intersected with European society's more formal and legal divide between those who were free and those who were not. The un-free could not join armies at even the lowest level of soldiering, and ordinary soldiers were keen to maintain a clear difference between their own status as free men and the mere labourers of the countryside. That strenuous assertion by the lowest ranks of serving men shows the extent to which large numbers of once-free peasants had been coerced into serfdom.

## THE NOBILITY AND PATRONAGE

The great territorial lords often had a family history extending back to the Carolingian period, and the term 'noble' was used to describe kinship groups whose names and distinguished ancestry were known and widely respected. Noble groups intermarried and recognized, initially, the importance of both the female and the paternal line of ancestry when it came to establishing their identity, rights and inheritances. Charlemagne used this international nobility to rule his empire, and its descendants included the aristocracy of the central Middle Ages. By then however noble status had changed substantially. Aristocratic families were now defining themselves exclusively in

terms of the patrilineal line, and they were strongly identified with a particular piece of property which, handed down through the generations, often supplied the family's name. Titles such as 'count' and 'duke' were originally handed out in recognition of royal service, but although they increased a family's prestige these honours were not intrinsic to noble status. In early medieval Europe not even kings could turn those who were not noble by birth into members of the nobility.

Great territorial lords identified themselves as warriors, and their material needs in that regard grew during the central Middle Ages. Technological advances in warfare, such as the heavy cavalry, meant new costs, and since war had gained in complexity the nobility needed more time to train and prepare for battle. Europe's reorganized countryside produced the wealth that helped to meet these aristocratic requirements. Some nobles also asserted themselves by seizing territory that, along with its inhabitants, was then controlled from a castle. The very greatest of these aristocrats administered vast estates acquired through inheritance and by land grants from the king. Closely governed territorial principalities evolved as a result and, in the case of France, these were eventually absorbed by the Crown and redistributed to younger members of the royal family. As territorial monarchies increased in power during the later Middle Ages so the aristocracy adapted to new circumstances and decided to accept more royal offices, titles and patronage. The adoption of an elaborate system of ranking for groupings within the nobility demonstrated the aristocracy's determination to maintain itself as a separate and privileged cast. Nonetheless, they were all subordinated to the ruler, who could now ennoble whoever he wanted.

Knights started to appear on the European scene from the 11th century onwards, and the spread of knighthood as both an institution and an ethical code affected the warrior group in profound ways. Early medieval armies were composed of free men who differed widely in terms of their wealth, and knights likewise differed greatly in terms of their material riches as well as in social status. Great aristocrats called themselves knights, and so did lords whose lands could be decidedly modest. It was, however, the professionalism of the knight that established his distinctiveness as a specialist warrior – a category of the fighting man which was new in European history and thought. All knights moreover, whether possessed of broad acres or not, were equally bound by the code of chivalry. Despite the extreme diversity between the lesser knights and minor nobles on the one hand, and great aristocrats on the other, the common warrior-culture, expressed in the literature and ideology of chivalry, was a real social bond that excluded those who did not share it.

The exchange of loyalties between superiors and inferiors was a fundamental feature of European social order in the central Middle Ages. Its expression was various. Aristocrats, lesser nobles and knights asserted themselves by promising to protect inferiors who undertook vows of obligation. Myriad relationships of power were thereby asserted between, for example, the great nobles of the warrior class and fighting men of lower status who depended on them for support, with grants of land and income drawn from the lord's resources carrying with them the hope of social advancement. Some knights of a modest social standing were therefore owed loyalty from their 'vassals' while in turn incurring obligations to great territorial lords. Similarly, the territorial lords were themselves vassals of monarchs as a result of receiving royal favours – most typically in the form of land grants. The recurring link in all these relationships is 'lordship', and that institution provided the context for the reciprocal transmission of respect and obligation that was such a defining feature of European society between the 11th and 14th centuries.

The '*feudum*' (also called a 'fief') – a form of property holding common in France and England – provided a localized and specific application of lordship, and its tenures could be either free or un-free. Knight service was the principal form of a free tenure, with military duties being performed for the king or another lord, although by the mid-12th century this service was usually commuted in England on payment of a tax called *scutage*. *Socage* was another free tenure, and its principal service, provided usually by tenants of more modest standing, was frequently agricultural – such as performing a certain number of days' ploughing for the lord. All these tenures were subject to a number of conditions such as *relief* (the payment made on transferring a fief to an heir) and *escheat* (the return of the fief to the lord when the tenant died without an heir). The main type of un-free tenure was *villeinage*, which started as a barely modified form of servitude. Free tenants' duties were predetermined, but those who were un-free never knew in advance what they might be asked to do for their lords, although the legal ruling that *villein* tenants could not be ejected in breach of existing custom eventually came to apply.

## TRANSCENDING TRAGEDY

By the mid-14th century the effects of famine and plague were starting to drive down Europe's population levels. But those who survived could also prosper. Competition for labour drove up wages in real terms, and the scarcity of workers depressed rural

rents. A falling population led to a drop in the cost of basic foodstuffs such as wheat, and workers could therefore diversify their diets. The increased consumption of dairy products and meats was a feature of the subsequent population increase, and the greater purchasing power enjoyed by workers also meant they could afford the manufactured products developed in the towns. That level of demand therefore benefited the urban economies, and despite the overall decline in Europe's population levels during the 14th and 15th centuries the number of European towns with more than 10,000 inhabitants increased.

ABOVE *The Black Death, which peaked in the mid-14th century, killed up to half of Europe's population. This illustration of plague sufferers is from the 1411 Toggenburg Bible.*

The European recovery of the 15th century saw a cycle of growth re-establishing itself with increasing population levels, civic development and governmental activity producing a renewed demand for goods, food and services. The manorial system had long since been in decline, and it was further undermined by the period's emphasis on large-scale commercial crops such as wool and grain, as well as by the emancipation of servile labour. Manufacturing boomed, especially in areas geared to supplying armies and fleets with cloth, armour, weapons and ships. Technological advances produced labour-saving devices – such as the printing press – that increased worker productivity. Central Europe's large deposits of iron, copper, gold and silver were intensively worked by new mining techniques, and metalworking technology attained greater levels of refinement. All these economic developments gave new opportunities for the substantial capital investment that was fast becoming the defining feature of the European economy and the basis for its future sustained growth.

# York: 16 March 1190

*Until the late 11th century Jews in Europe had faced little persecution. Adherence to Judaism was regarded as an inexplicable rejection of the Christian gospel, but papal commands forbade the use of force to convert Jews and they often pursued the same careers as Christians. However, from the time of the First Crusade onwards hostility to Judaism became very widespread in Europe as the continent's culture started to define itself in an increasingly aggressive Christian fashion.*

Jews had always been seen as stubborn, but they were now also viewed as a malevolent force bent on destroying society from within. It was the increasing restrictions on their professional careers that turned so many Jews to money lending, a practice forbidden to Christians, and their prominence in that trade gave a new and vicious twist to anti-Semitic sentiment.

In 1170 William the Conqueror invited a number of Jews to move from Rouen in Normandy and settle in England, where they became the kernel of the country's earliest substantial Jewish community. The financial skills of English Jews served the Anglo-Norman Crown well in subsequent decades, and they enjoyed special privileges as a result. A royal charter issued by Henry I (r. 1100–35) gave Jews the right to move around the country without paying tolls, to buy and sell property, and to swear on the Torah rather than the Christian Bible. For most of the 12th century Jews enjoyed greater security in England than on the continent, and their numbers increased through immigration after the expulsion of French Jews in 1182 by King Philip Augustus.

Preparations for English participation in the Third Crusade, however, exposed the country's Jews to new levels of danger. Houses in the City of London's Jewish quarter ('Old Jewry') were attacked in the days following the coronation of Richard I ('the Lionheart') on 3 September 1189,

*Jews wearing identifying pointed hats and* yellow rouelle *badges are burned at the stake in 1348, in this illustration from the* Lucerne Chronicle *of 1513.*

and after the king's departure on crusade anti-Semitic violence spread to the counties of Essex and Norfolk. The city of York had seen extensive anti-Jewish rioting in early March 1190, and Jewish families were granted refuge within York Castle by its constable. Congregated within a central wooden tower, the Jews were then surrounded by a mob outside the castle walls who demanded their immediate conversion to Christianity on pain of death. When the warden left the castle the Jews, fearful of the consequences of opening the gates, refused to readmit him and a siege by the local militia followed. On 16 March the tower caught fire and most of the Jews killed themselves rather than face the Christian mob. Those who did surrender were then killed, despite having received assurances of their safety. At least 150 Jews died. The ringleaders of the massacre subsequently burned documents kept in York Cathedral which specified the local debts owed to the dead Jews. English Jews were supposed to come under the king's special protection and the murders did not go unpunished. But it was the harm to its financial interests that really motivated the Crown, since an attack on Jews was also an attack on its own revenue resources. Some 50 of York's citizens were fined, and King Richard I introduced a system whereby debts held by Jews were duplicated to the Crown.

# c.400 — 1300 | MEDIEVAL CULTURE

*Medieval European culture reflected the dominant role of the Christian Church as arbiter of human conduct and as authoritative guide to the truths revealed by God in the person of Christ. The* magisterium *or teaching authority claimed by the clergy expressed orthodox belief, and the Church's disciplinary powers, based on scriptural interpretation and formulated in canon law, prescribed correct behaviour. Astrology retained a widespread appeal despite its implicit contradiction of the Christian doctrines that asserted God's sovereign omnipotence. Predictions concerning the future persisted therefore, and a belief in magic, witchcraft and the powers of good and evil spirits subsisted beneath the official structures of ecclesiastical order.*

Christianity was also the filter through which a selective interpretation of ancient Roman culture was transmitted to Europe's evolving medieval civilization. Latin was used for the celebration of the Mass, and it was also the medium of communication used by both the Church's officialdom and that of secular princes. As a result, the language acquired a new lease of life – albeit one that was prone to bureaucracy's stiff jargon. When it came to preaching sermons a good deal of pragmatism was needed by priests if they were to communicate with a largely illiterate population. Most, therefore, opted for a kind of rustic Latin patois (*rustica Romana lingua*). Alternatively, they used one of the vernacular European languages that were acquiring a distinctive form by the eighth century – such as *Theotiscam*, a form of early German.

## GOVERNING IN THE ROMAN STYLE

RIGHT *An image from the 15th cenury* Très Riches Heures du Duc de Berry *depicting young Parisian aristocrats on horseback.*

The kings of early medieval Europe ruled in a Roman style after establishing themselves in the former imperial territories. They issued laws for their own people and for their newly acquired subjects who had been Roman citizens, and the coins they struck were modelled on imperial currency. Although these kingdoms – Frankish, Lombard, Anglo-Saxon, Visigothic in Spain and Ostrogothic in Italy – were newly formed, they

## MEDIEVAL CULTURE

**c.731** The English monk Bede has finished writing his *Ecclesiastical History of the English People.* The *anno domini* order of chronology that he adopts will become the European norm.

**910** Foundation of Cluny Abbey, Burgundy. An international federation of monastic houses, all under the ultimate authority of Cluny's abbot, develops subsequently.

**c.1127** Hugh of Saint-Victor writes the *Didascalicon*, a pioneering example of the medieval encyclopedia.

**c.1150** Emergence of coats of arms: heraldic devices are unique to the bearer and painted on the shield carried by a knight or lord.

**c.1200** The Gothic script has evolved: consistency of style and legibility promote standardized and reliable texts for teaching purposes.

**1204** The sack of Constantinople during the Fourth Crusade: Europe's cultural divide between Greeks and Latins becomes a chasm.

**1256** Thomas Aquinas starts to teach at the University of Paris.

**1300** Secular love poetry is being set to music in the form of the *motet*, and pastoral subjects are evoked in madrigals.

preferred to be considered as old. Antiquity lent authority, just as it had done in ancient Rome. The officially sponsored histories of these peoples, such as Paul the Deacon's *History of the Lombards* written in the 790s, claimed therefore that the kingdoms had a longer established, and more exclusive, ethnic foundation than was in fact the case.

Christianity's cultural influence on medieval European life and thought was continuous with its status in the civilization of late antiquity. Following Theodosius I's adoption of Christianity as the empire's official religion in 380 the clergy became aligned with the grades of the imperial civil service, and the religion was largely shorn of its earlier pacifist tendencies. Early medieval Christian culture built on this establishment status and was attuned to the pragmatic needs of warrior-kings who saw themselves as agents of a sacral and divine power. Many kings and aristocrats were converted by their wives. Queen Clotilda (*c*.474–*c*.545), the Burgundian and Catholic wife of Clovis, persuaded him to abandon the ancestral paganism of the Franks. The Bavarian princess Theodelinda (*c*.570–628), who married Agilulf, king of the Lombards, influenced his decision to abandon Arian Christianity in favour of Catholicism. The warrior ethic of previously pagan leaders acquired thereby a new focus, and the Church sanctioned the authority of Christian kings whose campaigns of conquest waged against hostile neighbours and dissidents led to new, and mostly enforced, conversions. Some of the monarchies, especially those of the Franks and of the Spanish Visigoths, adapted ancient Jewish rituals on the basis of a reading of the Old Testament. Kings were anointed liturgically with holy oil and reminded in sermons, prayers and Church councils of their responsibilities to God, who had chosen them to rule. The new culture of kingship was a potent mixture of public power and spiritual self-confidence. Underpinned by successful generalship, it spread to regions of Europe that had never been ruled by Rome, such as Ireland, northern Britain and areas to the east of the River Rhine.

## EVANGELIZING EUROPE

Irish missionaries were especially active in converting Europe's non-Roman peoples and Columbanus (*c*.543–615), the most celebrated evangelist, also founded new communities in Luxeuil in Burgundy and Bobbio in north Italy. The spread in Europe of the penitential practice of confession made individually to a priest – a distinctive feature of Celtic Christianity – owed much to Columbanus's pioneering example. Within the island of Britain earlier forms of Celtic Christianity clashed with the more hierarchical Roman form until the Synod of Whitby (664), when Roman Christianity's regulations were adopted for the kingdom of Northumbria with the other Anglo-Saxon kingdoms falling into line subsequently. It was therefore a very Romanized English Church structure that produced its greatest missionary in Boniface (*c.*675–754), who became archbishop of Mainz and spent most of his career evangelizing on the borders of the kingdom of the Franks.

The 'secular clergy' served the needs of the laity through the parish-based system, while monks and religious women lived in communities set apart from the world. Monasticism's earliest exponents were ascetics who had withdrawn to the deserts of Egypt and Syria, and the transmission of their influence to Western Europe, especially by the monk and traveller John Cassian (360–435), was a rare example of how the earlier communication networks across the Mediterranean could still operate in late antiquity. The rules prescribed for the monastic life varied, but the most influential were composed by Benedict of Nursia (*c.*480–*c.*547), who structured the day into periods of prayer, contemplation and work. The Order that followed his rule was named after him and the Benedictine elevation of manual labour in God's service marked a real shift in cultural attitudes, since the élites of classical antiquity had long since scorned such work as a sign of servility. Great monasteries such as the one at Cluny in Burgundy enjoyed a close association with the secular nobility, who endowed them with lands. The Cistercians, an Order of reformed Benedictines, were particularly active in cultivating and developing Europe's marginal lands during the 12th century. Monks constituted a disciplined, self-reliant, and unpaid labour force which could therefore develop farming practices in an innovative way and without having to rely on manorial customs.

ABOVE *Saint Columbanus, who founded monasteries in France and Italy in the late sixth century, is portrayed in this fresco in the 12th- century cathedral at Brugnato, near Genoa.*

Christianity's rituals, liturgies and sacraments gave structure to European culture at both an individual and social level, with seasons of penitence, Advent and Lent, preceding the joyful feasts of Christmas and Easter. Priests blessed harvests, animals and ships, and offered up prayers of intercession in the face of natural and man-made disasters. The Christian culture's chronology gave a new dimension to the passing of time and separated it from the pagan past. Earlier chronologies had been varied. Some dated the years according to the number that had elapsed since the foundation of the city of Rome, and others were structured by the regnal years of different emperors. In the early sixth century, however, the Syrian monk Dionysius Exiguus had established a sequence of years based on what he took to be the date of Christ's birth. After the English monk and historian Bede (673–735) used that *anno domini* system in his *Ecclesiastical History*

*ABOVE Farmers in Gimpelsbrunn celebrate a* kermis *in this woodcut (c.1530) by Sebald Beham. Popular in the Low Countries and northern France during the later Middle Ages, the* kermis *celebrated the anniversary of a local church's foundation and often honoured the church's patron saint.*

*of the English People,* it became the norm in Latin Christendom. The division of the year itself also changed. Although the months still had Roman names they were now divided into the seven-day week borrowed from the Jewish calendar, and that unit replaced the Romans' tripartite division of *Kalendae, Nonae* and *Ides.*

## THE PROMINENCE OF THE LAITY

The distinction between clergy and laity that gave structure to European society was interpreted with a new zeal by the Church reform movement of the 11th and 12th centuries. Clerical freedom from subordination to lay authority was, of course, central to the Investiture dispute, but the Church's new sharpness of tone also enhanced lay status in many ways. The new teaching stated, for example, that lay authorities could legitimately perform certain judicial actions that were now forbidden to the clergy, such as the shedding of blood and administration of physical punishment. Clerical authorities from the 11th century onwards also gave a new validity to lay activities that earlier and more monastic forms of Christianity had either ignored or scorned. Commerce, marriage and family life were now regarded in a positive light rather than being viewed as a sign of humanity's fallen condition. And the emergence in the central Middle Ages of theories sanctioning 'just war' – military action approved by the Church in specific circumstances such as a response to aggression – gave a new ideological underpinning to the battlefield excursions of Christian princes and generals.

Lay vitality was also evident in the universities founded in the Middle Ages and which were granted imperial, papal and royal privileges. The first guilds of university teachers had emerged in the late 12th century, with their members insisting on the professional right to set the standards that applied in admitting and examining students. Effective teaching and transmission of knowledge presupposed readable styles of writing, and the Carolingian script had been a huge ninth-century breakthrough in standards of legibility. Standardization took another leap forward with the Gothic script which was developed in the 12th century and whose consistent style for abbreviations and literary expression provided teachers and students with texts that were as identical as possible.

## SCHOLASTICISM AND MUSICAL ADVANCES

The dispute between the empire and the papacy was medieval European culture's first major public debate about the basis of authority, and its polemical energy resulted from rival interpretations of certain key texts – especially in the field of law. By the 1140s documents relating to Church law and discipline had been assembled together in the *Concordia discordantium canonum* attributed to the Benedictine monk Gratian who taught law at Bologna. More generally known as the *Decretum Gratiani,* the treatise combined jurisprudence with the analytic style typical of scholasticism – the technique of classifying knowledge and structuring arguments that was now the hallmark of medieval Europe's intellectual life. The sheer scale of scholasticism's ambitions set it apart from the earlier monastic culture's more contemplative and discursive approach to faith and knowledge, and the system's dialectical method was applied to medicine and the arts in general as well as theology and law. Hugh of Saint-Victor (1096–1141), based at the Paris abbey of that name, produced in *c.*1127 the *Didascalicon*, a wide-ranging encyclopedia of current knowledge, and Peter Abelard (1079–1142) taught the dialectical method of investigation to the many students who flocked to Paris to be instructed by him. A similarly analytical emphasis is evident in the *Four Books of Sentences* (*Sententiarum libri iv*), a highly influential work of theology written by Peter Lombard (*c.*1100–60).

Europe's musical culture also acquired new styles of elaborate expression at this time. The early medieval liturgy's most characteristic sound was that of the Gregorian plainchant whose differing styles, based on the Jewish tradition of singing psalms, were all monophonic. From the 12th century onwards, polyphonic styles started to diversify both sacred and secular music. Early motets were exclusively liturgical, but by the end of the 13th century the genre was accommodating secular love poetry. The madrigal, written usually for two voices and often based on a pastoral subject, had acquired its typical form in Italy by *c.*1300.

## THE CULTURE OF CHIVALRY

Religious and secular impulses co-existed within chivalry – a code of honourable conduct associated with the mounted knights (*chevaliers*) of French military culture and whose fashionable reputation led to its widespread diffusion among the landed classes from the 11th century onwards. The chivalric ethic fashioned the norms of social behaviour that applied in the courts of kings and princes, but the military dimension remained important throughout chivalry's four centuries of influence within European high society. Heraldry, for example, acquired increasingly elaborate rules that dictated the designs of coats of arms painted on warriors' shields. The wearing of heraldic emblems allowed individual knights and nobles to proclaim pride in their ancestry when taking part in jousts, tournaments and the formalized hunting of wild animals. But the shield and its designs never lost their primary role of identifying a combatant in the battlefield mêlée, and heraldic emblems became increasingly important during the later Middle Ages, since by that stage a nobleman's entire body was encased in armoury when he went into battle.

Chivalry, however, also encompassed a whole set of mental attitudes quite apart from the military expertise involved in adroit horsemanship and the handling of

*BELOW The Gutenberg printing press, as shown in this undated woodcut, revolutionized the production of books. After its introduction in the mid-15th century, texts no longer had to be copied by hand individually.*

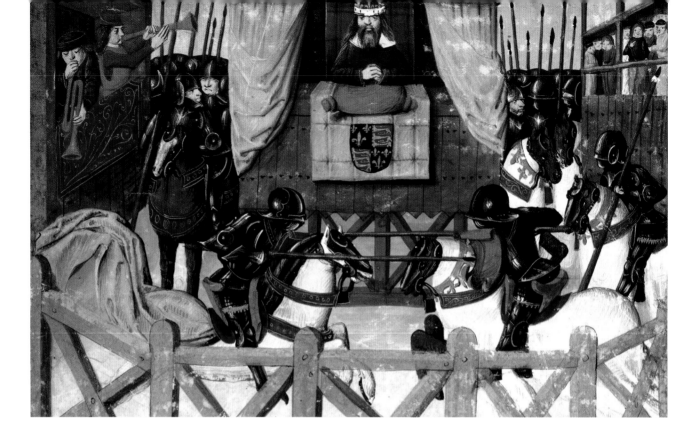

ABOVE *Richard II of England (r. 1377–99) presides over a courtly tournament in this 15th-century Flemish manuscript. Two mounted knights are jousting in the arena while, in the pavilion to the left, musicians play trumpets. Spectators view the scene from the safety of the pavilion on the right.*

lances and swords. Valour, honour and loyalty were supposed to be shown not just on the battlefield but also during peacetime and in domestic settings. Islamic society had its own traditions of chivalric behaviour in all these dimensions of life, and European knights may well have been influenced by the conduct of the warriors they encountered during the crusades waged in Syria and Palestine. Spain's Muslim commanders, encountered by many an adventurous Christian knight during the *reconquista*, produced their own influential examples of the Islamic warrior's gallantry. Christianity's social teachings were fundamental to European chivalry. The Peace and Truce of God was a Church-inspired movement that sought to limit the effects of both public warfare and private violence, and from the late-tenth century onwards popes and senior clergy would announce, and try to enforce, regular periods of amnesty when knights were expected to display mercy towards weaker members of society. Chivalric attitudes engendered a markedly individualized way of looking at the world, as can be seen in the code's association with the cult of love, both human and divine. Medieval Christianity's increased devotion to the Virgin Mary involved a new emphasis on redemptive suffering, and the chivalrous knight's duty of honour obliged him to play a self-denying and courageous role in warfare that was designed to defend and advance the Church's interests as guarantor of the faith. But chivalry's idealization of femininity was also present in the devotion shown by knights to certain aristocratic women, whose honour they defended and whose graciousness could then be extolled in the suitably decorous language of 'courtly love'.

## THE EXPANSION OF EUROPEAN CULTURE

Medieval Europe's encounters with its neighbours led to a tighter definition of what counted as 'European', with previously pagan civilizations being conquered, converted and assimilated into Christian cultural norms. That process led to Scandinavian society becoming the northern frontier of medieval Europe, and by the 11th century the previously nomadic Magyars, once so ferociously pagan, were settled in the kingdom of Hungary that had become a central European bastion of Catholic Christendom. The late tenth-century conversion of the aristocratic (and mostly Swedish) leadership of the principality of Rus, centred on Kiev, was the basis for Russian Christianity's subsequent evolution. Medieval Rus therefore provided a new eastern frontier that marked the boundary between European and Asiatic culture. Russian Christianity's allegiance to the patriarchate of Constantinople placed it however within the Orthodox Church's orbit of influence, and European culture's most significant internal division during the Middle Ages was the one between Latin and Greek Christianity.

Other cultures resisted the European tide or mounted offensives against its advance, and the climate of opinion associated with the First Crusade gave a new focus to Islamic-Christian hostility. The crusades led by Christian kings ended in failure in the Middle East, but the crusading ideal remained an important feature of European social attitudes until the 16th century, when Ottoman Turks threatened to advance through the Balkans and into central Europe. Despite its cultural and religious antipathy to Islam, Europe nonetheless imported many features of the Muslims' material culture – especially their maritime, technological and agricultural innovations. Europeans became aware of a dimension other than the Islamic one to their eastern borders with the arrival of the Mongols, whose savagely effective campaigning in the mid-13th century, especially in Poland, Hungary and Bulgaria, exposed the continent's east and centre to hitherto unimagined levels of danger. The diminution of that threat allowed Christian Europe to direct some of its missionary energy towards Mongol-dominated Asia – a vast territory extending to the Chinese border – and by the 1290s Franciscan friars were running missions in China.

ABOVE *A late-15th-century Flemish illustration, from the* Chroniques de France et d'Angleterre, *of the duke of Burgundy landing in Africa. Such explorations led to the global expansion of Christianity and European culture.*

From the 10th to the 15th century Europeans exported their culture to the continent's northern and eastern borders, and the idea of a common European society extending from the Atlantic shores to the frontier zone of the Eurasian steppes had acquired both a territorial reality and an imaginative power. From the 13th century onwards Europeans could also cross their local seas more rapidly, and map them more accurately, as a result of improved techniques in maritime engineering and navigation. It was that accumulated expertise and body of knowledge that enabled European mariners to embark on their subsequent explorations of the West African coasts and of the Atlantic and Pacific seas. The great age of discovery originated in the outward-looking curiosity of Europeans during the later medieval centuries, and by 1500 the continent's culture was being transmitted across vast oceans and to continental regions in the west and south of a newly discovered world.

# THOMAS AQUINAS

*The system of philosophical theology called Thomism was raised on the foundations laid by Tomasso d'Aquino (c.1224–74), the most original and influential thinker of medieval Latin Christendom. In the post-medieval centuries Thomas retained his authority as the philosopher who had reconciled the teachings of Aristotle with Christian theology.*

From the late 19th century onwards a revived form of Thomism became the voice of Catholic orthodoxy in its confrontation with secularism. However, emphasis on Thomas the saint (he was canonized in 1323), the scholastic system-builder and Doctor Angelicus – whose teaching was divinely inspired – obscures the reality of a creative intellectual whose work alarmed many contemporaries.

A scion of the southern Italian nobility, Thomas was educated as a boy at the Benedictine monastery of Monte Cassino and subsequently at the University of Naples, which had become a centre for the study of philosophical and scientific texts translated from Arabic and ancient Greek. His decision to join the Dominican Order, whose members embraced poverty and begging as a way of life, rather than the more venerable Benedictines, upset Thomas's family. The Dominicans however were involved in the cut-and-thrust of contemporary life as preachers and teachers who lived in the world – and most often within the fast developing townscape of 13th-century Europe – rather than existing in monastic seclusion. Thomas's decision was a conscious rejection of the two narrow forms of life in which he had been raised: the daily regime of Benedictine spirituality – ordered, beautiful but dull – and the social milieu of the landed estate as lived by his parents in the district around the town of Aquino. The mental and spiritual life that he craved instead was one capable of responding creatively to the contemporary European scene. Mendicancy (or begging) was central to the Dominicans' radical involvement, just as it was for Francis of Assisi and his followers.

By the autumn of 1245 Thomas was in Paris, having been sent there to study by his Order, and the intellectual excitement he could generate as both teacher and writer was immediately apparent once he started to lecture at the University of Paris

in 1256. Arabian-Aristotelian science and thought were now acquiring a widespread appeal in Europe, and the Church had responded initially with a panic-stricken condemnation. Aristotle in particular was deemed guilty of an arrogant rationalism and of naturalism – a creed equating nature with God. His reputation took a profound knock when the work of Averroes, the great Spanish-Islamic interpreter of Aristotle, became known in Paris and other university centres. The Averroist notion of a double truth, with the conclusions of reason and faith both being valid but also capable of contradicting each other, disturbed the Christian consensus. Other teachings by Averroes, and attributed by him to Aristotle, included the notion that the world is eternal (and not therefore created in time), and that the soul consists of two parts: an individual element which is not eternal and dies with the human body, and a divine element which links up all of humanity as common partakers in an eternal and universal consciousness.

The commentaries written by Thomas sought to show that Aristotle's thought was consistent with the Christian teaching that the individual soul is immortal and that God had intervened to create the world at a particular moment in time. Thomas's position, expounded in a dazzling series of over 80 works that include the celebrated *Summa Theologiae* (1265–73), was exposed to attack from two directions. Averroism was the most exciting form of wisdom in 13th-century Europe and its elevation of 'nature'– a category that included both the physical world and human society – appealed to many at a time of material advance and intellectual progress. Traditional Christianity on the other hand, harking back to St Augustine, emphasized the 'fallen nature' of mankind that was subordinate to God's grace – a divine freedom that obeyed its own imperatives. Thomas, by contrast, chose to relate reason to faith: the theologian accepts the insights of faith as a starting point and then expounds them by following the distinctive rules of reason. His re-evaluation of nature – the sum total of the material world's events and developments – proved particularly provocative. Matter was not distinct from spirit but its inevitable and appropriate setting, and human existence is defined by the thoroughgoing fusion of the two categories. 'Spirit', therefore, is not remote and supernatural. It exists in the here-and-now, and can be investigated, explained and enjoyed.

By the time Thomas returned to teach at Naples in 1272 he enjoyed a Europe-wide reputation. Nonetheless, the Masters of Arts at Paris, the Church's supreme body when it came to defining truths of theology, decided to condemn some of his most characteristic teachings in 1277. The Catholic Church took a long time to make up its mind about Thomas theologically, and it was only in 1567 that he was eventually named a Doctor of the Church.

*St Thomas Aquinas is flanked by Aristotle and Plato in this 14th-century tempera on wood, while Averroes reclines below him. Christ looks down from above, along with Saints Matthew, Mark, Luke, and John, Moses and Saint Paul. In this hierarchy of knowledge, philosophy is subordinated to theology. (Triumph of St Thomas Aquinas by Francesco Traini, c.1340, Church of Santa Caterina, Pisa.)*

# c.796 | MEDIEVAL

# 1450 | WARFARE

*Warfare was a near-constant preoccupation for medieval Europe's governing élites. Chroniclers then, and subsequently, drew a distinction between 'public' wars fought by rulers and 'private' wars, which were contests between individuals. In reality, however, both these kinds of medieval conflict overlapped. 'Public' wars between kings may seem to be* par excellence *the arena in which established political authority and the assertion of legal rights really came into operation by sanctioning violence. But the many powerful individuals who fought each other with armies – barons, counts, margraves and dukes – enjoyed a quasi-monarchical authority in the regions they dominated. They, too, appealed to ancestral political and legal rights when fighting their own internecine battles, and the medieval evolution towards territorial monarchies whose rulers enjoyed a monopoly of force was a very long-term development.*

Medieval European society tolerated very high levels of violence as a fact of everyday life. Men (and some women) resorted to force without much compunction in order to achieve their goals, and highly personal motivations could lead to war. In the later Middle Ages monarchs still used the language of honour to justify war after they or their dynasty had been slighted. And at all stages in its evolution, medieval European warfare found it easy to accommodate the very personal reasons that lead human beings to inflict pain on each other. Medieval warfare therefore includes the blood lust of the vendetta and the revenge sought by feuding families as well as the honour code of knights and the ambitions of Christian princes. The key to all these forms of conflict was the warrior code. Its dominance and persistence meant that violent motivations could be institutionalized and expressed in warfare's varied forms.

The Germanic warriors who took over the former Western empire and divided it into kingdoms set the medieval military pattern. Ties of loyalty to the leader and a strongly personal code of honour established a resilient *esprit de corps*. Fighting was the proper

RIGHT *Knights engage in hand-to-hand combat in defence of an English-held castle in this detail from a 14th-century manuscript.*

**796** Charlemagne's commanders discover the central European Avar confederation's treasure, some of which is then redistributed by the king as largesse.

**955** Battle of Lechfeld: Otto the Great's defeat of the nomadic Magyars is a victory for physically bigger warriors sustained by protein-enriched diets made possible by north European agricultural advances.

**1066–1141** Battles fought in England and Normandy show infantry's continuing relevance despite the novelty of cavalry's major role.

*c.*1180 German conflicts have spilled over into north Italy where local factions acquire the Guelph and Ghibelline labels as a consequence. The alliances linking originally separate theatres of war makes medieval warfare hard to contain.

*c.* 1200 Europe's mercenary market is expanding. Italian city states use mercenaries rather than local militias in their internecine wars.

**1272–1307** The reign of Edward I of England who deploys his military household, a permanent and professional fighting unit,

*continued*

occupation of an able-bodied, early medieval European male. Death in battle was glorious – although the shock recorded by chroniclers and writers of annals when great leaders fell in battle suggests that nobles were rarely exposed to high levels of personal danger. Social status mattered, and the humbly born were not supposed to engage their superiors in combat. The physical suffering and material losses inflicted on non-combatants were regrettable but unavoidable by-products of war. These mental attitudes were established as warrior kingship became the standard form of European leadership, and their authoritative appeal persisted throughout the medieval period.

## THE CONTAGION OF WAR

Medieval kings gained their authority by winning wars, and a sovereign who was consistently unsuccessful in warfare did not keep his throne for long. Early medieval monarchs in particular needed to gain land and booty that they could then redistribute to their retinue. As boundary zones became more established from the ninth century onwards there were less opportunities for raiding in Western Europe, but the frontiers of Christendom still provided opportunities for plundering in the high Middle Ages. The same is true of lands where territorial rights were disputed, such as France during the Hundred Years' War. Well into the central Middle Ages, therefore, kings embarked on annual campaigns partly in order to plunder, and they took care to reward their retinue.

Some wars were clearly defensive. Anglo-Saxon and West Frankish leaders were forced to respond to Viking attacks in the ninth and tenth centuries, and East Francia's campaigns against the Magyars in the 950s were wars of retaliation. The Norman thrust into England and southern Italy during the 11th century was straightforwardly aggressive. The same is true of the German kingdom's expansion at the same time into Slavic territories beyond the River Elbe. Islamic societies in Syria and Palestine saw the crusades as a series of offensive campaigns. But European rulers justified them as wars of liberation, since their aim was to re-occupy territories that had been Christian-held before being conquered by Islamic armies. The *reconquista* adopted a similar liberationist motivation, though its leaders in northern Spain frequently manoeuvred against each other in a shifting pattern of alliances before uniting in an anti-Islamic coalition.

Modern warfare has entailed major battlefield confrontations between armies paid for by sovereign states whose declared military aims are mutually incompatible. The more spectacular medieval conflicts have something in common with these later wars. Papal-imperial hostilities waged during the Investiture crisis – and renewed subsequently during the age of the Staufen rulers from Barbarossa to

Frederick II; the Franco-Spanish wars that developed after the Sicilian Vespers of 1282; the century of intermittent campaigning between England and France from 1337 onwards: these were all international conflicts between sovereign princes whose war aims were clearly defined. They were, however, extremely expensive to sustain, and the obvious solution was to turn to allies who could help bear the cost. Such allies tended to be already engaged in the types of conflict that were in fact much more characteristic of medieval warfare. Individuals of similar social standing – counts, dukes, royal princes and leaders of opposing cities – usually fought each other over titles and territories, as the Welf dynasty of Bavaria did in its contest against the Staufen. Rebellious groupings moreover attacked their superiors: nobles raised their standards against kings (as witnessed during the English baronage's reaction against King John), and leagues of cities fought their nominal imperial suzerain (as occurred in northern Italy when the Staufen tried to enforce their rights).

More regional conflicts therefore spread out into the international arena once local dynasts had formed alliances with kings, emperors and popes. Normans on the make in southern Italy were operating a long way from their domestic bases in northern France, and so they turned to the papacy, which was happy to have them as allies. And since the papacy hated the German empire these Norman princelings were an occasionally reliable source of papal support in the anti-imperial cause. Italian city-state conflicts illustrate a similar story of war's contagion, with local factions acquiring the labels 'Guelph' and 'Ghibelline' once they became the partisans of, respectively, the papacy and the empire. But the Italian combatants were, and remained, people who wanted to kill each other in any event – and quite regardless of the larger conflict to the north. The Guelphs and Ghibellines were therefore still engaging in Italian warfare long after the empire had been forced to concede defeat to the papacy in late 13th-century Germany.

## THE CALL TO ARMS

Most men went to war on the command either of their superior lord or of an employer who paid them to fight. Those destined to be élite soldiers were habituated to bloodshed: literature listened to and read from a young age was an important de-sensitizing element since lays, poems, romances and epics laid such stress on exemplary ferocity in battle. If the 'age of chivalry' meant the honour code of courage, modesty and loyalty, it also involved the ability to be an expeditious killer. The tournaments that were such an entertaining chivalric spectacle were also an important form of training in combat techniques.

Rulers refined methods of raising money from their own resources and kingdoms in order to pay for war. From the 12th century onwards bureaucratic systems run by professional clerks enabled royal households to tax and plan ahead. Courts acquired

permanent headquarters, and kings could also start to borrow against anticipated revenue – a very radical innovation. Kings and their officials could now intervene in local conflicts of interest and mediate (or enforce) a resolution. Armies were provisioned more effectively, and campaigns could be planned in greater detail. All of this should have brought greater order to the art of war from c.1200 onwards. But for at least another two centuries notions of containment within agreed limits remained irrelevant to European military campaigning. The search for greater resources in terms of men and materials made medieval warfare almost uncontainable, and the formation of alliances linked up the separate theatres of war in a pattern of interlocking disputes.

Warfare's incidence was reflected in the Church's ambiguous stance. Warriors who had killed their enemies, even in a cause supported by the Church, still had to do penance well into the high Middle Ages, since a sin had been committed. But even while it treated successful warriors as murderers, the Church was still blessing certain campaigns. 'Holy war' existed long before the 'just war' theories being advanced in the 13th century. The *reconquista* and the various crusades – those fought against the Prussians in the Baltic and the Cathars in southern France as well the Middle Eastern campaigns – were all regarded as holy wars. Penitential exercises, such as the prayers and fasting observed by crusading warriors while on campaign, recognized warfare's sacred nature and the need to prolong it until the day was won.

Although medieval warfare was endemic, most of it consisted of short-term raids whose aim was the capture of booty, especially livestock, slaves and prisoners. Raids of this kind could also yield tribute payments. The English monarchy introduced a tax later known as Danegeld, in the 990s, and some of the revenue raised was sent to Scandinavian rulers in order to keep Viking marauders away from England. Even serious long-term offensives often amounted to a series of raids rather than continuous campaigning. The Teutonic Knights structured their campaigns against the Lithuanians and the Baltic Prussians in the 13th to the 15th centuries around twice-yearly military interventions in February and August. Having set up base inside hostile territory the knights would send out daily raiding parties, and then withdraw and move on to a new area before the enemy's army could engage them in battle.

Earlier medieval armies had a heterogeneous composition, with every noble being obliged to respond to the military summons by providing troops, equipment, archers and infantry. Few of these serving lower ranks were trained soldiers. Nonetheless, such armies often incorporated mercenaries, and the medieval role of the professional standing army pre-dates the later Middle Ages. The military household of Edward I for example supplied his army with the permanent and professional element that made his Welsh and Scottish campaigning extremely effective. The same household component served in earlier Anglo-Norman royal campaigns in Wales and Scotland. Central levies of the free peasantry were certainly a major source of amateur recruitment for medieval armies in the high Middle Ages, and in England all free men had an obligation to serve 40 days a year. But Englishmen could avoid military service on payment of the tax called *scutage*, and the money thereby raised allowed English kings to pay professional soldiers, including mercenaries. By the 12th century there was a large mercenary market throughout Europe, and medieval Italian city-states in particular relied on mercenaries rather than the citizen militias of the past. Money provided warfare with its sinews, and those who could pay acquired the destructive capacity they wanted. Such people tended to be kings, and the history of medieval warfare in Europe is the story of their continuous, and increasing, influence in determining the aims of war.

ABOVE *Ludovico il Moro, duke of Milan, is handed over to French forces (right) by his band of Swiss mercenaries (left) at Novara in April 1500. French forces laid siege to the city of Novara after Ludovico attempted to recapture Milan, following his expulsion in 1498 (from the* Luzernerchronik *of 1513, written and partly illustrated by Diebold Schilling the Younger).*

## WEAPONS AND BATTLE STRATEGIES

By the 15th century the medieval army's dominant element was once again the infantry, just as it had been in the early Middle Ages. The cavalry and the institution of knighthood – central to war in the high Middle Ages – both lost pre-eminence. But

*continued*

## MEDIEVAL WARFARE

in his wars against the Welsh and Scots.

**1346–47** English forces besiege Calais for 11 months. Sieges, often lengthy, are basic to medieval warfare until the 15th-century spread of efficient cannonry.

***c*.1400** Knights sometimes dismount to deal with the threat posed by archers whose longbows shoot arrows rapidly. Cavalry is losing its former dominance.

**1420s** The Hussite wars waged by the followers of Jan Huss (*c*.1372–1415) against the nobility of Bohemia show how fighting men of lower social rank can outmanoeuvre and defeat aristocratic warriors.

***c*.1450** Decline of the galley, powered by oarsmen. It is replaced by bulkier, sail-powered ships mounted with cannon.

infantry had consistently played an important element in battle: the series of campaigns in England and Normandy between 1066 and 1141 show a typical combination of cavalry, infantry and archery. The pike and the longbow played a decisive role in the infantry warfare of the central and late Middle Ages. Long pikes deployed in flexible formations and complex manoeuvres were a particular feature of the Swiss mercenaries who were employed by most European princes by that stage. Although the longbow is particularly associated with the English and Welsh soldiers who used it to dramatic effect at the battles of Crécy and Agincourt, archers had a long warrior history and were present, for example, at Hastings in 1066. Enemy archers inflicted serious casualties on Edward I's armies of conquest in late-13th-century Wales, and their presence *en masse* in the armies subsequently led by the king against the Scots signifies the start of a new emphasis on archery's destructive power. Arrows shot from the longbow – used in a defensive configuration with rows of bowmen being protected by pits and trenches dug before them – could penetrate plate armour and mail. And a rapid rate of shots (possibly 12 arrows a minute for a highly skilled archer) gave the weapon its edge over the more clumsy crossbow. In the later Middle Ages even knights were beginning to dismount in order to deal with this new form of warfare, especially since advances in plate armour construction were giving a greater protection against arrows.

Some features of military strategy were constant. Maintaining sieges and inflicting famine, for example, were more effective ways of attacking the enemy than pitched battles – forms of military engagement that medieval commanders tended to avoid if possible. Communication systems in battle relied on flags, messengers and musical signals, and their inefficiency contributed to the battlefield mêlée. It was the capture of fortified locations that mattered rather than the unconditional surrender of the defeated. Capturing an opposing knight was preferable to killing him, since the prisoner could then be ransomed for booty. Command of territory came through occupying strongholds, and the definitive conquest of a disputed region could only be achieved by the occupation or destruction of its castles. The balance of power lay with the besieged if they were well provided with supplies, although some battles of note resulted in a besieging army's defeat of a relief force, as happened at Tinchebrai, Normandy, in 1106. Major fortifications needed lengthy sieges: that of Rouen in 1418–19 lasted six months and Calais took 11 months to fall in 1346–47. Warfare therefore was not just concentrated in the 'campaigning season' from spring to autumn, though foraging (living off the enemy's land) was easier during the summer months when crops were readily available. Supply trains were a vital resource in extending the (invariably brief) period when a medieval army could maintain a real front, but their slow speed of travel

inevitably impeded the force's rate of advance. Ravaging and plundering provided an army with additional resources, but their chief objective was the reduction of the enemy's fighting capacity and the infliction of famine was a conscious strategy rather than an opportunistic diversion.

## THE NEW ARTILLERY

Cannon using gunpowder to launch projectiles were first seen in European warfare during the *reconquista* in the 13th century, and the English used them at the Battle of Crécy in 1346. They initially had a poor rate of fire and were very cumbersome to deploy until one-handed cannon were developed. Nonetheless, the introduction of cannonry heralded the end of the siege as a method of warfare and would also play a decisive role in the development of naval warfare – a phenomenon that contributed in its own way to the displacement of cavalry and the diminution of knighthood. The galley propelled by oarsmen enjoyed a long dominance in medieval naval battles: missile fire would be exchanged and the combatant crews would then board the enemy's ships and fight on deck. Bulkier and sail-powered ships were then introduced, with cannon being mounted on their decks by the 15th century. Although here again the weaponry's bulk initially

ABOVE *The Siege of Orléans in 1428, shown here in a 15th-century illustration from* Les Vigiles de Charles VII, *was a major turning point in France's favour during the Hundred Years' War. The cannon used by the English were ineffective against the walls of Orléans.*

RIGHT *At the Battle of Sluys (1340) Philip VI's French fleet was destroyed by Edward III's naval force. England's command of the channel meant that the rest of the Hundred Years' War was fought on French soil. This late-15th-century illustration appeared in Jean de Wavrin's* Chronique d'Angleterre.

counted against it, the subsequent development of anti-personnel, hand-held cannon proved highly effective at sea. But it was the introduction of the gun deck – created by the insertion of an opening in the ship's side and below the main deck – which really transformed naval warfare by *c*.1500.

Monarchs with extensive revenue-raising powers could afford to buy the new artillery, and the nobility found it more difficult to wage war independently. A strong association with national identity, evident in the case of English and French monarchies from the 14th century onwards, underpinned the public role of kings as enforcers of domestic authority and war-leaders. Patriotism's call to the drum therefore meant not just more taxes but also a greater willingness to pay the tax demand, since monarchs now associated their territorial and dynastic objectives with the 'national interest'. Governments, especially in France and Spain, were now relying on paid and standing professional armies rather than occasional levies, and the improved weaponry led to more nobles being killed than in the past. During the Hussite wars, waged by the followers of Jan Huss against the nobility of Bohemia in the 1420s, fighting men in the lower ranks displayed great skill in outmanoeuvring and slaughtering aristocratic

# AMAZONS

*The medieval female warriors who played an important role in military strategy and even as commanders in the field were mostly either aristocrats or of royal blood.*

Matilda of England (1102–67) was her father Henry I's sole legitimate heir to survive to adulthood. Following Stephen of Blois's seizure of the throne in 1135 she led a series of military campaigns in an attempt at securing the English Crown for herself. Matilda of Tuscany (1046–1115), who ruled the region in her own right as its countess, is a major figure in the military and diplomatic history of the Investiture crisis, since she was Pope Gregory VII's chief supporter in Italy. Medieval warfare's most famous female warrior, however, was of peasant stock. Jeanne d'Arc (*c*.1412–31) inspired the military engagements that led to the relief of the town of Orléans in 1429 and the subsequent capture of Rheims – previously held by the Burgundian faction who were English allies during this late stage in the Hundred Years' War.

Gwenllian ap Gruffudd (*c*.1097–1136) was the daughter of Gruffudd ap Cynan (1055–1137), a dominant figure in Welsh politics and military strategy during his 62-year reign as prince of Gwynedd in north Wales. She married Gruffudd ap Rhys, ruler of the kingdom of Deheubarth, which extended across the southwest of Wales, and became the chatelaine at his castle in Dinefwr, near the town of Llandeilo. The royal house of Dinefwr, a cadet branch of the dynasty of Aberffraw that ruled Gwynedd, was already venerable by the

time of Gwenllian's arrival at its court. Hywel Dda ('the Good') (*c*.880–950) had expanded the early medieval kingdom of Dyfed to form Deheubarth in the 920s, and the codification of Welsh law in a single volume was achieved under his patronage in the 940s. By the early 12th century, however, Deheubarth was under sustained attack and Gruffudd ap Rhys, joined by his princess-consort, launched several retaliatory raids against the Norman, English and Flemish colonists who had established themselves within the kingdom. The years of 'the Anarchy' during the reign (1135–54) of King Stephen of England were an opportunity to recover Deheubarth's authority. Gruffudd raised the banner of revolt, and in 1136 he travelled to Gwynedd where he debated terms of alliance with his wife's father. Norman raiding in Deheubarth continued in his absence, and Gwenllian raised an army that she then led into battle at a site near Cydweli. Although defeated, captured and then beheaded by the opposing Norman force, Gwenllian's action proved the catalyst for a major Welsh rebellion that spread to the south of Wales. The memory of her exploits inspired Welsh military commanders, and the highly successful campaigns led by her son Rhys ap Gruffudd (1132–97) against Henry II in 1164–70 made Deheubarth the dominant power in late-12th-century Wales.

warriors. Earlier such military insurrections by the lower orders, such as England's Peasant Revolt (1381) and the Parisian *Jacquerie* led by Étienne Marcel in 1358, had been markedly ineffective by comparison.

The combination of social grievance with religious dissent, witnessed during the Hussite wars, recurred to explosive effect during the early 16th-century Protestant reformation. An idealized view of Christendom, and a belief in its unity, had been a defining feature of Europe's medieval civilization. But a world in which Protestants and Catholics killed each other also witnessed the progressive dissolution of the medieval world view, and the grave of 'Christendom' is to be found in the battlefields of early modern Europe.

# INDEX

# PICTURE CREDITS

# ACKNOWLEDGEMENTS

I would like to thank my literary agent Georgina Capel who provided me with invaluable support and advice in the course of writing *The Age of Chivalry*. Among others involved in the book's production I am grateful to Wayne Davies, Emma Heyworth-Dunn and Slav Todorov at Quercus Publishing, to Steve McCurdy and Graham Bateman of BCS Publishing for their work as designers, and to the cartographer William Donohue.

Quercus Publishing Plc
21 Bloomsbury Square
London
WC1A 2NS

First published in 2011

A catalogue record of this book is available from the British Library

ISBN: 978-0-85738-338-9
Printed and bound in China

10 9 8 7 6 5 4 3 2 1

Designed and edited by BCS Publishing Limited, Oxford.